THE SECRETARY'S HANDBOOK

THE MACMILLAN COMPANY
NEW YORK · BOSTON · CHICAGO · DALLAS
ATLANTA · SAN FRANCISCO

MACMILLAN & CO., Limited
LONDON · BOMBAY · CALCUTTA
MELBOURNE

THE MACMILLAN COMPANY
OF CANADA, Limited
TORONTO

THE
SECRETARY'S HANDBOOK

A Manual of Correct Usage

BY

SARAH AUGUSTA TAINTOR

DEPARTMENT OF ENGLISH, THEODORE ROOSEVELT HIGH SCHOOL, SECRETARIAL
CORRESPONDENCE, UNIVERSITY EXTENSION, COLUMBIA UNIVERSITY

AND

KATE M. MONRO

ADMINISTRATIVE ASSISTANT, HAAREN HIGH SCHOOL, NEW YORK CITY

FOURTH EDITION
REVISED

NEW YORK
THE MACMILLAN COMPANY
1932

Printed in the United States of America by
J. J. LITTLE AND IVES COMPANY, NEW YORK

TO THE SECRETARIES OF AMERICA
TO WHOSE UNTIRING AND OFTEN
UNHERALDED WORK THE WORLD
OF BUSINESS OWES MUCH OF ITS
SUCCESS, THIS BOOK IS GRATE-
FULLY DEDICATED

PREFACE

The number of good handbooks on English published during the last few years almost forbids the writing of another. Indeed, it would be futile if a new one should approach the subject of good usage from the same point of view or should offer no different material. This handbook is intended primarily for secretaries whose duties include the writing of letters and other business forms. Not a day passes in a business office that some question of usage does not arise. Secretaries have desired a book planned from their point of view, stressing their problems. With this in mind, the manual has been written as a reference book containing authoritative usage.

The material is divided into two parts: the first containing rules with illustrations of correct form in English; the second consisting of various types of letters relating to business, social, and official usage, as well as other forms of business writing often required of the secretary. These include, among other types, the making of resolutions, the writing of minutes, the framing of petitions, and the compiling of reports.

With particular problems of the secretary in mind, specific directions have been given for the preparation of manuscript for publication and the reading of it in proof, for the making of indexes, and the compiling of bibliographies. Other chapters contain sources of information for the secretary, and a number of citations used in conferring honors upon individuals. These will prove interesting and suggestive both for their content and for their manner of expression.

While the problems of the secretary have been emphasized, it is hoped the manual will prove helpful to all who are seeking concise information on points of correctness.

PREFACE

The authors have consulted freely other style books to which they acknowledge their indebtedness. Among these are: *A Manual of Style of the University of Chicago Press; A Style-Book for Writers and Editors,* compiled by C. O. Sylvester Mawson; *Text, Type, and Style,* published by The Atlantic Monthly Press; and *The Style Manual of the Government Printing Office.* Where usage is divided, the authors have endeavored to record such differences for the benefit of the secretary.

Special acknowledgment is made to the following persons who have offered helpful suggestions in making the book practical or who have made it possible to use valuable illustrative material: Nicholas Murray Butler, President of Columbia University; Professor John H. H. Lyon, Professor Ernest Hunter Wright, Miss Mildred Loxton de Barritt, of the English Department of Columbia University; Judge John J. Freschi; Mr. Augustus Loring Richards; Colonel Theodore Roosevelt; H. C. Major, Captain U.S.M.C.; L. G. Caton, Acting Secretary of the Library of Congress; Professor James C. Egbert, Columbia University; John A. Lynch, President of the Borough of Richmond; Mr. Eugene F. McLaughlin, Secretary of the Borough of Manhattan; Mr. E. F. Austin, Chief Engineer of the Borough of the Bronx; Mr. Peter McArdle, Secretary to the President of the Borough of Brooklyn; Julia M. Wilkinson, Executive Secretary, University of Wisconsin; Miss Ella Banks, Secretary to the President of Boston University; Mr. Hermann Hagedorn, Director of the Roosevelt Memorial Association; F. M. Wilmot, Manager of the Carnegie Hero Fund Commission; Mr. Cameron Beck, Director of the Personnel Department of the New York Stock Exchange; Congressman Sol Bloom; Mr. Andrew Keogh, Librarian of Yale University; Dr. Lawson Purdy, Secretary of the Charity Organization Society of New York; Mr. Hiller C. Wellman, Librarian of the City Library Association of Springfield, Mass.; Mother M. Corrigan, Instructor in the College of the Sacred Heart, New York; Dr. Otto

PREFACE

Zobel, Research Department of the American Telephone and Telegraph Company; Miss Isabel Stevenson Monro, New York Public Library; Mr. William R. Hayward, Principal of the Theodore Roosevelt High School; Mr. John B. Opdycke, Chairman of the Department of English of Haaren High School; Miss Katherine Morse, of the English Department of the Manhattan Training School; Dr. Charles R. Gaston, Chairman of the English Department, Mrs. Alice Butler Richards, Mrs. Edna B. Kerr, Dr. Bruno Fedter, Mr. H. S. Leonard, Mr. Jack Silverman, Mr. Harold Fields, of Theodore Roosevelt High School; Miss Olive Carter of The Macmillan Company; Miss Madeline Lane, Secretary, The Dorr Engineering Company; Miss Alice Ames, Secretary, The International Telegraph and Telephone Company; Miss Rose Wolcott, Architect; Miss Margaret Hanna, Washington, D. C.; Miss Marie Konzelman, student in Columbia University, and the classes of 1928 and 1929 in Secretarial Correspondence.

To Miss Katherine Spencer, who read the manuscript in proof, the authors wish to express their grateful appreciation.

They also wish to acknowledge their indebtedness to the following organizations which have allowed them to use illustrative material: The National Education Association, The Vocational Guidance Association, The Young Women's Christian Association, Rogers Peet and Company, and Lord and Taylor.

SARAH AUGUSTA TAINTOR
KATE M. MONRO

CONTENTS

PART I

PART II

CONTENTS

THE SECRETARY'S HANDBOOK

THE SECRETARY'S HANDBOOK

CHAPTER I

CAPITALIZATION

1. Capitalize the first word of every sentence.

Much may be made of a Scotchman if he be caught young.
SAMUEL JOHNSON

Modern writers often capitalize the first word of detached phrases and clauses used in place of sentences.

These essays are the records of moods and sometimes contradict each other. So much the better.
JOSEPH WARREN BEACH

Islands, islets, and mere rocks; some jutting high up, some nestling low. A dangerous coast, and a splendid fishing-ground.
HUGH S. SCOTT

2. Capitalize the first word of every line of poetry.

To the glory that was Greece,
And the grandeur that was Rome.
EDGAR ALLAN POE

In some modern English poetry forms, only the first word of the first line is capitalized, and sometimes even this is written lower case.

The sky
is that beautiful old parchment
in which the sun
and the moon
keep their diary.
ALFRED KREYMBORG

3. Capitalize all proper nouns that are names of individuals.

Jane Addams   Herbert Hoover

(1) Capitalize epithets added to proper names or applied to people.

The Lone Eagle	George the Fifth
The Commoner	Louis the Well-Beloved
The Pretender	Catherine the Great
William the Conqueror	Richard the Lion-Hearted

(2) Capitalize *father* and *mother* when used in address; but do not capitalize such nouns when a possessive pronoun is used with them.

> Yes, Mother, I am going.
> My father is at home.

(3) Capitalize *uncle, aunt,* and other family appellations when used with a proper noun.

I met Uncle John who told me of my aunt's good fortune.

4. Do not capitalize particles in *foreign* names if they are preceded by a forename or by a title of nobility or courtesy.

Marquis de Lafayette, Count von Moltke, Charles de Thou, Guy de Maupassant, Gabriel d'Annunzio, Leonardo da Vinci.

The *Style Manual of the Government Printing Office*[1] states the following in relation to the capitalization of particles in foreign names:

The prepositions "d," "da," "de," "della," "di," "l'," "van," "von," etc., in names from foreign languages if preceded by a forename, a title of nobility, a professional title, or one of courtesy, must be lower-cased; as Charles de Blé, Cardinal da Ponte, Marquis de Lafayette, Mr. de Thou, M. d'Orbigny, Señor da Yznaga, General della Santa Maria, Dr. d'Ouvillier, Captain di Cesnola, Admiral van Tromp, Count von Moltke, etc.

This rule of lower-casing "de," "van," "la," etc., does not apply to most American names. These usually take the capitalized form, as Martin Van Buren, Mr. Justice Van Devanter, William Henry Van Allen, etc.; De Koven, De Forest, De Witt, etc.; La Forge, La Follette, etc. Whenever the usual form of

---

[1] Hereafter called the *Style Manual.*

such names, either lower-case form or capitalized, one-word form or two words, is known or can be readily ascertained, such usual form should be followed.

Prepositions in names from foreign languages, without a forename, a title of nobility, a professional title, or one of courtesy, such as "van" in Dutch, "von" in German, "de" or "d'" in French, or "da," "della," or "di" in Italian, should be capitalized; as Van Tromp, Von Humboldt, De Thou, D'Orsay, Da Ponte, Della Crusca, Di Cesnola.

Some persons prefer, however, the foreign usage:

> Henry van Dyke   Robert de Forest
> Mrs. Norman de R. Whitehouse
> Mildred Loxton de Barritt

References for authoritative capitalization: *Who's Who, Who's Who in America,* etc.

5. Capitalize all academic degrees following the name whether abbreviated or written out.

> John H. Finley, LL.D.; Dorothy Scarborough, Ph. D.; Kate Douglas Wiggin, Litt. D.; Katherine Morse, Master of Arts.

(1) When writing more than one degree after a name, arrange according to their importance, the most important last, or, when they are of the same rank, as various doctoral degrees, according to the time of their being granted. (See p. 131.)

> Arthur Sutton Corbin, LL.B., M.A.
> James Rowland Angell, Ph. D., Litt. D., LL.D.
> Alexander William Evans, M.D., Ph. D.

6. Capitalize all academic and religious titles, as, *Doctor, Reverend, Professor, Dean,* when preceding a name. (See pp. 129-130.)

> Dr. Mary Morton, The Reverend Daniel Russell, Professor Ernest H. Wright, Dean Gildersleeve.

(1) With *Reverend,* other academic titles and abbreviations for academic degrees may be used, as they do not repeat the title:

3

The Reverend Professor Hugh Black, D.D.
The Reverend President Henry Sloane Coffin, D.D.

(2) Do not capitalize the following when they stand alone:

director (member of a board)	pastor
professor	priest
cantor	rabbi
elder	rector
minister (of religion)	vicar

7. Capitalize all titles of rank, honor, or respect when preceding the name.

President Hoover	Assemblyman Westall
Vice President Curtis	Mayor Walker
Queen Mary	Alderman Keller
the Earl of Denbigh	Cardinal Gibbons
General Pershing	the Rt. Hon. Winston
Captain Mackenzie	Churchill
Senator Borah	the Duchess of Athol
Congressman Sanders	the Hon. James Wadsworth
Speaker Longworth	Chief Justice Taft
Governor Smith	

8. Capitalize all Government titles when referring to definite persons or offices, and all titles of honor or nobility when referring to specific persons.

the Secretary of the Treasury	the Speaker of the House
the Assistant Secretary of the Treasury	House Chaplain
	Solicitor of Internal Revenue
the Secretary of Foreign Affairs	Superintendent of the Coast and Geodetic Survey
the Under-secretary of State	the King of England
the Under-secretary	the Prince of Wales
Acting Secretary of State	the President of the French Republic
Alien Property Custodian	
the Architect of the Capitol	the Premier of Italy
Associate Justice of the Supreme Court	the Archbishop of Canterbury
	the Mayor of Southampton
Chairman of the Committee of the Whole	His Honor the Mayor
	Your Grace
Chief Justice of the Supreme Court	Your Royal Highness
	Fellow of the Royal Society of Canada
Director General of Railroads	

4

CAPITALIZATION

DIFFERENCE IN USAGE OF CAPITALIZATION OF TITLES

9. When the title follows the name, there is no standard rule. The general tendency, however, is not to use capitals for titles in this position; as, A. Lawrence Lowell, president of Harvard. *Style-Book for Writers and Editors,* MAWSON.

It is customary to write *the President of Harvard,* but *the janitor of Haviland Hall,* the capital for *President* being out of respect for the higher office. *Modern Punctuation,* GEORGE SUMMEY, JR.

NEWSPAPER USAGE OF CAPITALIZATION OF TITLES

Some persons get in because of their official positions, such as the President, his Cabinet, members of Congress, federal judges, army officers above and including colonel, naval officers above the rank of captain, members of learned societies, educators, ecclesiastics and the like.

New York Evening Post

Others participating in the national conference at the Hotel Astor include Norman H. Davis, Acting Secretary of State in the Wilson Administration; Gov. Roy A. Young of the Federal Reserve Board; George W. Wickersham, Attorney General of the United States in the Cabinet of President Taft; Walter Lippmann of The World; James T. Shotwell, professor of history, Columbia University; W. Randolf Burgess of the Federal Reserve Bank of New York; Parker T. Moon, professor of international relations, Columbia University; David Hunter Miller, former special assistant of the State Department; William E. Lingelbach, professor of modern European history, University of Pennsylvania; Joseph P. Chamberlain, professor of public law, Columbia University, and Prof. Benjamin B. Wallace of the Georgetown School of Foreign Service, Washington.

The World

ACADEMIC USAGE

Henry Solon Graves, LL.D., Provost, Dean of the School of Forestry, and Stirling Professor of Forestry. *Bulletin of Yale University*

10. Capitalize *president* when referring to the President of the United States, or any synonymous title referring to him.

His Excellency   Chief Magistrate

Note the manner of writing the following:

ex-President Taft   Former-President Roosevelt

11. Capitalize *governor* when preceding the name of any state; as, the Governor of Wisconsin.

12. Capitalize *commissioner* when used definitely with a title, but do not capitalize it when standing alone.

Commissioner of Education of the State of New York.
Commissioner General of Immigration.
Commissioner of Patents.
Commissioners of the District of Columbia.

But write *civil service commissioner, interstate commerce commissioner*. The *Style Manual*.

13. Titles are sometimes used instead of the names of those who bear them. In such cases, when a definite person is referred to in the singular number, the title is to be capitalized. *Proof-Reading and Style,* DOBBS.

(1) In the second person if used as synonyms of proper names.

Mr. Secretary, please examine the report.
You will report, Captain, to Headquarters.
Do you think, Senator, this bill will pass?

Do not capitalize *sir, madam, monsieur,* and such expressions used alone in address.

What's that to you, sir?
Why, madam, look what it means.

And so, my fellow citizens, the reason that I came away from Washington is that I sometimes get lonely down there.

WOODROW WILSON

(2) In the third person.

When the Governor, escorted by local Democrats, appeared at the door of the station, there was a roar from the crowd.

The New York Times

CAPITALIZATION

14. The *Style Manual* presents the following rules in referring to the Army:

Capitalize the United States Army, the Army, the Army Establishment, the Regular Army, the Volunteer Army, the Regular and Volunteer Armies, the Regulars, the Volunteers.

Capitalize standing alone and also if used as an adjective, as the Army, an Army officer, etc.

Capitalize its organizations and branches, as the Cavalry, Infantry, Field Artillery, Coast Artillery, Engineer Corps, Nurse Corps, Pay Corps, etc.; also if used as an adjective, as Infantry or Cavalry officer, a Regular or Volunteer officer, Marine Corps man, National Guard man, Engineer Corps work, etc.; but lower-case artilleryman, infantryman, cavalryman; also regular or volunteer if used in the general sense, as a regular, a volunteer. Similar capitalization to apply to State organizations.

Capitalize the names of foreign organizations, as British Army, the Royal Guards, Gordon Highlanders, Eighty-eighth Connaught Rangers, etc.

Foreign: Lower-case army, navy, cavalry, etc., unless name is given.

Lower-case organizations bearing names of persons, as Robinson's brigade, Wheat's regiment, etc.

15. The *Style Manual* presents the following rules in referring to the Navy:

Capitalize United States Navy, the Navy, the Naval (or Navy) Establishment, Navy Regulations (book), the Marine Corps, etc. Capitalize Navy as an adjective, as Navy officer, Navy expenditures, Navy regulations (general use of word "regulations"), etc.

Lower-case naval if used generally, as naval expenditures, naval station, naval constructor.

Capitalize foreign navies only if preceded by name, as British Navy, French Navy, Royal Navy, etc.

Capitalize plurals, as the Navies of America and France, French and English Navies, etc.

Lower-case navy yard, navy-yard employee, etc.; but capitalize navy yard following proper name, as Washington Navy Yard, etc.

7

16. Capitalize the words *department, bureau, service* and *station* if referring to a bureau or executive department of the United States Government if the name is given.

the Bureau of Pensions	the Naval Retiring Board
the Pension Office	the National Board of Health
the Bureau of Education	the Office of Indian Affairs
the Department of State	Newport Naval Station

Do not capitalize *department, office, bureau, service,* and like words when used without a name or if used as an adjective.

> I am going to the office.
> He belonged to one of the Government bureaus.
> The department clerk filed the report.

17. Capitalize *Federal* and *State Courts* when used with a definite name. Do not capitalize *city* and *county courts.* *(Government usage)*

> the United States Supreme Court
> the Supreme Court of the United States
> the United States Circuit Court
> the State Court of Appeals
> the Supreme Court of the State of New York
> Federal Grand Jury
> the police court
> the magistrate's court

Capitalize *Court* meaning a judge or judicial tribunal in direct personal reference to such a judge or tribunal. *The New York Times Style Book*

18. Capitalize the word *Cabinet* when referring to the Cabinet of the President of the United States.

> Cabinet Officer
> The President's Cabinet

19. Capitalize *Federal* when referring to the United States Government.

> He was in the service of the Federal Government.

8

20. Capitalize *Government* when used synonymously with the United States Government or when referring to that of any foreign nation.

a Government official   the Italian Government
Federal Government   Imperial Government
National Government   His Majesty's Government
Government ownership

Do not capitalize *government* when referring to that of a State in the United States or to that of any possession of the United States.

21. Capitalize *Constitution* when referring to that of the United States.

James Madison wrote the Constitution.
James Madison was called the Father of the Constitution.
The Constitution of the United States of America was adopted in 1789.
The Constitutional Convention of Philadelphia set up the Federal Government of the United States.
Constitutional Committee, Constitutional Amendment.

Note the "down" style of capitalization in the following news item:

The nullification of the fourteenth amendment in congress has given the United States a form of representative government for which the constitution does not provide.

Chicago Tribune

22. Capitalize any United States Government commission when it is designated by its name.

Interstate Commerce Commission
Commission of Fine Arts
International Waterways Commission
National Forest Reservation Commission
U. S. Tariff Commission
Reciprocity Commission
Commission on Country Life

Also capitalize *commission* when standing alone, if it refers to a commission already named.

9

23. Capitalize all names of state legislatures when used with the name of the state and all names of national legislatures and their branches.

> the Assembly of New York
> the Ohio House of Representatives
> the General Court of Massachusetts
> British Parliament
> Chamber of Deputies
> Reichstag
> the Sixty-ninth Congress

But do not capitalize *assembly, general court, the legislature,* if they stand alone without the name of the state to which they belong. Do not capitalize *national legislature,* meaning the United States Congress, or *city legislature,* meaning City Councils or Board of Aldermen; or *executive session, special session.*

24. Capitalize *nation* when used as a synonym for the United States, or when used with a name to designate a definite nation.

> What are we going to do with the influence and power of this great Nation?   WOODROW WILSON
> *But,* What great nation in such circumstances would not have taken up arms?   WOODROW WILSON
> The Six Nations lived within the boundaries of New York.

Capitalize *national* when preceding a capitalized word.

> National Capital
> National Academy of Sciences
> The National Government
> *But,* national ideas, national pride
> The national defence demands not merely force but intelligence.   ELIHU ROOT

25. Capitalize *state* when used with a name or when used in place of the name.

New York State	State ticket
the State of Ohio	State government
the State leaders	State Democratic headquarters

Capitalize *state* in the following:

State prison	State's evidence
State rights	State banking division
State's attorney	

26. Capitalize all names of political parties and their adherents; names of royal families and dynasties.

Democrats	Non-Partisan
Republicans	Wets
Fascisti	Drys
House of Windsor	Socialists
Soviet	House of Stuart

Usage varies as to capitalization of *party*. Mawson in *Style-Book for Writers and Editors,* the *New York Times,* and the *New York World* capitalize *party,* as, Republican Party; the *Manual of Style,* the *New York Herald Tribune,* and the *New York Sun* do not capitalize it, as, Republican party.

27. Capitalize names of clubs, associations, institutions, orders, and companies.

> Union League Club
> Tammany Hall
> University Club of New York
> American Association of University Women
> American Association for the Advancement of Science
> Young Women's Hebrew Association
> American Academy of Arts and Letters
> English Speaking Union
> Knights of Columbus
> Order of the Sacred Heart
> American Ice Company

Do not capitalize *club, association, union, college,* or *university* when used alone, unless it has the value of a proper name.

> I will meet you at the Club this afternoon.
> The clubs and associations of this city are numerous.
> He belonged to a carpenter's union.
> The Association voted on the question of dues.

Note the following illustrations of the "down" style of capitalization in regard to names of clubs, associations, etc.

> The Chicago chapter of the Connecticut College Alumnae *association* is to meet for dinner this evening at the Chicago College *club,* after which the annual election of officers will take place. Mrs. Clarence Silber is now the president. *Chicago Tribune*

> Dr. Nicholas Murray Butler, President of Columbia University, was elected President yesterday of the American Academy of Arts and Letters. He succeeds William Milligan Sloane, who died in office. Archer M. Huntington nominated the Columbia President at a meeting of the Board of Directors of the *academy* in the Academy Building, No. 633 West 155th Street.
>
> *The World*

28. Capitalize names of squares, parks, towers, monuments, statues, buildings, thoroughfares.

Union Square	Trinity Church
the Tower of London	the Washington Monument
Park Row	or the Monument
Gramercy Park	the House (National)
the Mall	Halls of Congress
Eiffel Tower	the Capitol Grounds
the Capitol (Washington)	the Lincoln Memorial
the Congressional Library	Capitol Halls of Congress
the Library of Congress	the Senate (National)
El Bethel Synagogue	Governor's Mansion
Avery Library	Kingsway
the Hall of Fame	the Lincoln Highway
the Executive Mansion	Capitol Chamber
Mansion House (London)	Westminster Abbey
the Guild Theater	Champs Elysées
the White House	

But, the statue of Lincoln, the tomb of Washington.

In some telephone and city directories, and in many newspapers the words *avenue, street, boulevard, square, place* and *court* are not written with initial capitals, even when used to indicate particular places. *English Grammar and Composition* CLARENCE STRATTON

CAPITALIZATION

Construction of a new Y. M. C. A. building at Grove *street* and Elmwood *avenue,* Evanston, will begin this week, it was announced yesterday by Edward Sherman, chairman of the building committee. *News Item* from *Chicago Tribune*

Mr. Augustus Dinkler, of Waterbury, Conn., formerly of Narberth, is the guest for a few days of Mr. and Mrs. Newlin Wismer, of 210 Essex *avenue,* Narberth. *News Item* from *Public Ledger*

When such words as *street, boulevard, river,* etc., are pluralized and used with a proper noun, they are not capitalized unless they precede the proper noun. *Stratton*

The men were overtaken by Detectives Benjamin, Cocozza, and Bechtel at 11th and Fitzwater *streets* after the detectives had followed them from 11th and South *streets. News Item* from *Public Ledger*

> Avery and Law libraries
> Trinity and Grace churches
> Union and Pershing squares

Place references when merely descriptive and preceded by *the* and a definite name are not capitalized.

the river Dee   the valley of the Susquehanna

(1) The *Style Manual* lists the following geographical terms to be capitalized in the singular or plural, immediately following the name:

aqueduct	glacier	park
archipelago	group	passage
basin	gulch	peninsula
bend	harbor	plateau
branch (stream)	hill	pond
butte	hollow	range (mountains)
canal	inlet	reef
channel	island	ridge
county	light	run (stream)
crater	mesa	shoal
creek	mountain	sound
draw (stream)	narrows	township
flats	nation (Oklahoma)	tunnel
fork (stream)	ocean	
gap	parish (Louisiana)	

(2) The *Style Manual* lists the following to be capitalized, singular or plural, when they stand before a name or after it, or when they are used as a part of a name:

bay	lake
bayou	mount
camp (military)	oasis
cape	pass
Dalles (the)	peak
desert	port (but port of New York)
falls	river
fort	sea
head	strait
isle	valley

(3) Capitalize the following when used with a name, a number, or a letter (*Government Usage*):

breakwater	levee
chute	light
dam	lighthouse
dike	light station
dock	lock
dry dock	pier
dune	reservoir
ferry	slip
forest	weir
jetty	woods
landing	

29. Capitalize special names of countries or regions of countries, cities or sections of cities, countries, rivers, bays, oceans, mountains, islands, and other geographical words.

New World	the Continent (but, the continent of Europe)
Old World	
the Levant	Greater New York
Middle West	the Southland
Orient	the West End (London)
Occident	the Stock Yards (Chicago)
the Northwest Pacific States	the North End (Boston)
Far East	the North Drive (Chicago)
Near East	the Right and Left Bank
the Empire State	(Paris)

Beacon Hill (Boston)	Bay of Biscay
the Border (Scotland)	Atlantic Ocean
South America	Isle of Man
New Orleans	Strait of Gibraltar
Livingston County	English Channel
Hudson River	

In the South and in the Border States the Democrats rest their claims upon past majorities. *New York Evening Post*

30. Capitalize points of the compass when they designate geographical parts of the country.

The South has increased its manufactures.
Election returns from the East are eagerly awaited.
The North took a decided stand on the question.
The West has never understood the Orient, and it has been reserved for a few of our great scholars to penetrate to an understanding of the beliefs and convictions that have so long ruled the life of the Oriental peoples.

NICHOLAS MURRAY BUTLER

Do not capitalize such words when used merely to indicate direction.

—in Virginia and the colonies to the north and south of her.

WOODROW WILSON

(1) Do not capitalize adjectives derived from regional names when they are merely descriptive in character.

continental customs	oriental life
western hospitality	southern cooking
eastern fashions	

(2) Capitalize *northern, southern, western, eastern*, etc., when used as a part of proper names to designate a world division; do not capitalize such words when used to indicate parts of states.

Central and Southwestern Europe	western New York
	eastern Pennsylvania
Eastern Asia	southern California
West South Africa	northern Idaho
Northern Italy	

15

(3) Capitalize nouns referring to the inhabitants of different sections of the country.

Northerner	Westerner
Easterner	Southerner

31. Capitalize all proper names denoting political divisions.

British Empire	the Papal States
French Republic	the Pine Tree State
the Dominion of Canada	Ward Ten
the Commonwealth of Massa-chusetts	Nineteenth District
	Fourth Precinct
the Republic (United States)	Thirteenth Congressional District
the South American Republics	trict
Thornton Township	

32. Capitalize *college, university, seminary, school, high school,* when used with a proper name; but when such words are used alone do not capitalize unless the word stands for a definite college or university and has the value of a proper name.

Elmira College	Oak Park High School
the College of Fine Arts	Bacon Academy
the School of Philosophy	the Academy (Athens)
the Graduate School	Students Hall

33. Capitalize *church* when used with a name to designate a body of religious belief or a building and also when it designates the Church Universal; capitalize *cathedral, synagogue,* and *chapel* when used with a name.

the Roman Church	the Cathedral of St. John the Divine
the Church of England	
High Church	St. Patrick's Cathedral
Low Church	the National Cathedral
Protestant Episcopal Church	Beth-El and Emanuel Syna-gogue
the Presbyterian Church	
the dignitaries of the Church	Free Synagogue
Church and State	

When *church, cathedral, synagogue, chapel* are used without a name or in a general sense, do not capitalize them.

church history
church altars
cathedrals of France

synagogue services
chapel exercises

34. Capitalize all names for the Bible, for parts and versions of the Bible, and all names of other sacred books.

Bible
Scriptures
Holy Writ
Word of God
Holy Bible
Breeches Bible
Old Testament
New Testament
Pentateuch
the Ten Commandments
Gospels (*but,* gospel teachings)

Lord's Prayer
Twenty-third Psalm
Gospel of Mark
King James Version
Authorized Version
Septuagint
Vulgate Version
Revised Version
Koran
Talmud
Apocrypha

Do not capitalize adjectives derived from such nouns.
Manual of Style

biblical
koranic

apocryphal
scriptural

Text Type and Style, however, capitalizes *Biblical* and *Scriptural.*

35. Capitalize all names for the Deity.

Father
Almighty
Judge of Nations
Jehovah
Supreme Being
First Cause
Divine Providence
Lord God of Hosts

Messiah the Comforter
Son of Man
King of the Jews
Holy Ghost
Holy Spirit
Holy Trinity
Redeemer
Saviour

Do not capitalize *fatherhood, sonship, messiahship, messianic.*

36. Capitalize the *Virgin Mary,* the *Virgin,* the *Blessed Virgin, Madonna,* the *Holy Mother, Our Lady.*

17

37. Do not capitalize the word *goddess* when referring to heathen deities.

> When the daughter of Jupiter presented herself among a crowd of goddesses, she was distinguished by her graceful stature and superior beauty.
>
> ADDISON

38. In the Bible and in the Book of Common Prayer, pronouns relating to the Deity are not capitalized.

> O Lord, thou hast been our dwelling-place in all generations. And he looked up and saw the rich men that were casting their gifts into the treasury.

Opinions of publishers of other books differ in regard to the capitalization of pronouns relating to the Deity.

The nominative and the accusative of the personal pronouns—He and Him, Thou and Thee—are capitalized in this connection, but not the possessives, his and thine. *Text, Type and Style*

All pronouns referring to the same (the Supreme Being, or any member of the Christian Trinity) when not closely preceded or followed by a distinct reference to the Deity should be capitalized.

> "Trust Him who rules all things" (but; "When God worked six days, he rested the seventh.")
>
> *Manual of Style*

39. Capitalize *Heaven* when referring to the Deity, and *Paradise* and *Heaven* only when referring to a future abode; also *Hades,* but not *hell. New York Times Style Book*

> Her prayers, whom Heaven delights to hear.   SHAKESPERE
> New Thoughts of God, new hopes of Heaven.   KEBLE
> O bed! bed! bed! delicious bed!
> That heaven upon earth to the weary head.   HOOD
> He descended into hell.   *Book of Common Prayer*
> And in Hades, he lifted up his eyes, being in torment.
> *Gospel of Luke, Revised Version*

40. Capitalize the Pope, or the Popes, always; also Holy Father and Pontiff, meaning the Pope; Cardinal, Apostolic

Delegate, Archbishop, Bishop, Moderator and Presiding Elder before personal names; also when used separately after the person has been named or when used in direct reference to persons holding office. *New York Times Style Book*

> Every heart that has not been blinded and hardened by this terrible war must be touched by this moving appeal of his Holiness, the Pope. WOODROW WILSON

41. Capitalize all names of creeds and confessions of faith and general biblical terms.

the Apostles' Creed	the Westminster Catechism
Nicene Creed	Thirty-nine Articles
Athanasian Creed	Lord's Supper
Westminster Confession of Faith	

42. Capitalize *Devil,* the *Evil One,* the *Adversary,* the *Father of Lies,* and *Beelzebub* meaning Satan.

Do not capitalize when used in a general sense or as an expletive.

> "The beggar is in the saddle at last," cries Proverbial Wisdom. "Why, in the name of all former experience, doesn't he ride to the Devil?"
>
> JAMES RUSSELL LOWELL

> And the great dragon was cast out, that old serpent, called the Devil, and Satan, which deceiveth the whole world.
>
> *Rev.* 12:9

> The things, we know, are neither rich nor rare.
> But wonder how the devil they got there.
>
> POPE

43. Capitalize all names of holy days and holidays.

Christmas	New Year's Day
Easter	Thanksgiving Day
Good Friday	Fourth of July
Labor Day	Columbus Day
Yom Kippur	Passover
Feast of Tabernacles	All Saints' Day
Whitsuntide	Michaelmas
Memorial Day	Lincoln's Birthday

44. Capitalize the first word of every complete quotation.

In one of his letters, Franklin K. Lane wrote, "To be gay one must see how very little some things are."

(1) Do not capitalize the first word of a direct quotation if this quotation is introduced indirectly in the text.

Lincoln ended his famous speech at Gettysburg with a plea for government "of the people, for the people, and by the people."

It was said by Roosevelt that "no people on earth have more cause to be thankful than ours."

(2) Do not capitalize that part of a quotation resumed within the same sentence.

"Nature," said Lowell, "abhors the credit system."

(3) Capitalize the first word of a question made in direct form but not quoted.

1789 asked of a thing, Is it rational? 1642 asked of a thing, Is it legal? or, when it went further, Is it according to conscience?—Sir M. Foster (Quoted in *Text, Type, and Style*)

(4) Do not capitalize the first words of an indirect question or statement.

He asked what was the meaning of the party's steady growth in power.

Stevenson says that it is charm which is the basis of enduring art.

(5) Do not capitalize a partial quotation when this quotation is used as a motto on a title page or as a heading of a chapter; as,

. . . a letter may be written upon anything or nothing just as that anything or nothing happens to occur.

William Cowper

On introductory page to Part V, Letters, in *Harper's Anthology of Prose*

(6) Do not capitalize a parenthetical statement that occurs in the middle of a sentence.

The enclosed matter either falls between the parts of a sentence or follows a sentence. When within a sentence the enclosed matter does not begin with a capital letter even though a full sentence, unless the first word is a proper noun, nor does it take a period at the end. If, however, the language is either interrogative or exclamatory, it takes the proper mark to show this; and such mark is placed within the parenthesis or brackets. *Why We Punctuate,* W. L. KLEIN

The clanging of the ambulance bell (for I had been brought to the hospital in an ambulance) was still ringing in my ears as the attendants tied me to a bed.   *Scribner's Magazine*

"We're going to annoy you, Worth!" (He kept on reading.) "We've invented a new game." (At this he appeared interested.) "It's called 'Eenie, meenie, minee, moe'—you get out and I go to Central Islip, or vice versa." Worth actually smiled.

Scribner's Magazine

45. Capitalize the first word of exclamatory or of interrogative sentences used in a series.

Not believe in Santa Claus! You might as well not believe in fairies!

FRANCIS R. CHURCH in *The New York Sun*

The pale nymphs dancing at dawn, in a landscape of Corot's, —are they not formed from the dawn itself, from the first shafts and glimmerings of light on the forest's edge? And may not myths have been evolved in the same manner?

SOPHIA KIRK

46. Capitalize *Whereas* and *Resolved* in resolutions and generally the first word following them. (See pp. 260-273.)

Whereas, The United States Tariff Commission————
Be it *Resolved,* That the President of the Senate————

47. Capitalize the definite article *the* when it is a part of a proper name or of a title belonging to a person, to a book, or to a work of art, or when incorporated as part of the legal name of a company, a corporation, or an institution.

The Hague
The Right Reverend Bishop Manning
The Honorable William E. Borah
The Prisoner of Zenda
The Sistine Madonna
The Federal Sugar Refining Company

Most authorities do not, in referring to the title of a newspaper, capitalize the article *the* even when it is a part of the actual title.

> Do you take the *Chicago Tribune?*
> You will find the *Boston Transcript* a conservatively edited newspaper.

The New York Times, however, capitalizes the article *the* when it is a part of the actual title.

> The owner of *The New York Times* is Adolph S. Ochs.

Note also that the article *a* is capitalized when it is part of the title.

> A Tale of Two Cities
> A Midsummer Night's Dream

48. Capitalize all references to divisions or parts of a specific work.

> The Preface of the textbook is interesting.
> Look in the Table of Contents.
> The Index is well arranged.
> The Introduction to the text presents biographical information.
> Look in the Appendix for further information.

Do not capitalize these when used in a general sense; as,

> We learned how to make an index.

49. Capitalize the names of the seasons only when they are personified or when they are referred to specifically.

> If Winter comes, can Spring be far behind?   SHELLEY
> We are going in the spring.
> The Spring of 1930.

50. Capitalize words personified.

> Sport that wrinkled Care derides,
> And Laughter holding both his sides.
>
>   MILTON

CAPITALIZATION

For emphasis in advertisements and in journalistic writing and for humorous effect, many writers capitalize important words.

A Married Couple possessed two Boys named Joseph and Clarence. Joseph was much older. His Parents brought him up on a Plan of their Own. They would not permit him to play with other Boys for fear that he would soil himself, and learn to be Rude and Boisterous.

GEORGE ADE

As the practice of capitalizing personified terms gives rather an old-fashioned appearance, some modern writers disregard it.

51. Capitalize the pronoun *I* and the interjection *O*; also Roman numerals and letters used separately as abbreviations or to indicate paragraphs or divisions in a subject.

OK, Paragraph B, Article II

52. Capitalize nouns followed by a capitalized Roman numeral; as,

Act I, Vol. V.

Often *in references* such nouns and Roman numerals are not capitalized.

53. Capitalize all principal words (that is, nouns, pronouns, adjectives, adverbs, verbs, first and last words) in titles of books, pictures, plays, musical compositions, documents, reports, papers, proceedings, captions, display lines, headings.

Books	The Son of the Middle Border
	Mark Twain's Letters
Pictures	Raphael's Madonna of the Grand Duke
	The Last Supper
Plays	The Merchant of Venice
	They Knew What They Wanted
	She Stoops to Conquer
Musical Compositions	
	Beethoven's Fifth Symphony
	The Moonlight Sonata
	The Pirates of Penzance
	Chopin's Nocturne, Opus 37, No. 2

Documents, Reports, and Proceedings
>> The Covenant of the League of Nations
>> The Report of the Committee on Vocational Education
>> The Proceedings of the Modern Language Association

Captions   Aloft They Soar in Their Air Taxis
>> At the Flying Fields Adventurers of All Types Get New Thrills

A style has sprung up lately of printing book catalogues without capitals—sometimes, even, words which should be printed with a capital occurring in any other place. No advantage whatever is gained by this, and the common practice is always the best.

>> *Proof-Reading and Style,* JOHN FRANKLIN DOBBS

Do not capitalize subdivisions and their abbreviations in literary references.

article—art.	line—l.	page—p.	verse—vs.
chapter—chap.	note—n.	section—sec.	volume—vol.

54. Capitalize scientific names of the world's eras, common names for historical epochs, periods in the history of literature or language, and important events.

the Neolithic age	the Wars of the Roses
the Paleozoic period	Colonial days
the Fourth Glacial age	Revolutionary period
the Dark Ages	the days of the Empire
the Christian Era	the Civil War
the Crusades	the World War
the Middle Ages	the Louisiana Purchase
the Renaissance	the Battle of Bull Run
the Exile	Armistice Day

55. Capitalize all names of the bodies of the solar system except the words *earth, moon, stars,* and *sun* unless they are personified.

the Milky Way	Orion
the Great Bear	Cassiopeia's Chair
the Big Dipper	the North Star
Venus	the Southern Cross

CAPITALIZATION

56. Capitalize in botanical and zoological matter the names of species if derived from proper names of persons or when the specific name is or has been used as a generic name. *Manual of Style*

Cedrus libani	Styrax californica
Felis leo	Lythrum hyssopifolia
Cocos nucifera	Phyteuma Halleri
Carex Halleriana	

57. In geological and medical matter the names of species are never capitalized. *Manual of Style*

Pterygometopus schmidti	Conodectes favosus

58. Do not capitalize such abbreviations as *e.g., i.e., viz.,* etc.

59. Abbreviations for forenoon and afternoon may be written as follows:

A. M.	or	a. m.
P. M.	or	p. m.

60. Do not capitalize units of measurements such as 6 *ft.,* 4 *lbs.,* 3 *qts.*

61. Capitalize the trade names of manufactured products.

Bon Ami	Nash car
Force	Pears' soap
Hudson Super Six	Quaker Oats

62. Capitalize most adjectives formed from proper nouns

British	Olympian
Canadian	Pan-American
Chesterfieldian	Pan-German
Ciceronian	Pan-Hellenic
Darwinian	Papal
Elizabethan	Parisian
Gregorian	Romanist
Hellenic	Rooseveltian
Homeric	Semitic
Johnsonian	Swiss
Latin	Victorian
Napoleonic	Wilsonian

63. A list of words and expressions showing their generally accepted capitalization follows:

American history	india rubber
Americanism	Iroquois nation
Americanization	italicize
Anglo-French entente	italics
anti-Romanist	lyonnaise potatoes
artesian well	macadamized roads
Axminster carpet	mansard roof
Basque customs	mercurial
boycott	morocco leather
Breton lace	pagan belief
Caucasian race	plaster of paris
Cheshire cat	Pompeian red
Cheshire cheese	poor whites
china (the ware)	pro-British
chinaware	Pullman car
colored people	Red Man
delftware	Roentgen rays
English literature	roman type
French leave	Romanize
Georgian architecture	tantalize
Georgian era	Venetian blinds
Gothic type	Wedgwood ware

REFERENCE BOOKS

Handbook of Style, A. Compiled by Frank D. Halsey. Princeton University Press.

Manual of Style with Specimens of Type, A. The University of Chicago Press.

Style Manual of the Government Printing Office, The.

Style Book, The New York Times.

Style Book for Writers and Editors. C. O. SYLVESTER MAWSON. Thomas Y. Crowell Company.

Text, Type, and Style; a Compendium of Atlantic Usage. GEORGE B. IVES. The Atlantic Monthly Press.

DE VINNE, THEODORE L., *Correct Composition.* The Century Company.

HART, HORACE. *Rules for Compositors and Readers at the University Press.* Oxford.

HOTCHKISS and KILDUFF. *Handbook of Business English.* Harper and Brothers.

KLEIN, WILLIAM LIVINGSTON. *Why We Punctuate; or, Reason versus Rule in the Use of Marks.* The Lancet Publishing Company, Minneapolis, Minn.

SUMMEY, GEORGE, JR. *Modern Punctuation.* Oxford University Press.

CAPITALIZATION

Woolley and Scott. *College Handbook of Composition*. D. C. Heath and Company.

Who's Who. A. & C. Black, Ltd.

Who's Who in America. Edited by Albert Nelson Marquis. Chicago, The A. N. Marquis Company, 1928-1929.

The Social Register.

CHAPTER II

PUNCTUATION

THE PERIOD

1. Place a period at the end of a declarative sentence.

The pure scientists are the advance guard of civilization.

2. Place a period after a request.

Will you please give me a copy of the Summer Session Catalogue of Columbia University.
May I have your answer by next Friday.
May I not help you with your problem of reorganization of the Advertising Department.

A technically interrogative sentence—disguised as a question out of courtesy but actually embodying a request—does not need the interrogation point. *Manual of Style* [1]

Will you kindly sign and return the inclosed card.

In the following sentence interrogative form is merely a form of courtesy. The period is better than the question mark would be.

Will you please quote prices for (1) 200 copies in paper, (2) 300 copies in regular cloth binding, and (3) 25 copies in library binding. *Modern Punctuation,* GEORGE SUMMEY

3. Do not place a period after MS [1] (manuscript); after Mme and Mlle in French (American usage, Mme. and Mlle.); after letters of technical matter of well-known publications; as PMLA (Publications of Modern Language Association) or after abbreviations for linguistic epochs, as OE (Old English), MHG (Middle High German).

[1] *Manual of Style:* p. 85, (*b*); p. 72.

4. Do not place a period after Roman numerals unless they are in a table of contents, or other enumerative parts of a list.

Vol. X   George V
    I. The Development of the Letter
   II. Letter Arrangement
  III. What Enters into the Making of a Letter

5. Do not place a period after letters when they designate a person, as *Mr. A has paid his monthly interest;* but place periods after letters when they mark the chief division of a subject.

  I. The Nationalizing Influences in Greece
      A. Common Race
      B. Common Language
      C. Religious Institutions
        1. Oracles
        2. Delphic Amphictyony
        3. National Games
        4. Festivals
      D. Political Leagues

6. Place a period before a decimal; and after pounds, shillings, and pence.

24.55   £10.   5s.   10d.

7. A period may be used between figures denoting hours and minutes; as, 10.15. (See pp. 47, 83.)

8. Place the period inside the parentheses when they inclose an independent declarative sentence.[1] (See p. 58.)

"Orchestra?" repeated Ben, in a puzzled voice.
"The crickets." (She tried not to make it sound like an explanation.) "I'd forgotten that nights on the Island were like this."

CHRISTOPHER MORLEY

9. Place the period outside the parentheses when the enclosed matter forms a part of the preceding statement.

[1] *Manual of Style:* p. 83, 172; *College Handbook of Composition,* Woolley and Scott; p. 206, (*b*).

H. Poincaré, *Science and Method* (trans., pp. 54-55) (Footnote in *The Art of Thought*).

GRAHAM WALLAS

The base, ribbed and scarred by the lava flows of centuries, stood out boldly in support of the whole, like the flying buttresses of a Gothic cathedral (see illustrations, pages 57-60).

Orator, statesman, philosopher, rhetorician, and letter writer was the great Marcus Tullius Cicero (B. C. 106-B. C. 43).

JOHN B. OPDYCKE

10. Place a period inside quotation marks. (See p. 53.)

I am going to read Tomlinson's "Gifts of Fortune."

"I am not afraid of work," said Gissing. "But I'm looking for horizons. In my work, I could never find any."

CHRISTOPHER MORLEY

11. Omit the period after all display lines; after running heads; after centered headlines; after side-heads set in separate lines; after cut-in heads; after box-heads in tables; after superscriptions and legends that do not make more than a single line of type; after items in enumerated lists; after date lines heading communications; and after signatures. *Manual of Style*

12. Do not place a period after chemical symbols, the words indicating size of books, or the words "per cent." *Manual of Style*

H_2O 16mo   10 per cent

THE COMMA

1. Use a comma to separate words and phrases in a series.

The ground, the turf, the atmosphere of an old orchard, seem several stages nearer to man than that of the adjoining field.

JOHN BURROUGHS

Present usage advocates the use of the comma before *and* connecting the last two words of a series.

If we would cultivate ourselves in the use of English, we must make our daily talk accurate, daring, and full.

GEORGE HERBERT PALMER

Chess players, mathematicians, and organists are clannish, as all are workers in mysteries.

The Atlantic Monthly

I recall the covered bridge across the Androscoggin at Bethel, with ancient circus posters flaring from the dusty walls, with tin placards on every beam proclaiming some magic spavin cure, with bits of hay hanging from the cobwebs, pulled from a towering load recently passed through, and finally with exquisite landscapes of the great curve of the river, the green fields, and the far blue peaks of the Presidentials, framed through the square windows—for every covered bridge is lighted by square windows at orthodox intervals.

WALTER PRICHARD EATON

(1) Do not use a comma when the conjunction connects all the words in a series.

Men and puppies and dolphins and baby lions, it is true, obedient to a kind of play principle in the universe, have disported themselves since the beginning of time.

ROBERT L. DUFFUS

The soul of the largest and wealthiest and proudest nation may well go half-way to meet that of its poets.

WALT WHITMAN

There was in it (the song of a thrush) youth and hope and spring and glories of dawns and sunsets and moonlight and the sound of the wind far away.

SAMUEL SCOVILLE, JR.

(2) Do not use a comma between the last two adjectives preceding a noun if the last adjective more closely relates to the noun than do the others.

A State road runs northward by my door, dropping at length, through rolling fields, to a *pretty little* valley threaded by a *clear mountain* brook, and swinging across a neat bridge into an elm-shaded village.

WALTER PRICHARD EATON

2. Use a comma to separate pairs of words in a series.

Arbutus and violets, crocuses and snowdrops, daffodils and jonquils bloom early.

3. Use a comma to separate the name of the person addressed or his title from the rest of the sentence.

I believe, Mr. Cameron, that insurance is advisable for protection.

Certainly, sir, no one will assert that Henry Clay in that transaction performed an obscure, or even a common part.

W. H. SEWARD

Keep up your spirits, my boy, until I write you another letter.

T. B. ALDRICH

4. Use a comma to set off words in apposition.

Brigadier General Hugh A. Drum, Commander of the First Division, U. S. Army, formerly War Plans Officer of the General Staff, addressed reserve officers of the Metropolitan district last night at the De Witt Clinton High School.

News Item

Kessler and Alder, great tragedians both, once trod the board with no more than a sentimental notice from the world uptown.

The American Mercury

(1) The compound personal pronouns (myself, himself, herself, etc.) are not set off from words which they emphasize.

Stevenson himself confesses, but with no trace of egotism, that it is charm which is the basis of enduring art.

(2) Also do not use the comma when the word or phrase is in italics or is set apart by some other device.

The word *caprice* is derived from the Latin word *caper*.

Some few years ago painters coined the word "expressionism."

JOHN GALSWORTHY

(3) Omit the comma in the following:

    a. When the appositive has become part of the proper name.

Cedric the Saxon   William the Conqueror

    b. When the connection is unusually close between the appositive and the word it modifies.

        My sister Isabel paid the mortgages.
        My friend Mary called yesterday.

5. Use a comma to set off inverted names in bibliographies, in directories, or in other reference lists. (See p. 313.)

Cleveland, Grover   Lane, Franklin K.
Eliot, Charles W., LL.D.   Taylor, Howard C., Dr.

6. Use a comma to separate a name from a title that follows it.

Glenn Frank, President of the University of Wisconsin
Simon Flexner, M.D.

7. Use a comma to set off a contrasted word, phrase, or clause.

Idling, in the true sense, is a gracious, not an inane thing.
HELEN COATE CREW

In regard to inspiration man is passive, not active.
ROBERT W. S. MENDL

Unlike the builders of the Renaissance, our engineers are not yet artists.
WALTER PRICHARD EATON

The rule works both ways: The higher the yield, the less the safety; the greater the safety, the less the yield.

8. Use a comma to set off a transitional word or expression.

Moreover, a series of short unrelated problems does not sustain the interest.
ABBOTT LAWRENCE LOWELL

On the contrary, it is very clear that native good judgment and good feeling are not proportional to education.
CHARLES WILLIAM ELIOT

Of course, the subway has its incidental charms—its gay fresco of advertisements, for instance, and its faint mysterious thunder when it runs near the surface of the street on which we stand.
JOYCE KILMER

In conclusion, then, let it be stated again that the secretary in going into a new position has a vast amount of information to acquire.
EDWARD J. KILDUFF

We need not wonder, then, if perfect sentences are rare, and perfect pages rarer.
R. L. STEVENSON

All that we can say, therefore, as to the choice of words, is that we should use the words which fit the thought, whether they are Saxon or Latin.

GEORGE PHILIP KRAPP

9. Use a comma to set off parenthetical words, phrases, and clauses.

1. He, however, hurried forward, led by instinct towards an unknown goal.

HANS CHRISTIAN ANDERSEN

2. The foreign born, in fact, compose only fifty per cent of the East Side population.

News Item

3. All students, except aliens, are required to attend exercises in military drill.

University Bulletin

4. A recent writer, it is true, has done much to show that the general reader daily indulges in poetry of a kind without knowing it.

HENRY SEIDEL CANBY

5. Travel, we are often told, gives light to the mind.

H. M. TOMLINSON

10. Use a comma to indicate the omission of a word.

The former lead to the degree of Bachelor of Science or Bachelor in Architecture; the latter, to the degree of Master in Architecture, Master in Science, Doctor of Philosophy, Doctor of Science, Doctor of Public Health.

Bulletin, Massachusetts Institute of Technology

Often, however, commas are omitted, if the meaning is clear without them.

The Englishman's virtue is wisdom; the Frenchman's is reason; the Spaniard's serenity.

SALVADOR DE MADARIAGA

11. Use a comma to set off light exclamations.

Ah, if it were only the ocean to cross, it would be a matter of small thought to me—and great pleasure.

R. L. STEVENSON

12. Use a comma to set off a phrase denoting residence or position.

> Mr. Alexander Vanderpoll, of Larchmont, New York, addressed the meeting.

Also written:

> Mr. Alexander Vanderpoll of Larchmont, New York.
> Miss Gertrude Mitchell, 420 West 116 Street, New York.
> The plans will be placed on exhibition today at the present headquarters of the museum in the Gracie Mansion, East River and Eighty-eighth Street, and will remain there until April 16.
> *News Item*

13. Use a comma in dates.

> The book was published on February 25, 1920.

A comma usually separates the month from the year when the day of the month is omitted, as June, 1927; but modern usage permits June 1927.

14. Use a comma to set off figures in groups of more than four; as, 1,000,000; 31,842. (See p. 79.)

15. If such introductory words as *as, for example, for instance, e.g., namely, viz., that is, i.e.,* and the terms following form parenthetical expressions and do not introduce enumerations, a comma precedes and follows the introductory word. (See p. 43.)

> Many of our American universities, for example, Harvard, offer excellent courses in business.

> You know that our November holiday, that is, Thanksgiving, was a New England institution.

> Perhaps the most important factor of all is the psychological one, namely, the charm of aviation, for this means that the whole weight of American sentiment is behind this industry.

16. Use a comma to mark off phrases of the following kinds:

(1) Introductory adverbial phrases out of their natural order or phrases not closely connected with the rest of the sentence.

In the beginning, I know there was nothing more unusual in the things about me than a motor-car standing by the entrance to a dull, palatial, and expensive hotel on the Devon coast.

H. M. TOMLINSON

Here—in this excellent civilized, antipodal club smoking-room, I have just read the first part of your *Solution*.

R. L. STEVENSON in a letter to Henry James

Like a spear of silver piercing the velvet dusk, the Graf Zeppelin nosed her way to rest on the landing field.

News Item, Boston Herald

To be happy, we all need a certain tenacity and continuity of aim and view.

A. C. BENSON

(2) Introductory absolute phrases.

The matter being decided, the President continued his report.

Generally speaking, a ship outranged is a ship defeated.

To quote your heading to my wife, I think no man writes so elegant a letter.

R. L. STEVENSON in a letter to Henry James

(3) Descriptive phrases following the noun they modify.

The stock, having reached 175, remained there for three weeks.

The child, pale with fatigue, waited for her mother.

17. Use a comma after a dependent adverbial clause which precedes the main clause.

Although that immense country house was empty and for sale, and I had got an order to view it, I needed all my courage to walk through the lordly gates, and up the avenue, and then ring the door-bell.

LOGAN PEARSALL SMITH

If nature did much for Athens, it is undeniable that art did much more.

JOHN HENRY NEWMAN

Note that when the subject of the dependent clause is the same as that of the independent clause following it, the comma is sometimes omitted.

Before I began to write novels I had forgotten all I learned at school and college.

JOHN GALSWORTHY

Note that when the dependent clause follows the main clause, the comma is usually omitted.

He was always at hand when there was difficult work to do. He saw that some causes of international jealousy and of war would be removed if the grosser forms of exploitation of labor and the more distressing kinds of competition in this field . . . were eliminated.

The New York Times

18. Use a comma to precede dependent clauses introduced by *for, since, as,* showing reason.

It was that smile of Lindbergh's, for in it there was that terrible wisdom of youth, a wisdom baffling their arithmetic.

W. O. McGEEHAN

Students are strongly advised to make payments by mail, as they will find it greatly to their convenience to do so.

University Bulletin

19. Use commas to separate the members of a compound sentence when the clauses are short and closely connected and contain no commas.

Annoyances were laughed at, our noisy behavior was overlooked, conversation took an agreeable turn, and a delightful air of cheerfulness and good humor pervaded the entire household.

AGNES REPPLIER

20. Use a comma to separate similar or identical words standing next to each other, even when the sense or continuation does not require it.

Whatever is, is right.

21. Use a comma to set off a non-restrictive adjective clause. Such a clause is one that is not needed to make the meaning clear.

37

Engraved letterheads, which convey the impression of dignity and reliability, add to the attractiveness of letter pictures.

22. Do not use a comma to set off a restrictive adjective clause. Such a clause is one that is needed to make the meaning clear.

(1) Every student who enters the Institute is given a physical examination.

(2) A man who beats his wife is shocking to us, and a colonel who cannot manage his soldiers without having them beaten is nearly equally so.

ANTHONY TROLLOPE

(3) Tall and slender of figure, with sharply cut features, and with a nervous quickness of manner; a fisherman who had taken a high place in his sport; an editorial writer who never tired of his work, and whose work never grew stale; a tireless reader, and a master of the art of quotation; a critic who was often keen but never malicious, Mr. Lang will stand as a type of writer more familiar to the French than to the English; a man whose national gifts would probably have stood out in clearer perspective had it not been for his immense industry and the wide range of his knowledge.

The Outlook

23. Use a comma to set off informal direct quotations.

"Isn't it remarkable," marvelled Tonseten, "that such things can spring up out of the very ground? This is truly a Promised Land."

O. E. RÖLVAAG

"Let our object be our country, our whole country, and nothing but our country," said Webster in his *First Bunker Hill Oration*.

Washington declared, in his *Farewell Address,* "Harmony and liberal intercourse with all nations, are recommended by policy, humanity, and interest."

Note that in an indirect quotation no comma is needed.

Washington said that we should not enter into political alliances with foreign nations.

24. Do not use a comma after a verb followed by an object noun clause introduced by *that, how, whether,* or *what.*

> They believed that such a system, in order to be efficient, must be carefully planned and controlled.
> Experience has shown how speed classes keep a stenographic force alert.
> The firm did not know whether or not it would be successful in its new venture.
> I learned what radio means to thousands of active-minded men and women, temporarily in drydock.
>
> *The New York Times*

25. Use a comma to set off numbers, words, phrases, and clauses that would otherwise not be clear.

> Wrong: For a dollar you can secure dinner or bed and breakfast.
> Right: For a dollar you can secure dinner, or bed and breakfast.
> Wrong: When I was about to begin the speech ended.
> Right: When I was about to begin, the speech ended.

26. For use of the comma with parentheses, see p. 58.

27. Notice the correct uses of the comma in the various parts of a letter.

FRIENDLY LETTER

WITH CLOSED PUNCTUATION [1]

Avon, New York,
April 10, 19—.

Dear Helen,

Sincerely yours,

(name)

[1] Closed punctuation means the use of punctuation after all letter parts.

BUSINESS LETTER WITH CLOSED PUNCTUATION

141 West 16 Street,
New York City,
April 6, 19–

Mr. Norman Read,
11 Cliff Way,
Larchmont, N. Y.

Dear Mr. Read:

Yours very truly,
HARRIET CHAMBERLAIN

BUSINESS LETTERS WITH OPEN PUNCTUATION

Modern usage, however, particularly in business letters where the block form is used, advocates open punctuation. The following illustrate accepted forms:

(1)

1700 Garfield Park
Chicago, Illinois
February 25, 19—

Miss Violet Powell
Gardner Terrace
Allston, Mass.

Dear Miss Powell

Yours very truly
Bessie McKenzie

(2)

Ripon, Wisconsin
602 Watson Street
June 30, 19—

Miss Emily Atkins
50 Jones Street
Jersey City, N. J.

Dear Miss Atkins:

Yours sincerely,
Rose Wolcott

(3)

1398 Main Street
Worcester   Mass
January 8   19—

Miss Maude Pfaffmann
437 Rochelle Terrace
Pelham   N. Y.

Dear Madam

Yours truly
Gladys Russell

THE SEMICOLON

1. Use a semicolon between the clauses of a compound sentence when the conjunction is omitted or when the connection is not close.

Some of us are wise in this way naturally and by genius; some of us never become so.

WILLIAM JAMES

A man of action may be thinking; a man of passion may be acting.

SALVADOR DE MADARIAGA

The sky was cloudless; the sun shone out bright and warm; the songs of birds and hum of myriads of summer insects filled the air; and the cottage garden, crowded with every rich and beautiful tint, sparkled in the heavy dew like beds of glittering jewels.

CHARLES DICKENS

He is at home in any society, he has common ground with every class; he knows when to speak and when to be silent; he is able to converse, he is able to listen; he can ask a question pertinently, and gain a lesson seasonably, when he has nothing to impart himself; he is ever ready, yet never in the way; he is a pleasant companion, and a comrade you can depend upon; he knows when to be serious and when to trifle with gracefulness and to be serious with effect.

JOHN HENRY NEWMAN

2. Use a semicolon to separate coordinate clauses when they are long or when they contain commas.

In writing about himself, he may assume a serious or semi-serious attitude; but more frequently he deals with his subject in a humorous, mock-serious, or even playful, personal gossip.

WILLIAM TURNER

3. Use the semicolon in lists of names with titles or addresses and in other lists which would not be clear if separated by commas. (See p. 5.)

Other speakers on this program were L. R. Alderman, Specialist in Adult Education in the U. S. Bureau of Education; Miss Willie Lawson, Deputy State Superintendent of Public Schools, Little Rock, Ark.; Edward L. Thorndike, Teachers College, Columbia University; and Reed Lewis, Director of Foreign Language Information Service, New York City.

News Item

In addition to foreign affairs, American life in cultural and political aspects will be covered by the ten regular staff lecturers of the league and by visitors to the league's platform. representing the following subjects: American poetry, Edna

PUNCTUATION

St. Vincent Millay and Christopher Morley; literature, John
Cowper Powys and William Lyon Phelps; stage, E. H. Sothern
and Peggy Wood; press, Walter Lippmann and Will Irwin;
social philosophy, Jane Addams and Will Durant; colleges,
William Starr Myers (Princeton) and Curtis Hidden Page
(Dartmouth); army, Major Gen. William R. Smith, West
Point; pulpit, Rev. S. Parkes Cadman.

News Item, The World

The earlier translations were the work of T. Nugent, 1771;
T. Roscoe, 1822; and J. A. Symonds, 1888.

Bibliographical References.

Political Conditions in the South in 1868.—Dunning, *Recon-
struction, Political* and *Economic.* (American Nation Series),
pp. 109-123; Hart, *American History Told by Contemporaries,*
Vol. IV, pp. 445-458, 497-500; Elson, *History of the United
States,* pp. 790-805.
    Psalms 23:1-4; 37:2-5; 91:1-10

4. Use a semicolon to separate groups of words, whether
phrases or clauses, dependent on a general term or statement.

We hold these truths to be self-evident,—that all men are
created equal; that they are endowed by their Creator with
certain inalienable rights; that among these are life, liberty, and
the pursuit of happiness.

THOMAS JEFFERSON

5. Use a semicolon to precede *for example, namely, for
instance, viz., to wit, as, i.e.,* when they come before "an
example or a classification of particulars or subjects enumerated." (See p. 35.)

Designs for decoration of chinaware have also been copied;
for example, the famous willow-tree pattern, a copy of Nanking
blue China, introduced to England in 1780 and now a collec-
tor's prize.

Boston Evening Transcript

Periodic reports, which are invariably administrative, may be
either public or private; that is, they may deal with the affairs
either of a community or of a business organization.

RAY PALMER BAKER

The qualities of the examination report are those which have been stressed in connection with the report as a type of literature; that is, completeness, clearness, and conciseness.

RAY PALMER BAKER

The course in Mechanical Engineering prepares the student to enter any one of the various branches of the profession; i.e., engine design, automatic design, locomotive construction, etc.

Boston Evening Transcript

The Catholic Church lays down rules and regulations; to wit, the Canon Law and the regulations made by the bishops of the several dioceses throughout the world for the conduct of its members.

Boston Evening Transcript

6. Use a semicolon to separate clauses joined by such words as *hence, moreover, however, also, therefore, consequently.*

The principles are almost universally accepted; hence you should learn them.

Altogether, the style of a writer is a faithful representative of his mind; therefore, if any man wishes to write a clear style, let him first be clear in his thoughts; and, if any would write in a noble style, let him first possess a noble soul, and live a noble life.

GOETHE

7. Place a semicolon after the parentheses when the parenthetical matter is explanatory of something that precedes.

Example: All marks (proofreader's) should be made in the margin on the same line as the error, and if there is more than one correction in a line, they should appear in their order separated by a slant line (i.e., cap/wf/tr/); if there are many, both margins may be used for marks.

Manual of Style

THE COLON

1. Use a colon to introduce a list.

In the preparation of every report, there are three distinct steps:

1. Formulating the plan
2. Making the examination
3. Writing the report

RAY PALMER BAKER

Examples of the use of the colon in lists taken from news items:

The final scores of the meet are: Manual Training, 20; DeWitt Clinton, 17; George Washington, 13; Stuyvesant, 9; Erasmus Hall, 6; Boys' High, 5; Brooklyn Tech., 3; Townsend Harris, 2; Flushing, 2.

These ocean liners are due from Europe today: The United States liner President Roosevelt from Bremen, Cherbourg, and Southampton, at Second Street, Hoboken; the Italian liner Roma from Genoa and Naples, at West Forty-seventh Street; the French liner Rochambeau from Havre, at West Fifteenth Street.

The matches resulted as follows:

The County Club No. 1 defeated Detroit Curling Club No. 2, 18 to 9; St. Andrews Golf Club defeated Caledonia Curling Club No. 1, 14 to 12; and the County Club No. 3 won from Detroit Curling Club No. 3 by default.

2. Use a colon to introduce a formal or long direct quotation.

The writer recalls a grocer who said: "Of course I can pay my bills now; instead of the pay check going to the saloon, the housewife gets it, pays cash for what she buys, pays a little on her account, and I am able to meet my obligations, something I have never been able to do before, since being in business here."

News Item

3. Use a colon after a formal salutation in a letter. (See p. 40.)

Dear Sir: Gentlemen:

4. Use a colon after the first item in such references as the following:

Boston: Houghton, Mifflin & Co.
Scribner: New York, April, 1928.

45

5. Use a colon preceding a restatement of an idea.

Special intensity of silence seemed to emanate from Ben and Ruth, who sat close together on the top step. In the general pause theirs was like a hard core: it was not true silence but only repressed speech.

CHRISTOPHER MORLEY

6. A colon is often used to precede an extended explanation.

True democracy presupposes two conditions: first, that the vast majority of the people have a genuine opinion upon public affairs; secondly, that electors will use their power as a public benefit.

ANDRÉ SIEGFRIED

Summer night cannot be shut out: it is heavier than thin lamp-shine, it spreads along the floor, gathers beneath chairs, crowds up behind pictures, makes treacherous friendship with the gallant little red-headed bulbs.

CHRISTOPHER MORLEY

Two tendencies can be observed in the way American policy is evolving: first, we have the men who, having reasoned out the situation, are preparing their country for an international economic future; and secondly, the public and most of the employers, who are only interested in their apparently insatiable home market, and whose optimism seems justified by events.

ANDRÉ SIEGFRIED

7. Capitalize the first word following a colon when it introduces an independent passage or sentence.

Of what use is a college training? We who have had it seldom hear the question raised; we might be a little nonplussed to answer it offhand. A certain amount of meditation has brought me to this as the pithiest reply which I myself can give: The best claim that a college education can possibly make on your respect, the best thing it can aspire to accomplish for you, is this: that it should help you to know a good man when you see him. This is as true of women's as of men's colleges; but that it is neither a joke nor a one-sided abstraction I shall now endeavor to show.

WILLIAM JAMES

PUNCTUATION

8. A colon may be placed between figures denoting hours and minutes. 11:30. (See pp. 29, 83.)

1. Use an interrogation point at the end of a direct question.

> "What are you going to do about it?" she asked.
> She asked, "What are you going to do about it?" in a sarcastic manner.

Note that an indirect question is followed by a period.

> They asked what we were going to do about it.

2. Use an interrogation point to indicate the end of a parenthetical question.

> There are some odd laws to watch out for, even if one be "Jenkins, sir," butler to the Vice President of the United States. They arrested Jenkins (do butlers have first names?) for riding a bicycle without a light on it. "I'm Jenkins, sir," he said, "butler to Vice President Dawes, sir." The police went into a huddle, gave him a good talking to and let it go at that.
>
> *News Item, Associated Press*
>
> They wanted to know (would you believe it?) whether we should go by airplane. (See p. 59.)

Note also that a request is usually followed by a period, rather than by an interrogation point. (See p. 28.)

> Will you send me these articles by parcel post.
> May I ask you to come early.

3. An interrogation point in parenthesis is sometimes used to indicate doubt or irony.

> Booker T. Washington was born in 1858 (?).
> The necklace consisted of real (?) emeralds.

4. Place the interrogation point inside the quotation marks when it belongs to the quoted matter. (See p. 54.)

47

"Page," said Mr. McClure, "there are only three great editors in the United States."

"Who's the third one, Sam?" asked Page.

Life and Letters of Walter Hines Page

But place the interrogation mark outside the quotation marks when it is not a part of the quoted matter.

Have you heard "Carmen"?
Were you ever "Way Down South in Dixie"?

THE EXCLAMATION POINT

1. Use an exclamation point to mark an exclamatory word, phrase, or sentence.

Eastward Ho!
New Hampshire! historic state of scenic beauty, enshrined in the hearts of Americans! [Advertisement]
Simplicity, simplicity, simplicity! I say, let your affairs be as two or three, and not a hundred or a thousand; instead of a million count half a dozen, and keep your accounts on your thumbnail.

HENRY DAVID THOREAU

This is a pretty state of things, seven o'clock and no word of breakfast!

R. L. STEVENSON

2. If the whole sentence is exclamatory in form, place an exclamation point at the end.

And I awoke in struggles, and cried aloud, "I will sleep no more!"

THOMAS DE QUINCEY

3. Use an exclamation point at the end of sentences, interrogatory in form, but exclamatory in meaning.

What could have been better than our supper, cooked in the open air and eaten by firelight!

HENRY VAN DYKE

4. When the exclamation is not emphatic, place a comma instead of an exclamation point after it.

48

Well, well, Henry James is pretty good, though he is of the nineteenth century, and that glaringly.

R. L. STEVENSON

5. Use an exclamation point to express irony, surprise, and dissension.

What if words are doomed—merely to be used to fill in the interstices of architecture, the intervals between jazz music, or just written on a board! What if the dramatist is to become second fiddler, a hack hired and commissioned!

JOHN GALSWORTHY

THE APOSTROPHE

1. To form the possessive singular of nouns add 's: the *woman's* child, the *secretary's* report, the *professor's* book, *Dun's.*

2. To form the possessive plural of nouns add an apostrophe if the plural ends in *s*: *girls'* coats, the *Ladies' Home Journal.*

If the plural does not end in *s*, add an apostrophe and *s* ('s): *children's* games, *women's* clubs.

3. In proper nouns ending in *s*, add an apostrophe and *s* ('s) to indicate the possessive:

Keats's poems, *Dickens's* stories, *Brooks's* composition. This usage is advocated by *Text, Type, and Style;* by *A Handbook of Style of the Princeton University Press;* and by *Rules for Compositors and Readers at the University Press,* Oxford; *College Handbook of Composition,* Woolley and Scott.

(1) Some authorities allow the omission of *s* after the apostrophe in singular nouns ending in *s; as, Keats'* poems, *Dickens'* stories, *Brooks'* composition; but modern usage, as quoted above, prefers *Keats's, Dickens's, Brooks's.*

(2) Notice the omission of apostrophes in some titles: *Teachers College, Governors Island, Citizens Bank.* (Reference: *The Style Book of the New York Times*)

4. Do not use an apostrophe in possessive forms of pronouns: *its, hers, ours, yours, theirs.*

5. The *'s* is used to form the plural of figures and of letters of the alphabet. Some authorities, however, prefer omitting an apostrophe in such cases.

> Your *a's* look very much like your *o's*.
> In our grandmothers' days the three *Rs* (or *R's*) formed the basis of education.
> The *8's* are to be placed in this column.
> They marched by *twos* (or by *two's*).
> Why do you have so many *and's* and *but's* in your paragraphs?
> The children are learning their *abc's*.
> In the *1800s* (or in the *1800's*) business made great strides.
> Julian Hawthorne recalls the *70s and 80s*.

6. An apostrophe is used in expressions like the following:

> I. W. W.'s, OK'd, William Madison Jr.'s garage.

7. Use an apostrophe to denote the omission of a letter:

> *can't, couldn't, didn't, it's, isn't, o'clock, they're, 'tis, won't.*

QUOTATION MARKS

1. Use double quotation marks to enclose a direct quotation.

> "The truth is," says Roland Hall in *Business Writing,* "that business and industry are full of romance, adventure, and interesting pictures if the observer will only train his mind to see and appreciate."
> Weseen states in *Everyday Uses of English,* "Speaking and writing are done, not for the sake of the speaker or writer, but for the sake of other persons."
> "Page could reject a story with a letter that was a compliment," O. Henry said, "and make everybody feel so happy that you could take it to a bank and borrow money on it."
>> *Life and Letters of Walter Hines Page*

Do not use quotation marks to set off indirect quotations.

> Wrong: He remarked "that he was tired."
> Right: He remarked that he was tired.
> Right: He remarked, "I am tired."

Do not capitalize the first word of a quotation introduced indirectly in the text. (See p. 20.)

> Field Marshal Lord Allenby praised the Kellogg anti-war pact as the "finest achievement of modern times."
>
> *The Christian Science Monitor*

> Mr. Humphrey expressed confidence that the commission would have the coöperation of "practically every publisher in the country" in its attempt to suppress fraudulent advertising.
>
> *The Monitor*

2. When two or more paragraphs are quoted, quotation marks should be placed at the beginning of each paragraph, but only at the end of the last.

In *Writing of Good English,* Manly and Rickert state the following:

> "The chances are that on almost any subject, if you have done your bibliographical work well, you will have many references. Where shall you begin to read?
> "It is usually best to begin with the most recent books and articles, for the reason that they often include summaries of earlier work on the same subject and may save you the trouble of looking that up.
> "As between two recent writers on the same subject, choose the one of better reputation."

Modern usage advocates the omission of quotation marks around single extracts quoted in smaller type or placed in paragraphs indented on both sides.

John Burroughs, who had plenty of time and leisure to read and think about books and nature, said of writing:

> One thing is certain: where there is no distinct personal flavor, we soon tire of it. The savor of every true literary production comes from the man himself. The secret is not in any prescribed order or words—it is the quality of mind and spirit that warms the words and shines through them.

If Burroughs had written these words in regard to letters, he could not have spoken more truly, for one of the requisites of great letters is the revelation of personality.

> *Training for Secretarial Practice,* S. A. TAINTOR

3. Use single quotation marks to enclose a quotation within a quotation. When it is necessary to use the quotation marks within these, use double marks again.

> "Fourth 'world's greatest movie' this season on at the Manzanita tonight," Nat said.
>
> "'Did you ever know,' said the indignant Mr. Balfour, turning to me, 'of such a thing as a minister not even being informed of his Government's decisions?' 'Yes,' I said, 'if I ransack my memory diligently, I think I could find such cases.' The meeting went into laughter."
>
> *Life and Letters of Walter Hines Page*

4. Use quotation marks or italics to set off from the context any quoted or emphasized word or short phrase.

> "Inquiry" and "address" are words often mispronounced by secretaries.
>
> We are sorry, but we'll probably go right on using "we." In the first place, it's a nicer pronoun. "I" is so bare, so uncompromisingly perpendicular, that it embarrasses us continually. "We" is a more comfortable, neighborly word. We can employ it with small discomfort.
>
> F. F. Van der Water

> "Hoping to hear from you soon," is a stereotyped ending to many a business letter.
>
> People never cease to marvel at the so-called "suddenness" of fate. In the next street a house "suddenly" falls down, an old neighbor "suddenly" dies, a famous European dynasty is "suddenly" wiped out. As a matter of fact, as all scientists, most newspaper men, and a few historians know, nothing ever happens "suddenly."
>
> Hendrik Van Loon

> The phrase, "A hundred per cent American," is often carelessly used.
>
> The publishers have repudiated the attempt to "stereotype the American mind."
>
> The government is "playing with fire" in sending troops.

5. Quotation marks are ordinarily used to enclose titles of books.

> My favorite? It is "Joan of Arc." My next is "Huckleberry Finn," but the family's next is "The Prince and the Pauper."
>
> *Mark Twain's Letters*

Underline in manuscript what is intended to be in italics in print.

In the best present usage titles of whole printed works and periodicals are italicized and titles of parts are inclosed in quotation marks. (See p. 314.)

A Dictionary of English Grammar, MAURICE WESEEN

QUOTATION MARKS WITH REFERENCE TO OTHER PUNCTUATION MARKS

6. The following usage of quotation marks represents modern practice in writing.

Quotation marks are always set *outside* the comma and the period; always *inside* the colon and the semicolon; *outside* or *inside* the marks of exclamation and interrogation according as those marks do or do not belong to the quoted matter; *outside* the dash when it stands for something left *unsaid*, and *inside* when it is used as an ordinary punctuation mark; *inside* parentheses when the parenthetical clause is quoted, otherwise *outside*.

Text, Type, and Style, Atlantic Monthly Press

With the comma:

Never were "we, the people of the United States," so thoroughly united as in that vast coöperation.

HENRY VAN DYKE

With the period:

Elbert Hubbard's essay bore the title of "A Message to Garcia."

With the semicolon:

"Punctuality," says the proverb, "is the courtesy due to kings"; and the saying has an extra super-diplomatic force when the sovereign happens to be a very beautiful young lady.

HENRY VAN DYKE

There are Americans who appear to love their country for much the same reason that Stevenson's "child" loves the "friendly cow";

"She gives me cream with all her might
To eat with apple tart."

AGNES REPPLIER

Newspapers unsparingly denounced "trade union politicians" as "demagogues," "levellers," and "rag, tag and bobtail"; and some of them, deeming labor unrest the sour fruit of manhood suffrage, suggested disfranchisement as a remedy.

History of the United States, BEARD

With the dash:

He asked Christopher if he would like to leave St. Benedict's and come back to Mr. Porteous.

"No,—I'm all right there now, pater. Now—that I've had these talks. It is not being sure about things——"

"Work is the cleanest of all things, the game you are playing or the job you are going to do."

"I see that in a sort of way. But I suppose one has feelings——"

"Get your feelings to back up your job."

Sorrell and Son, WARWICK DEEPING

With the exclamation and interrogation points:

O, if I could only write my own biography from beginning to end—without reservation or false colouring—it would be an invaluable document for my countrywomen in more than one particular; but "decency forbids"!

JANE CARLYLE

"Mother!" he appealed. "Tell the truth. It's awfully important. Cross your heart, and hope to die. Do you have a good time?"

CHRISTOPHER MORLEY

Why should we be told that "the world gapes in wonder" as it contemplates "an Aladdin romance of steel and gold"?

AGNES REPPLIER

But who shall say that a hundred dollars a minute is beyond the "order of reason"?

AGNES REPPLIER

THE DASH

1. Use a dash to indicate an abrupt change in a sentence.

July 25—your birthday!

"We haven't found out yet, but—here comes the doctor," Mother replied.

2. Sometimes a dash is used in place of the parentheses to set off interpolated explanatory matter.

Care should be exercised in the construction of any sort of insert—be it notice or announcement or frank sales appeal—to make it comply with the general principles involved in writing good advertising copy.

JOHN B. OPDYCKE

Then there is the never-failing crop of birds—robins, goldfinches, king-birds, cedar-birds, hair-birds, orioles, starlings—all nesting and breeding in its branches.

JOHN BURROUGHS

3. Use a dash to indicate an unfinished sentence.

"Oh, but I can't," I said. "They're the most interesting letters I've read this year. In fact, she is the most alive and compelling personality I've met since—since—" I hesitated for a worthy comparison.

"You surely wouldn't give a present of books you didn't like," Gretta interrupted. "If you can't give away the poor ones, and won't give away the good—" She raised her eyes in despair.

4. A dash is sometimes used in appositive expressions.

They sit there forever on the dim horizon of my mind, that Stonehenge circle of elderly disapproving Faces—Faces of the Uncles and Schoolmasters and Tutors who frowned on me in my youth.

LOGAN PEARSALL SMITH

5. Use a dash to indicate hesitancy in speech.

"You're—you're fine!" she said admiringly. "Just—just fine!"

"Think, for instance, of—well—of Helen's foolish extravagance or Paul's selfishness."

"Never to marry!" exclaimed Anne, "To be—to be an old maid—why—why that would be tragic."

6. Use a dash instead of the word *to* in reference to dates, pages, paragraphs, verses, and cantos.

1455–1485	Genesis 2:10-14
pages 10–49	verses 5–10
paragraphs 1–14	cantos I–IV

7. Use a dash under names in a catalogue to indicate repetition.

> Galsworthy The Forsyte Saga
> ———————— The Silver Box
> ———————— Justice

Note that the dash for this purpose must never be used at the top of a page.

PARENTHESES

1. Use parentheses to denote all parenthetical matter not necessary to the grammatical structure of the sentence.

> The French (and I never could write a book without some reference to that peculiar wisdom of the French people which seems to harmonize whatever it touches), the French long ago gave us a recipe for the writing of history.
>
> HENDRIK VAN LOON

> But, my dear fellow, a gout (the most obscure of diseases) of thirty-two years standing (and when the patient is sixty-five years old) is not to be driven off by the Medicine-men incantations.
>
> *Letters from Joseph Conrad*

> The old New England covered bridge, (covered, of course, to protect the traffic from the winter blasts during the long crossing) had the box-like simplicity of the New England farmhouse and barn.
>
> WALTER PRICHARD EATON

> Sentiment (so far as literature is concerned) may be defined, I suppose, as the just verbal expression of genuine feeling.
>
> JOHN GALSWORTHY

2. Use parentheses to enclose figures or letters marking the divisions of a subject.

Alexander Hamilton believed that Washington's *Farewell Address* should include among other topics the following:

> (a) The Union
> (b) Relation of the parts of the Union to each other
> (c) Morals, religion, industry, commerce, economy
> (d) Good faith with all other nations

Webster spoke on the following subjects at Bunker Hill: (1) the significance of the occasion, (2) honor to the dead, (3) the principle of popular government.

Modern usage, however, omits parentheses with Roman numerals.

3. Use parentheses to enclose *sic* following an error in spelling or usage in copied matter.

4. Use parentheses to enclose matter interpolated by way of explanation.

A student entering the senior class by transfer from another institution will not be admitted to a combined course leading to an undergraduate and a higher degree, (e. g., B.S. and M.D., B.A. and LL.B., Ph.B., etc.).

University Bulletin

Others like Robert R. Livingston (of Declaration of Independence fame) decided that it was better not to put the cart ahead of the horse, (or the engine in this case) and they collected charters for the exclusive rights to ply steamboats on certain rivers and lakes and meanwhile waited with more or less patience for the day when the venture should have been commercially profitable.

Hendrik Van Loon

Yale University beneficiary funds (available in part for financial aid to undergraduates in addition to that provided by the above funds of the separate schools) include the University Loan Fund and those founded in memory of Francis Bacon, Joseph Lyman, and David Willcox.

University Bulletin

The Perfect Tribute (a story of Lincoln's Address at Gettysburg) by Mary Raymond Shipman Andrews, Charles Scribner's Sons.

5. Parentheses are sometimes used to indicate place and time of publication in bibliographical references. In making a list of such references, however, the parentheses are usually omitted. (See p. 316.)

The Spirit of St. Louis, ed., Charles Vale (New York, 1927).

6. Use parentheses around dates indicating the years of a man's life.

Robert Louis Stevenson (1850-1894).

7. Parentheses with other marks of punctuation.

(a) The mark of punctuation follows the second parenthesis of the pair when this mark applies to the sentence containing the parenthesis and not to the passage in parentheses.

WOOLLEY and SCOTT

(b) The mark of punctuation precedes the second parenthesis of the pair when this mark applies to the passage in parenthesis.

WOOLLEY AND SCOTT

With the period:

Outside the parenthesis: (See p. 29.)

The whole of this passage is worth studying. Part of it is quoted by H. Hazlitt (*loc. cit., pp.* 84-88).

GRAHAM WALLAS

The Headmaster of a London County Council secondary school, attended mainly by boys drawn at the age of 11$^+$ from the elementary schools, published a novel called *The Day Boy* (R. Gurner, 1924).

Ibid.

Inside the parenthesis: (See p. 29.)

The remark set me wondering to what extent dealers in other articles are perplexed by their customers' preferences. (Some milliners, I hope.)

E. V. LUCAS

With the comma:

If a State, spending fifty million dollars a year on its highways (or, like New York State, closer to seventy-five million dollars), should decree that all private accessories to those roads, especially in regions of natural beauty, should conform to some decent standard of cleanliness and architectural form, and should further decree that the taxpayers of the State, who use those roads, should be entitled to all possible recreational benefit that comes from scenic charm, hence abolishing entirely billboards and outdoor advertising, the sacred rights of private property would be no more infringed than they ever must be in a society that comes to civilized development through co-operation.

WALTER PRICHARD EATON

With the exclamation mark:

I find that on my list of loves, scents would take a very important place— . . . the leaves of the lemon verbena, the scent of pine trees, the scent of unlit cigars, the scent of cigarette smoke blown my way from a distance, the scent of coffee as it arrives from the grocer's (see what a poet I am!), the scent of the underside of those little cushions of moss which come away so easily in the woods, the scent of lilies of the valley, the scent of oatcake for cattle, the scent of lilac and, for reasons, above all perhaps the scent of a rubbish fire in the garden.

E. V. LUCAS

With the question mark:

He was vain (who would not be under the circumstances?) and loved to hear the applause of the multitude.

HENDRIK VAN LOON

BRACKETS

1. Use brackets to enclose words and phrases independent of the sentence, such as explanatory notes, omissions, and such comment as are not written by the author of the text.

I once asked him [John] what he thought.
The following year [1620] the Pilgrims landed at Plymouth.
Browning, Robert. [Armstrong, A. J.] Baylor University's Browning Collection and Other Browning Interests. Waco, Texas, 1927. The Baylor Bulletin, Vol. XXX, No. 4.

CHAPTER III

HYPHENATION AND DIVISION OF SYLLABLES

THE HYPHEN

General Uses

A hyphen is used to indicate the following:

1. Words compounded of two or more words to represent a new idea.

2. The division of a word into syllables.

3. The division of a word at the end of a line.

COMPOUND WORDS WITH THE HYPHEN

1. Use a hyphen as follows between words forming an adjective when preceding the noun modified:

semi-final examination	house-to-house search
first-class bond	long-distance telephone
world-wide fame	one-man job
deep-blue color	one-way street
four-year-old girl	up-to-date fashion

2. Foreign phrases used adjectively should not be hyphened; as, an *a priori* argument, a *noblesse oblige* attitude, an *ex cathedra* pronouncement.

3. An adverb ending in *ly* is not joined with a hyphen to the adjective with which it is compounded; as, a *highly* developed intelligence, a *fully* balanced ration, a *beautifully* told story.

4. Proper names used adjectively are not joined by a hyphen; as, *New England* winters, *Fifth Avenue* shoppers, *South American* Indians.

But notice such forms as *German-American, Anglo-Indian, Indo-European,* which are purely adjective in nature and always hyphened.

5. Use a hyphen in compound numerals; as, *forty-six, twenty-one* hundredths.

6. Use a hyphen when compounding numerals with other words; as, *five-o'clock* tea, *twenty-foot* pole, *150-yard* dash.

7. Fractions are hyphened only when the word is used as an adjective; as, They were entitled to ten and one-half shares of stock.

Note that when the fraction is used as a noun no hyphen is necessary; as, He invested one third of his money in real estate.

8. Use a hyphen in titles compounded with *ex, elect,* and *general;* as, *ex-president, president-elect, postmaster-general*.

Viceroy and *viceregent* are written solid.

Most titles beginning with *vice* may be written hyphened or with their components entirely separated. WOOLLEY

Right:	Right:
vice president	vice-president
vice admiral	vice-admiral
vice chancellor	vice-chancellor
vice consul	vice-consul

9. Use a hyphen in compounds made up of nouns and prepositional phrases.

sons-in-law	eau-de-vie
daughter-in-law	vis-à-vis
man-of-war	tête-à-tête
hand-to-hand	will-o'-the-wisp

10. Use the hyphen in compounds made up of prefixes joined to proper names and in compounds of unusual formation.

anti-American	un-American
mid-Atlantic	anti-suffragist
mid-August	anti-trust
neo-Platonism	ante-bellum
pan-Hellenic	pre-natal
pre-Raphaelite	pre-requisite
pseudo-Gothic	ultra-fashionable

11. Do not ordinarily use the hyphen between a prefix and the stem. If the prefix, however, ends with the same letter with which the stem begins, a diaeresis is usually placed over the second vowel or a hyphen between the two; as, *preëminent, pre-eminent; coöperate, co-operate,* also written *cooperate.*

12. In the following, use the hyphen to distinguish words spelled alike but pronounced differently:

> re-cover, to cover again
> recover, to regain
> re-create, to create anew
> recreate, to refresh oneself

13. Use the hyphen to form adjectives compounded with *well* preceding the noun; as, *well-bred, well-born, well-to-do, well-earned, well-expressed, well-known.*

> His *well-known* courtesy made him a favorite.

Do not use the hyphen with such expressions when they follow the word modified.

> She showed herself a woman *well versed* in the ways of the world.

14. Use the hyphen generally in words compounded with *self* as a prefix; as, *self-conceit, self-confidence, self-control, self-reliance, self-respect, self-starter, self-assured, self-explaining, self-governing, self-made, self-taught, self-willed.*

Do not use the hyphen in *selfsame* and *selfless* or in pronouns compounded with self; as, *myself, himself, herself, itself, oneself, ourselves, themselves.*

15. Use the hyphen in unusual words compounded with *non;* as, *non-contagious, non-interference, non-commissioned.*
In the following omit the hyphen: *nondescript, nonessential, nonplussed, noncombatant, nonconformist, nonpareil, nonsuit.*

16. Note the use of the hyphen in the following compounds with *cross*:

cross-banded	cross-examine
cross-country	cross-eyed
cross-examination	cross-fertilization
cross-fertilize	cross-purpose
cross-fire (v.)	cross-question
cross-grained	cross-reading
cross-interrogate	cross-refer

Write the following as one word:

crossbow	crossway
crosspiece	crosswise

Write the following as separate words:

cross action	cross reference
cross bill (law term)	cross section
cross fire (n.)	cross street
cross grain	

The following adjectives selected from a list included in the *Manual of Style,* take the hyphen:

able-bodied	broad-minded	cross-grained
absent-minded	clean-cut	deep-dyed
after-dinner	clear-sighted	deep-rooted
all-around	coarse-grained	dry-as-dust
all-round	cold-blooded	dry-eyed
awe-stricken	cold-hearted	dull-eyed
base-minded	color-blind	dull-sighted
book-learned	cream-colored	eagle-eyed
brand-new	cross-country	ear-splitting
broad-brimmed	cross-eyed	easy-going

egg-shaped
faint-hearted
fair-minded
fair-spoken
far-fetched
far-reaching
far-seeing
feeble-minded
first-born
first-rate
flat-bottomed
foul-mouthed
foul-spoken
four-footed
free-born
free-for-all
free-handed
free-hearted
free-spoken
gilt-edged
God-fearing
goggle-eyed
gold-filled
golden-eyed
good-humored
good-natured
great-hearted
half-and-half
half-breed
half-heartedly
half-hourly
half-witted
half-yearly
hard-favored
hard-headed
hard-hearted
hawk-eyed
heart-easing
heart-rending
heart-shaped
hit-and-miss
hit-or-miss
honey-tongued

hot-tempered
ill-advised
ill-humored
ill-mannered
ill-natured
kind-hearted
knife-plaited
labor-saving
large-hearted
law-abiding
left-handed
letter-perfect
life-giving
light-fingered
light-footed
light-headed
like-minded
lion-hearted
long-distance
long-suffering
loose-bodied
loose-jointed
low-lived
low-spirited
lower-case
man-eating
middle-aged
middle-class
middle-sized
money-making
moss-backed
moss-grown
moth-eaten
motor-driven
muddle-headed
namby-pamby
narrow-minded
near-by
neat-handed
noble-minded
non-stop
off-color
old-fashioned

old-maidish
old-womanish
old-world
on-coming
open-hearted
parti-colored
pepper-and-salt
poverty-stricken
powder-blue
quick-witted
rain-proof
rattle-brained
rattle-headed
red-breasted
red-handed
red-headed
red-winged
rose-colored
second-class
second-rate
sharp-witted
shock-headed
short-handed
shrill-tongued
side-splitting
silver-haired
simple-hearted
sky-high
slow-burning
square-built
tender-hearted
thick-and-thin
third-class
third-rate
three-bagger
top-heavy
two-decker
ultra-violet
uncalled-for
unheard-of
unhoped-for
unlooked-for
vine-clad

warm-blooded	word-blind	worn-out
warm-hearted	word-deaf	wrong-headed
wonder-working	worldly-minded	wrong-minded
wool-dyed		

COMPOUND WORDS WITHOUT THE HYPHEN

1. In the following compound words, authorities differ in regard to the hyphen: *goodby, today, tomorrow, tonight* (*Manual of Style*); good-by, to-day, to-morrow, to-night (Webster)

2. Write as one word two nouns used together to form another, when the prefixed noun consists of only one syllable; as, *cupboard, notebook, penknife, penholder, schoolroom, textbook, viewpoint.*

3. Write without the hyphen words compounded with *like;* as, *childlike, businesslike, ladylike.*

4. Write without the hyphen such words as *northeast, southwest;* but write with the hyphen *north-northeast, south-southwest,* and the like.

5. For personal pronouns compounded with *self,* see p. 32. For pronouns compounded with *any, every, no,* and *some,* see pp. 68, 145.

6. Do not use a hyphen when the following prefixes are used with a stem to form a word except when the added word is a proper noun; as, *Anti-Trust* Law, *Anti-Labor* League, *Anti-British.*

after	demi (*but,* demi-tasse)
ante	extra
anti	fore
bi	hyper
by (*but,* by-name, by-law, by-product)	inter
	intra
circum	intro
contra	mis
counter	mono

non	sub
off	super
over	there
post	thorough
pre	to
pro	trans
pseudo	tri
re	ultra
retro	under
semi	up
step	where

Co. Write words compounded with *co* as follows:

co-operate	coeducation
coöperate	co-workers
cooperate	coequal

The following common words according to Webster's *New International Dictionary* are written solid:

aircraft	beefeater	bookbinder
airman	beefsteak	bookcase
airship	beehive	bookcraft
antechamber	beeswax	bookkeeper
armchair	beforehand	booklore
autotruck	behindhand	bookmaker
backdoor	biannual	bookmaking
background	billposter	bookman
baggageman	birthday	bookmark
barberry	birthmark	bookplate
baseball	bittersweet	bookrack
basketball	blackboard	bookseller
bathhouse	blackmail	bookshop
bathroom	blindfold	bookstall
bathtub	bloodhound	bookstand
battleship	bloodthirsty	bookstore
bedcover	blunderbuss	bookworm
bedridden	boathouse	brakeman
bedroom	boldface	breadwinner
bedside	bombproof	breakneck
bedspread	bonbon	breastbone
bedtime	bondholder	breastpin
beechnut	bonfire	brickyard

bridesmaid
broadside
brotherhood
businesslike
busybody
bygone
byplay
bystander
byword
cabinetmaker
candlepower
cardboard
cardcase
caretaker
careworn
cashbook
castaway
causeway
cellarway
centerboard
churchgoer
churchman
churchwarden
churchyard
clapboard
claptrap
classmate
classroom
closefisted
clotheshorse
clothesline
clothespin
clubhouse
coeducation
commonplace
commonwealth
companionway
copperplate
copybook
copyright
corkscrew
courthouse
courtyard

craftsman
crossroad
cupboard
curbstone
customhouse
daybook
daybreak
daylight
daytime
downhearted
downpour
downtrodden
dressmaker
earache
earthquake
eastbound
elsewhere
evergreen
everlasting
everybody
everywhere
facsimile
farmhouse
farsighted
fellowship
ferryboat
fireplace
fireproof
flagpole
flagstaff
foghorn
foolhardiness
foolproof
foolscap
football
forasmuch
foreclosure
forever
freethinker
gangplank
gaslight
gatekeeper
godchild

godfather
godmother
handbook
handclasp
handiwork
handshake
handwriting
heartache
henceforth
henceforward
hereafter
hereby
herein
herewith
highball
horsepower
household
housekeeper
housetop
iceberg
inkstand
inkwell
innkeeper
keyboard
keyhole
kinsman
landholder
landlord
lawgiver
lawmaker
layout
letterpress
lifeboat
lifelike
lifetime
machinemade
mailman
mainland
mainsail
mainspring
masterpiece
mealtime
meanwhile

midday
midsummer
milestone
motorcycle
noontime
northeast
notebook
oneself
onlooker
onrush
onslaught
onward
otherwise
pawnbroker
paymaster
piecework
pocketbook
pocketknife
policeman
policyholder
postgraduate
postmark
postscript
praiseworthy
pressroom
presswork
railroad
railway
roommate
runabout
safeguard
sailboat
salesman
salesroom
saleswoman
schoolbook
schoolboy
schoolfellow
schoolhouse
schoolmaster
schoolmate
schoolroom
schooltime

schoolyard
scrapbook
seacoast
seafarer
seaman
searchlight
seashore
semiannual
semicircle
semicolon
semiofficer
shipboard
shipbuilder
sideboard
sidewalk
signboard
signpost
slaughterhouse
snowflake
snowstorm
somebody
something
sometimes
somewhat
somewhere
songbook
spoilsman
spokesman
spoonful
stockbroker
stockholder
stockjobber
storehouse
storekeeper
storeroom
straightforward
subdivisions
subnormal
subtreasury
sunshine
tablecloth
taxicab
teacup

teamwork
teaspoon
tenfold
textbook
thousandfold
timekeeper
timesaver
toothache
toothbrush
transatlantic
transoceanic
tricolor
turnover
typesetter
typewriter
viceroyal
viewpoint
warehouse
warship
waterproof
wayfare
wayfarer
waylay
weatherman
weatherproof
weathersail
whatever
whatsoever
whenever
whereabouts
wherefore
wherein
whereof
whereon
wheresoever
whereto
whereupon
wherever
whichever
whirlpool
whitewash
whoso
whosoever

widowhood	wonderland	workshop
windmill	woodwork	wrongdoer
windstorm	workaday	yachtsman
wintergreen	workingman	yearbook
wintertime	workman	yesterday
womanhood	workroom	

Note the correct ways of writing the following words:

all right	en route
any one	every day
anyone (*Manual of Style*)	every one
anybody	everyone (*Manual of Style*)
any time	everybody
any way (when *way* is a noun	ex dividend
	ex officio
anyway (an adverb meaning in *any way* or in *any case*)	ill at ease
	ill health
bank book	ill humor (but ill-humored)
by and by	ill temper (but ill-tempered)
can not (Webster)	ill will
cannot (*Manual of Style*)	no one (but nobody)
check book (*Manual of Style*)	per cent
check-book (*Style Manual*)	pro tempore

DIVISION OF WORDS INTO SYLLABLES

The following suggestions are founded on principles of division of words in Webster's *New International Dictionary*.

Avoid all unnecessary divisions of words. Pronunciation is usually the best guide in determining how to divide words into syllables. An important principle to follow is that the part of the word left at the end of the line should suggest the part beginning the next line.

1. Do not divide monosyllables: *friend, through, stopped.*

2. Divide words of two syllables at the end of the first: *pave-ment, Eng-lish.*

3. Do not divide words of four letters or, if avoidable, those of five or six: *item, index, supper.*

4. Do not divide a syllable that does not contain a vowel: *haven't, Jones's.*

5. Do not divide a word on a single letter or on two letters: *able,* not *a-ble; omit,* not *o-mit; ratio,* not *rati-o; only,* not *on-ly.*

6. In words beginning with prefixes divide, if possible, on the prefix: *mis-pronounce, sub-sidize.*

7. Never let more than two consecutive lines end with a hyphen if this can be avoided.

8. Do not divide such suffixes as the following:

cial	in	spe-cial
tial	"	pala-tial
cion	"	coer-cion
sion	"	occa-sion
tion	"	administra-tion
cious	"	falla-cious
geous	"	gor-geous
gious	"	conta-gious
tious	"	frac-tious

9. Separate suffixes, as a rule, from the stem of the word: *hop-ing, dear-est.*

10. Divide words containing the endings, *able, ance, ant, ence, ent, ible, ical, ive,* according to the sound:

lov-able	prefer-ence
consider-able	correspon-dent
practi-cable	forc-ible
appli-cable	poss-ible
atten-dance	logi-cal
assist-ant	crea-tive

Notice, however, this does not apply to such words as end in a double letter: *bluff-ing, fulfill-ing.*

HYPHENATION AND DIVISION

11. In general, when a word contains double consonants, divide between the two consonants: *pos-sessor, mil-lion.*

12. Words containing a single consonant or digraph are divided as follows:

(a) If the preceding vowel is short and the syllable accented, let the consonant end the syllable: *bal-ance, treas-ury.*
(b) If the preceding vowel is long, write the consonant with the following syllable: *beau-ti-ful, le-gal.*

13. When two or more consonants, capable of beginning a word or a syllable, come between two sounded vowels, they are joined to the following vowel if the preceding vowel is long: *peo-pled;* but divided if the preceding vowel is short: *mas-ter, advan-tage, finan-cier.*

14. Divide two or more consonants, not capable of beginning a syllable or word, when coming between two sounded vowels: *demon-strate, tech-nical, streng-then, mor-tality, bor-row.*

15. Unless absolutely necessary, do not divide names of persons or other proper nouns.

16. Do not separate such titles as *Capt., Dr., Esq., Mr., Mrs., Rev., St.,* or abbreviations for degrees, from names to which they belong.

17. Do not separate abbreviations for societies or parties: *Y.W.C.A., B.P.O.E.*

18. Do not divide initials preceding a name.

19. Do not divide a word at the end of a page or a paragraph if it is possible to avoid doing so.

20. Do not add another hyphen to words already hyphenated; not *self-con-trol,* but *self-control.*

21. When two vowels come together but are sounded separately, divide them into separate syllables: *gene-alogy, cre-ation.*

THE SECRETARY'S HANDBOOK

REFERENCE BOOKS

Dictionaries:
   Century
   New English
   Worcester
   Standard
   Webster

Style Books:
   Style Manual of the Government Printing Office, The.
   Style-Book for Writers and Editors, C. D. Sylvester Mawson.

CHAPTER IV

USE OF ITALICS

1. Italics are often used to give prominence or emphasis to words or expressions. To indicate italics in print, underline in manuscript the words to be so written.

When I was an undergraduate in Brown, it seemed quite out of order either to write or to read a *popular* book on science.

DALLAS LORE SHARP

If anything can make hard things easy to follow it is a *style* like Bergson's.

WILLIAM JAMES

2. Italicize the words *Continued, To be continued, Continued on page,* and *To be concluded.*

3. Italicize the words, *See also, See,* in writing cross reference for indexes; also the words *For* and *Read* in a list of *errata* placed at the beginning or at the end of a volume.

> *See also* Advertising.
> *Errata,* For Rosevelt *read* Roosevelt.

4. Abbreviations of Latin words in common use are not ordinarily italicized; as, *e.g., i.e., viz.,* and *vs.* Italicize *v.* or *vs.* as in Yale *vs.* Princeton, 5 to 0, when it stands between terms not italicized. (See pp. 77-78.)

5. Italicize the following abbreviations, words, and phrases used for reference unless they occur in italic matter.

ad loc. (to the place)	loc. cit. (place cited)
ante	op. cit. (work cited)
circa, c., ca. (about)	passim (here and there)
et al. (and others)	post (after)
ibid. (the same reference)	sc. (namely)
idem (the same person)	supra (above)
infra (below)	vide (see)

6. Italicize such foreign phrases and words as have not become a part of the English language.

à la carte
ancien régime
bête noire
bon vivant
comme il faut
de trop
embarras de richesses
entente cordiale
fait accompli
feu de joie
hors de combat

in re
jeu d'esprit
mise en scène
noblesse oblige
nom de guerre
par excellence
pièce de résistance
raison d'être
savoir vivre
tant mieux
tour de force

appliqué
artiste
beau monde
belles-lettres
bon mot
bon ton
bourgeois
boutonnière
casus belli
causerie
chic
cinquecento
coiffeur
comédienne
concierge
congé
cortège
coup
crème
danseuse
de facto
dégagé
déjeuner
distrait

dos-à-dos
double entente
écru
élan
émigré
empressement
en bloc
en masse
entourage
entre nous
ergo
fauteuil
faux pas
femme de chambre
foyer
garçon
gendarme
genre
imprimus
Konzertmeister
laissez-aller
maestro
mêlée
métier

naïveté
née
nisi
on dit
opus
pâté
peccavi
penchant
petite
pince nez
porte cochère
poseur
pourboire
prie-dieu
rapprochement
recherché
salon
sang-froid
soi-disant
soupçon
valet de chambre
Wanderlust
Zeitgeist

ante meridiem
a posteriori
a priori

de jure
Nunc Dimittis
post meridiem

rara avis
tabula rasa
Te Deum

7. Use italics when a word is spoken of as a word. (See p. 52.)

> The word *very* is incorrectly used in the expression *very pleased*.

When a word, however, is quoted, it is better to enclose it in quotation marks rather than to put it in italics.

> I said "minuteness" and "selfishness" of suggestion: but it would have been enough to have said "injustice" or "unrighteousness" of sensation.
>
> JOHN RUSKIN

8. The *Manual of Style* lists the following words and phrases as not to be italicized:

ad interim	cul-de-sac	litterati
ad lib (itum)	débris	mandamus
ad valorem	début	matinée
aide de camp	décolleté	mélange
alias	delicatessen	milieu
Alma Mater	demi-tasse	motif
anno Domini	dénouement	nom de plume
ante-bellum	de rigueur	onus
à propos	dilettante	parvenu
atelier	divorcée	patois
attaché	dramatis personæ	per annum
beau ideal	éclat	per capita
billet doux	élite	per cent
bona fide	en route	per contra
bouillon	ensemble	prima facie
cabaret	entente	procès verbal
café	entrée	pro rata
camouflage	entrepreneur	régime
carte blanche	ex cathedra	résumé
chargé d'affaires	ex officio	reveille
chef d'œuvre	exposé	soirée
clientèle	fête	señor
confrère	habeas corpus	tête-à-tête
contretemps	hors d'œuvre	vice versa
coup d'état	laissez faire	vis-à-vis
coup de grace	lèse majesté	viva voce
crèche	littérateur	

9. Use italics for titles of books, of music, and of periodicals, pamphlets, and newspapers. (See p. 52.)

My authority is *Text, Type, and Style*.
It appeared in the *Springfield Republican*.
Then from over the edge of the world appeared *The Popular Science Monthly, The Warfare of Science* by Andrew D. White, and the *Lay Sermons* by Huxley.

DALLAS LORE SHARP

I am going to hear Beethoven's *Symphonie Pathétique* tonight.

USE OF ITALICS AS SHOWN IN BIBLIOGRAPHICAL MATTER

"Some Neglected Characteristics of the New England Puritans"; *Annual Report of the American Historical Association for 1891.*

(1) Do not use italics, but use quotation marks, however, around titles of divisions of books and around titles of magazine articles and other contributions.

"How He Went to the Devil"; Two Tales, April 30,—From Bibliography attached to *Barrett Wendell and His Letters.*
"Were the Salem Witches Guiltless?" *Historical Collections of the Essex Institute,* February.
"The Dean at Bourges" (poem): *Scribner's Magazine,* January.

(2) Do not use italics, but use quotation marks around the titles of lectures, toasts, articles, sermons, and papers.

Russell H. Conwell's famous lecture, "Acres of Diamonds," was given hundreds of times.
Miss Jane Brown read her paper, "Women in Business," before the Business and Professional Women's Club.
"Francis Parkman"; *Proceedings,* American Academy of Arts and Sciences, May 9.

Notice, however, the following:

Review of *The Transit of Civilization from England to America in the Seventeenth Century,* by Edward Eggleston: *American Historical Review,* July.

(3) Do not use italics or quotation marks in long bibliographies where their use would detract from the appearance of the page. (See p. 316.)

(4) Do not use italics or quotation marks for the Bible, its books, or for titles of ancient manuscripts.

> The clergyman took the text for his sermon from Matthew 5:5.

To this list, the *Style Book of The New York Times* adds the following:

> Book of Common Prayer, Prayer Book, Blue Book, Scriptures, New Testament, Corporation Manual, Revised Statutes, Encyclopedia Britannica, Lippincott's Gazeteer, Almanacs, Annuals or similar publications.

10. Legal usage customarily places in italics the names of plaintiff and defendant in the citation of cases at law, and titles of procedure.

> *Brown* v. *Jones*
> *The Atlantic Pencil Company* vs. *Henry Taylor*
> *In re Sumner*
> *Ex parte John Chase*
> *In the matter of Elmer White for a writ of—*

The *Style Manual* uses italics for *v.,* in titles of cases referring to bills introduced into Congress and for contested election cases. It states, however, that Supreme Court records use roman for both titles of cases and for *v*: Jones v. Brown.

Under Court Briefs and under Court of Claims Opinions, the *Style Manual* presents the following to illustrate capitalization, italic, small caps, and abbreviations generally used in court work.

> The *Legal Tender* cases.
> In Clarke's case the court says.
> In the case of Clarke.
> In *Ex parte 74* the court said.
> In the *Fifteen Per Cent Rate Increase case* the court decided.
> In the case of Jones against Robinson (A general or casual reference to a case.)

In *Jones* v. *Robinson* (122 U. S. 329) (a specific citation of a case.)

(*Ex parte Robinson,* 19 Wall. 304).

(*Ex parte 74,* 58 I. C. C. 220.)

Bowman Act (22 Stat. L. ch. 4, § [or sec.] 4, p. 50).

Act 5th August, 1882 (Supp. Rev. Stat. 284; Stat. L. 28; R. S. 15).

Clarke's case (14 Hun, 14).

Wallace, J., delivered the opinion.

(31 Stat. 154.)

Follow Rev. Stat., Stats., Stat. L., Stats. L. or R. S., as written.

In *Roe* v. *Doe* the court ruled.

United States v. *12 Diamond Rings.*

The *United States* v. *Forty Hogsheads of Tobacco.*

In titles of cases, follow copy as to figures and abbreviations.

11. Modern usage differs widely as to the correct manner of indicating the names of ships in print or in typewritten manuscript.

The *Manual of Style* advocates the use of quotation marks; the *Style Manual,* italics; while most newspapers seem to prefer roman.

(1) The "Mauretania" has a record for speed.

(2) The *Leviathan* is one of the largest ships.

(3) The Olympic arrived in port early.

12. Italicize the scientific names of species and genera.

Sali babylonica, acer rubrum, liriodendron tulipifera.

13. Use italics for abbreviations for shillings and pence after numerals: 5*s.* 6*d.*

14. Use italics for address lines in speeches and in reports.

To the Honorable Senate and House of Representatives of the United States of America Now Assembled at Washington, D. C.

Mr. President, Ladies and Gentlemen:—

15. In preparing matter for publication, use italics for a title following a signature: William Hawthorne, *Secretary.*

CHAPTER V

FIGURES

1. NUMBERS IN ORDINARY TEXT.

In bookwork and other plain reading matter, as editorials and book reviews, usually spell out all numbers under one hundred.

Book

> For thirty-six years after the Treaty of San Stefano and the Berlin Conference, Europe maintained an uneasy peace within its borders.
>
> H. G. WELLS

Editorial

> Whether the Antarctic is one continent or two great bodies of land separated by a frozen sea, he may be able to determine.
>
> *The New York Times*

Business Letters

> When an isolated mention of a sum in round numbers is written, spell out the number if it can be done in one or two words; as, *six, three hundred, ten thousand, five million.* For other numbers, use the sign $ and figures; as $321; $4,425; $2,640,000. (See p. 35.)
>
> Please invest twenty thousand dollars for me in ————— stock.
>
> His shares depreciated over twelve hundred dollars.
>
> His estate amounted to $67,554.

When writing ordinal numbers to designate days of a month, figures or words may be used.

> I forwarded your order on the fourth of March (*or* March 4th).

Financial News Item

They frequently have risen as much as 10 points a day.

After selling as low as 75 this year, the debentures touched a new price yesterday at 92 7/8.

Sport News

Henri Cochet, ace of the French Davis Cup team, advanced into the semi-final round by defeating Gerald Stratford of San Francisco, 6—4, 6—1.

2. ROUND NUMBERS.

Usage differs as to the writing of such figures. The *Style Manual* states that in spelling out numbers greater than one thousand, write *one thousand eight hundred and fifty dollars,* not *eighteen hundred and fifty dollars; one thousand two hundred tons,* not *twelve hundred tons.*

The *Manual of Style* and the *Style Book of The New York Times* state that numbers of four figures, if spelled out, as in straight reading matter, should read *eighteen hundred and fifty dollars,* not *one thousand eight hundred and fifty dollars.*

(1) The word *and* may or may not be used between tens and units. Modern usage seems to prefer its omission; as *three hundred five.*

(2) Spell out all round numbers of approximate figures; as, four or five feet, six or seven hundred miles, a thousand reasons, almost a million slaves.

(3) Spell out round numbers of sums of money in general matter if this can be done in one or two words; as, two hundred dollars, seven thousand dollars, three million dollars. (See p. 84.)

In newspapers, however, figures are generally used for definite amounts:

The movement of gold from London to New York, which started in mid-September, was increased to $10,000,000 yesterday when it was announced that $5,000,000 of bars was being sent here on the Mauretania, steaming today.

At the start of the movement estimates were made by bankers that it would total $25,000,000 or so, and it is still believed this is a fairly accurate gaging of the situation.

In their feverish activity, however, may be seen pretty clear proof that the party managers are as doubtful about the outcome of the campaign, in which perhaps 40,000,000 votes will be cast, as are the rest of us.

3. FIGURES AT THE BEGINNING OF A SENTENCE.

Spell out all figures at the beginning of a sentence, even when other numbers in the sentence are expressed by figures.

Forty cows comprised his livestock.

Three years ago he left for South Africa.

Two cars of new sample grade corn were received here during the day and sold at 68 to 71 cents.

Twenty-four States retain the total amount collected in gasoline taxes for the State highway funds. Alabama, with a 2-cent tax and Georgia with one of 3½ cents, apportion 1 cent of the tax to the general fund, and Georgia applies ½ cent to the school fund. Twenty States distribute some portion of the tax to local communities.

4. FIGURES WITHIN A SENTENCE.

Numbers or amounts within a sentence should be expressed either entirely in figures or entirely in words unless this would result in lack of clearness.

They employed ten girls for three weeks at fifteen dollars a week. *Or,* They employed 10 girls for 3 weeks at $15 a week.

At the close of 1927, four States were collecting 5 cents a gallon, one State 4½ cents, eleven States 4 cents, one 3½, fourteen States 3 cents, and fifteen States and the District of Columbia 2 cents.

Note that it is better not to place next to each other two numbers referring to different things:

Incorrect:	In 1929 15 states ratified the law.
Correct:	In 1929 fifteen states ratified the law.
Allowable:	In 1929, 15 states ratified the law.
Incorrect:	2 3-room apartments.
Correct:	Two 3-room apartments.

5. DATES.

In decades and centuries. Spell out numbers referring to decades and to centuries; as, the *nineteenth century;* the gay *nineties.*

In years. For general purposes, in expressing years in words, write *nineteen hundred and forty;* but in formal and legal documents, write *one thousand nine hundred and forty.*

At the beginning of questions and answers, in testimony and hearings, use figures for years.

> Q. When did he arrive in this country?
> Ans. 1926.
> Q. 1926?
> Ans. Yes, 1926.

In letters. Use figures, as a general rule, in the heading of a business letter to express the date; as, *January 27, 1928.*

(1) Many business houses write out the day and the year in the headings of letters; as, *June sixth, Nineteen Hundred and Twenty-eight* or *June sixth, 1928.*

(2) According to European practice, the day precedes the month in letter headings; as, *12, May, 1928.*

(3) Do not write 12/11/1928 for the date in the heading of a letter.

(4) In legal documents, such as wills, deeds, and the like, dates are invariably written out; as, *the twelfth day of January, one thousand nine hundred and thirty. Style-Book for Writers and Editors.*

(5) In formal invitations, announcements, and acceptances, dates are invariably spelled out; as, *February Twenty-first Nineteen Hundred and Twenty-nine,* or, *February Twenty First, Nineteen Hundred and Twenty Nine.*

6. TIME OF DAY.

Spell out the time of day in text matter.

> They are coming at three.
> I expect to leave at a quarter to three.
> The boat leaves at twelve o'clock.

FIGURES

(1) Use *A.M.* or *a.m.*, *P.M.* or *p.m.* in connection with figures; as,

> 1:30 P. M. or 1.30 P. M.
> 1:30 p. m. or 1.30 p. m. (See p. 25.)

Note that when the time is spelled out, the abbreviations a.m. or A.M., p.m. or P.M., must not be used:

> The train left at three in the afternoon.
> Not: The train left at three P. M.

7. STREETS.

In the text spell out numbers of streets, avenues, wards, and districts; as, *Forty-second Street, Sixth Avenue, Thirteenth District, Ninth Ward*.

In writing streets and avenues, spell out the names of those up to twelve; as, *Fifth Avenue, Ninth Street*.

Express numbers above twelve in figures; as, *121 Street* or *121st Street*.

8. PAGE NUMBERS.

Use figures for page numbers; as, page 533.

9. REFERENCES IN FOOTNOTES.

In footnotes and in all bibliographical material abbreviate a word designating a part when followed by a number.

Chap. III	art. 14 (arts.)
Vol. II (pl. Vols.)	p. 1 (pp.)
Fig. 80 (Figs.)	col. 2 (cols.)
sec. 3 (secs.)	pp. 6 f. (page 6 and the fol-
No 1 (Nos.)	lowing page)
pp. 6ff (page 6 and the following pages)	
vs. (vss.) pp. 5-8 (pages 5 to 8 inclusive)	

Abbreviate *section* each time it is enumerated, except the first:

> Section 1
> Sec. 2
> Sec. 3

10. SUMS OF MONEY.

Write sums of money in general matter as follows:

$55,000 *not* $55,000.00.

They also announced September earnings were $650,000 equal to about $8 a share on the present stock, and sales of more than $4,000,000. Earnings for four months were said to be about $20 a share.

59 cents *not* $.59 *nor* 59¢.

The company declared a special dividend of 75 cents a share.

The heavy offerings of highway bonds by various States since the war have been made possible to a large extent by State gasoline taxes ranging from 2 to 5 cents a gallon. Only two States have not levied a tax on gasoline; they are Massachusetts and New York.

(1) In bills and in other distinctly financial statements the symbol for cents is used when given in cents only; as, *steers low, 25¢ to 40¢ lower*.

(2) Do not use both figures and words for sums of money except in commercial and legal documents. When both are used, parentheses follow the completed expression; as, thirty dollars ($30) or thirty (30) dollars *not* thirty ($30) dollars. The custom of using both figures and words for sums of money is seldom used today in letters. (See p. 169.)

11. DECIMALS.

Use figures for expressing decimals and percentages, but spell out percentages when they begin a sentence.

0.832; 10.5

The Saskatchewan official reports said 80 per cent of the wheat in that province had been threshed.

Ten per cent will be the profit.

12. FRACTIONS.

Spell out fractions when they stand alone; as, one third.

13. AGES.

In stating definite ages, usage differs. The *Style Manual* states figures should be used to represent ages; as, "My age is 52 years, 6 months, 10 days; a boy 6 years old; a boy about 6 years old; 3-year-old colt; 2-months-old child."

The *Manual of Style* rules that references to ages should be spelled out; as "eighty years and four months old; children between six and fourteen."

14. RESULTS OF BALLOTS.

These should be expressed by figures; as 38 for, 25 against. Yeas 56; nays 24.

15. DIMENSIONS.

In text write to represent dimensions, 10 by 15 inches, *not* 10 x 15 inches *or* 10″ x 15″.

16. DISTANCES.

Write in figures all measures of distances except a fraction of a mile; as, 16 miles, 12 yards, 3 feet; but, one-half mile.

17. MEASURES.

Enumerations of measure must be expressed by figures; as, 10 gallons, 4 quarts, and 3 pints; 60 bushels, 5 pecks.

18. TEMPERATURE.

Use *F*. for Fahrenheit preceded by the degrees in figures; use *C*. for Centigrade preceded by degrees in figures; as, 32° F., 45° C.

19. WEIGHTS.

Enumerations of weight should be expressed in figures; as, 2 tons, 40 pounds, 10 ounces.

20. METRIC SYSTEM.

Abbreviate after a numeral all designations of weights and measures in the metric system.

2 m.	8 kg.
4 c. m.	2 gm.

21. ROMAN NUMERALS.

The following table represents Roman numerals commonly used:

1—I	19—XIX	500—D
2—II	20—XX	600—DC
3—III	30—XXX	700—DCC
4—IV or IIII	40—XL	800—DCCC
5—V	50—L	900—CM
6—VI	60—LX	1000—M
7—VII	70—LXX	2000—MM
8—VIII	80—LXXX	3000—MMM
9—IX	90—XC	4000—M$\overline{\text{V}}$
10—X	100—C	5000—$\overline{\text{V}}$
11—XI	200—CC	1928—MCMXXVIII
14—XIV	300—CCC	1930—MCMXXX
18—XVIII	400—CCCC or CD	1,000,000—$\overline{\text{M}}$

CHAPTER VI

SPELLING

Doubling final consonants.

1. Monosyllables and words accented on the last syllable when ending with a single consonant preceded by a single vowel, double the consonant before a suffix beginning with a vowel.

bag	baggage	occur	occurred
begin	beginning	refer	referring
bid	bidden	remit	remittance
control	controlling	repel	repellent
equip	equipped	sad	sadden
impel	impelled	sit	sitting
man	mannish	wit	witty
plan	planned		

Exceptions.

gas	gaseous
transfer	transferable, *but*, transferring, transferred

2. Final consonants when preceded by two vowels are not doubled in adding a suffix beginning with a vowel.

beat	beaten
congeal	congealing
retail	retailing
soak	soaking
toil	toiled

3. Final consonants are not doubled when the word ends in more than one consonant.

conform	conformed	conforming
help	helped	helping

4. Final consonants are not doubled when the accent is not on the last syllable or when the accent is thrown forward in the case of a derivative.

benefit	benefiting	benefited
cancel	canceling	canceled
worship	worshiping	worshiped
travel	traveler	traveled

Note that the American and the British usage often differ.

5. Words ending with *l* keep that letter before a suffix beginning with *l*.

accidentally	exceptionally	occasionally
casually	finally	really
coolly	legally	unusually

Prefixes and suffixes ending in *ll* generally drop one *l* in combination.

although	always
altogether	helpful
already	wonderful

6. Words ending in *n* keep that letter before the suffix *ness*.

barrenness	meanness
greenness	plainness
keenness	suddenness

7. Words ending in a double consonant usually retain both consonants on adding suffixes.

assess	assessment	shrill	shrilly
embarrass	embarrassment	success	successful

Note the spelling of the following words according to American and British usage:

American	*British*
enroll	enrol
enrollment	enrolment

8. British usage authorizes the doubling of the final *l* when adding a suffix beginning with a vowel; American usage does not authorize the doubling of the final *l* in such cases.

SPELLING

The following show both American and British usage in the doubling of the *l*:

American	British
appareled	apparelled
appareling	apparelling
barreled	barrelled
beveled	bevelled
chiseled	chiselled
chiseling	chiselling
councilor	councillor
counseled	counselled
counselor	counsellor
dueling	duelling
enameled	enamelled
enameling	enamelling
equaled	equalled
equaling	equalling
impaneled	empanelled
impaneling	empanelling
imperiled	imperilled
imperiling	imperilling
jeweled	jewelled
jeweler	jeweller
jewelry	jewellery
kidnaped	kidnapped
labeled	labelled
labeling	labelling
leveled	levelled
leveling	levelling
libeled	libelled
marshaled	marshalled
marshaling	marshalling
marveling	marvelling
marvelous	marvellous
medalist	medallist
metaled	metalled
modeled	modelled
modeler	modeller
paneled	panelled
paneling	panelling
parceled	parcelled
parceling	parcelling

American	British
penciled	pencilled
penciling	pencilling
periled	perilled
periling	perilling
quarreled	quarrelled
quarreling	quarrelling
raveled	ravelled
raveling	ravelling
reveling	revelling
rivaling	rivalling
shoveled	shovelled
shriveled	shrivelled
shriveling	shrivelling
signaled	signalled
signaling	signalling
stenciled	stencilled
stenciling	stencilling
toweling	towelling
trammeled	trammelled
trammeling	trammelling
tranquilize	tranquillize
traveled	travelled
traveler	traveller
traveling	travelling
tunneled	tunnelled
tunneling	tunnelling
woolen	woollen
worshiped	worshipped
worshiping	worshipping

FINAL E.

9. Words ending in silent *e* usually omit the *e* before suffixes beginning with a vowel.

arguing	giving	pleasing
arrival	guidance	salable
blamable	hoping	separating
coming	judging	subduing
deplorable	lovable	truism
desirable	loving	typing
dining	managing	writing
excitable	notable	

British usage does not conform entirely to this rule.

10. When words end in soft *ce* or *ge*, keep the *e* before *able* and *ous*.

advantageous	noticeable
allegeable	outrageous
changeable	peaceable
chargeable	pronounceable
courageous	serviceable
enforceable	traceable (*but,* tracing)

11. Keep final *e* in the present participle of *singe, tinge, dye.*

singeing
tingeing
dyeing

12. When words end in *oe*, keep the *e* before a suffix beginning with any vowel except *e*.

hoeing
toeing

13. When words end in silent *e* keep the *e* before the suffix beginning with a consonant.

baleful	lonely
encouragement	lovely
movement	

Exceptions:

acknowledgment	duly
argument	judgment
truly	

14. Verbs ending in *ie* change the termination to *y* before adding *ing.*

die dying (*but,* died)   lie lying (*but,* lied)
tie tying (*but,* tied)

FINAL Y.

15. Words ending in *y* preceded by a consonant change *y* to *i* before a suffix, unless the suffix begins with *i*.

busy	busier	business
likely	likelihood	merciless
mercy	merciful	

But

carry	carrying
hurry	hurrying
study	studying

16. Words ending in *y* preceded by a vowel generally keep the *y* before a suffix.

buyer	buying	
gayest	gayety	gayly
	(gaiety and gaily sometimes used)	

Exception:

daily	said
paid	laid

17. Monosyllabic adjectives usually keep *y* when adding a suffix.

dry	dryly
sly	slyly

18. EI AND IE.

Follow the well-known rhyme in spelling words in *ie* and *ei*.

> I before E
> Except after C
> Or when sounded as A
> As in n*ei*ghbor and w*ei*gh

ei used after *c*:

receive, perceive, conceive
ceiling, receipt, deceit.

ie used after all letters but *c*:

achieve	fiend	niece	shriek
apiece	frontier	pierce	shrieve
believe	grief	relieve	sieve
chief	mischief	reprieve	yield

ei sounded as *a*:

feign	reign
heinous	weight
neighbor	their

Exceptions:

counterfeit	height
foreign	leisure
forfeit	seize

19. Words ending in *C*.

When words end in *c* add *k* to *c* when adding *ing* or *ed*.

frolicked
picnicking
trafficking

Variations in American and British Spelling

20. Note the variations in American and British usage in the following:

(1) Words ending in *or*.

American	British
arbor	arbour
ardor	ardour
behavior	behaviour
candor	candour
clamor	clamour
endeavor	endeavour
favor	favour
flavor	flavour
harbor	harbour
honor	honour
humor	humour
labor	labour
misdemeanor	misdemeanour
neighbor	neighbour
odor	odour
parlor	parlour
rancor	rancour
rumor	rumour
splendor	splendour
vapor	vapour
vigor	vigour

93

Note that *discoloration, horror, invigorate, mirror, pallor, tenor, terror,* and *tremor* do not take *u*.

Note that adjectives formed from *clamor, humor, labor, odor, rigor, vigor* do not take *u*.

clamorous	odorous
humorous	rigorous
laborious	vigorous

(2) Words ending in *er*.

American	British
caliber	calibre
center	centre
fiber	fibre
liter	litre
maneuver	manoeuvre
meter	metre
miter	mitre
niter	nitre
reconnoiter	reconnoitre
theater	theatre

(3) Words ending in *ise* and *ize*.

Most words ending in this sound take *ize*. Some may be spelled either *ize* or *ise*, but American usage generally prefers *ize*.

The following spellings are those given in Webster:

advertise	compromise
advise	criticize
anglicize	demoralize
apologize	despise
apprise	devise
authorize	disfranchise
baptize	disorganize
capitalize	dramatize
centralize	economize
characterize	enfranchise
chastise	enterprise
civilize	equalize
colonize	exercise
comprise	extemporize

familiarize	penalize
fertilize	recognize
franchise	satirize
harmonize	scrutinize
merchandise	specialize
mobilize	supervise
modernize	surmise
monetize	surprise
naturalize	sympathize
organize	utilize
patronize	visualize

(4) Words beginning with *in* and *en*.

American	*British*
inclose	enclose
indorse	endorse
inquire	enquire

Words Often Misspelled

(Divided according to Webster's New International Dictionary)

a bridg ment	as cend ant
a cad e my	ath let ic
ac ci den tal ly	aux il ia ry
ac com mo date	
a chieve ment	bal ance
ac knowl edg ment	ba zaar
ac quaint ed	be lieve
ac quit ted	be liev ing
a cross	bi ased
ad dressed	bound a ry
aer o drome	bou quet
air plane	Brit ain
all right	broad cast
al read y	buc ca neer
a lu mi num	busi ness
am a teur	
an es thet ic	car bu ret or
ap pa ra tus	cem e ter y
ar chae ol o gy	chang ing
ar gu ment	cli en tele
as cend an cy	col umn

95

com mit tal
con fec tion er y
con trol ler
cor rob o rate
coun ci lor
coun se lor

de bat er
de ceive
de ferred
de mean or
de scend ant
de scribe
de scrip tion
de spair
dex ter ous
diph the ri a
di rect
dis ap pear
dis ap point
dis patch
dis trib u tor

ear nest
ec sta sy
eighth
em bar rass
em i grant
en cour ag ing
ex ag ger ate
ex ceed
ex cel
ex cel lent
ex er cise
ex hil a rate
ex ist ence

fas ci nate
Feb ru a ry
fi nal ly
for eign er
fore tell

for ward
friend

gov ern ment
gov er nor
gram mar
grand daugh ter
griev ous
guar an tee
guard i an

hair breadth
har ass
he roes
hop ing
hun dredths
hy giene

ic ing
im ag i na ry
im me di ate ly
im mi gra tion
im mi nent
im ping ing
in ci den tal ly
in de pend ent
in dis creet
in fi nite
in noc u ous
in oc u late
in sist ence
in stil
in ter cede
ir i des cent

judg ment

keen ness
knowl edge

lab o ra to ry
le gion naire
li bra ry

li cense
light ning
lik a ble
liq ue fy

man i kin
man u al
mar riage
mat i nee
me di e val
mes sen ger
mil len ni um
mil lion aire
mis cel la ne ous
mis chie vous
mis spell
mis state ment
mon as ter y
mon eyed

ne groes
nick el
nine teenth
no tice a ble

oc ca sion al ly
oc cur rence
oc cur ring
om e let
o mis sion
o mit ted
op ti mis tic
out ra geous

pac i fist
paid
par al lel
par lia ment
pas sen ger
pas time
peace a ble
per ceive
per emp to ry
per se ver ance

per son nel
per spi ra tion
pic nic
pneu mo ni a
pol i ti cian
pol i tics
pos ses sor
pre ced ence
prep a ra tion
priv i lege
pro ced ure
pro fes sion
prof fered
prom is so ry
psy chol o gy

ques tion naire

real ly
re ceive
rec og nize
rec om mend
ref er ence
rep e ti tion

sec re ta ry
seize
ser geant
serv ice a bly
siege
sim i lar
sin cere ly
su per in tend ent

tend en cy
trace a ble

u nan i mous
un nec es sa ry
use ful

venge ance
vil lage

war rant
weath er

LIST OF WORDS ENDING IN *IBLE*

accessible
admissible
audible
collapsible
collectible
combustible
comprehensible
compressible
convertible
corruptible
deducible
destructible
dirigible
discernible
divisible
edible
eligible
exhaustible
feasible
forcible
horrible
illegible
imperceptible
inaudible
incompatible

incorrigible
incredible
indefensible
indelible
indigestible
infallible
inflexible
intangible
intelligible
invincible
invisible
irascible
legible
negligible
permissible
plausible
possible
reprehensible
resistible
responsible
reversible
susceptible
tangible
terrible
transmissible

CHAPTER VII

DICTION

WORDS OFTEN CONFUSED IN MEANING AND IN SPELLING

accede	to attain, to agree
exceed	to surpass
accept	to receive
except	to exclude
adverse	opposed
averse	disinclined
adapt	to suit oneself to
adept	proficient
addition	something added
edition	number of books printed at a time
advice	counsel
advise	to give counsel. Not used correctly for *inform*
affect	to influence, to change, to assume, always a verb
effect	to bring about, as a verb; a result, as a noun
ascent	act of rising
assent	consent
altar	a sacred place for worship
alter	to change
canvas	a coarse cloth
canvass	to solicit
capital	a chief city, a sum of money
capitol	a state-house
censer	an incense pan
censor	a critic, to criticize
censure	to blame

99

cite	to summon
sight	a view
site	a place
cession	a ceding, a yielding up
session	a meeting assembled
coarse	common, rough
course	a direction of going
complement	that which completes
compliment	flattery, praise
correspondent	one who writes letters
co-respondent	a third party in a divorce suit
council	an assembly or group for conference
counsel	advice; legal adviser
device (a noun)	a plan
devise (a verb)	to plan
desert	a barren place
dessert	a course at the end of dinner
decent	respectable
descent	act of descending
dissent	act of disagreement
elusive	baffling
illusive	unreal
eminent	prominent
imminent	threatening
fair	just; blonde
fare	sum paid for journey
formally	perfunctorily, ceremoniously
formerly	in times past
forth	away; forward
fourth	a number
farther	in space
further	in thought
guarantee	preferred in the verb sense
guaranty	preferred in the noun sense
ingenious	clever
ingenuous	frank

DICTION

instance	an example
instants	periods of time
its	pronoun
it's	contraction of *it is*
later	comparative of *late*
latter	the second of two mentioned
loath	adjective
loathe	verb
loose	free
lose	to free
miner	a workman in a mine
minor	one under age; lesser
ought	should
aught	anything
naught	a cipher
past	adjective, adverb, or preposition
passed	past tense of *to pass*
personal	individual, private
personnel	staff of an institution
persecute	to subject to persistent ill-treatment
prosecute	to pursue, to bring lawsuit against
precede	to go before
proceed	to begin
precedence	priority
precedents	previous examples taken for basis of present action
presence	state of being present
presents	gifts
prescribe	to lay down authoritatively a course of action
proscribe	to outlaw
principal	chief; head of a school; sum of money
principle	a general truth
prophecy	a noun
prophesy	a verb
quite	completely
quiet	not noisy

respectfully	manner of feeling
respectively	proper to each
	(not to be used at closing of a letter)
stationary	not moving
stationery	writing paper
statue	a piece of sculpture
stature	height
statute	a law
their	a pronoun
there	an adverb
they're	contraction of *they are*
therefor	to that end
therefore	for the reason
who's	contraction of *who is*
whose	pronoun possessive of *who*
your	pronoun
you're	contraction of *you are*

WORDS COMMONLY MISUSED

ability	power to do
capacity	power to receive
all right	Note this is the correct and only spelling. There is no such spelling as *alright*
almost	an adverb meaning *very nearly* (almost all)
most	an adjective, a pronoun, and an adverb of comparison: *most* people; *most* of them came; *most* beautiful
allusion	an indirect reference
illusion	an error of vision
delusion	an error of judgment
amount	the sum total referring to number
number	refers to something counted
quantity	refers to something measured
apt	suitable, appropriate, skilled
likely	possible
liable	implies undesirable consequences, legally bound
anywhere	There is no such word as *anywheres*.

DICTION

as—as	used in affirmative comparison
so—as	used in negative comparison
remainder	the comparatively small part left over
balance	the difference between the debit and credit side of an account
each	refers to the members of a group
both	two considered together
bring	to convey toward the speaker
take	to carry from the speaker
can	denotes ability
may	denotes permission
customer	person entering shop to buy, especially one usually dealing with a firm
client	person using the services of a lawyer or other professional man
due to	adjective modifier *Correct:* His failure, *due to* ill health, caused financial embarrassment. *Incorrect: Due to* the bad weather, we could not go.
because of	*Because of* financial embarrassment he could not go to Europe.
directly	never a conjunction; as, *Directly* he came, I left. *Correct: As soon as* he came, I left.
each other	Use *each other* of *two.* Use *one another* of *more than two.*
exceptional	unusual
exceptionable	open to objection
emigration	the moving out from a country
immigration	the moving into a country
expect	to regard as likely to happen
suspect	to doubt the truth of
few	used in reference to number
less	used in reference to quantity
first	both adjective and adverb. *Firstly* is not in good use.

hanged	of a person
hung	of an object
healthy	in good health or condition
healthful	health-giving, as of climate
wholesome	producing a good effect, as of food
hire	to employ, to obtain the use of
let	to give the use of
lease	to give the use of by lease
human	pertaining to mankind (an adjective, not a noun)
humane	benevolent
last	after all others
latest	the most recent
learn	to acquire knowledge
teach	to give instruction
luxuriant	profuse of growth
luxurious	self-indulgent, conducive to luxury
mad	insane. Do not use in the sense of *angry*.
angry	enraged
majority	receiving more than half of the number of votes
plurality	receiving a greater number than any other, but less than half of the votes cast
much	referring to quantity
many	referring to persons, or things
near	in proximity to time or space
nearly	almost
new	recent, not old
novel	unusual, strange
none (see p. 145)	may be singular or plural according to sense
noted	favorably known
notorious	unfavorably known
famous	celebrated
observance	rite, ceremonial
observation	act of observing
party	a body of persons; in law term, a person
person	an individual

DICTION

partake	to take a share, as of food
participate	to have a share in
practical	that which can be done advantageously
practicable	that which can be done
proposition	statement, assertion, something offered for discussion
proposal	something offered for acceptance or rejection
real	not counterfeit
quite	adverb of degree, meaning entirely
very	adverb of degree, meaning extremely. Do not use to modify a participle
raise	transitive verb, to lift
rear	to bring up, to train
rise	intransitive verb, to ascend
recipe	a statement of ingredients and procedure for a medicine or dish
receipt	a written acknowledgment of receiving money, a fact of receiving
salary	a fixed periodical payment made to a person employed in other than manual or mechanical work
wages	workman's or servant's periodical pay
some	an adjective or a pronoun
somewhat	an adverb of degree

Words Commonly Mispronounced

acclimate—ăk-klī′-māt, *not* ăk′-klĭm-āt
acumen—à-kū′-mĕn, *not* ăk′-yū-mĕn
address (n.)—ăd-drĕs′
address (vb.)—ăd-drĕs′
adept (n.)—ăd-ĕpt′, *not* ăd′-ĕpt
adept (adj.)—ăd-ĕpt′
admirable—ăd′-mĭr-à-bl, *not* ăd-mī′-rà-bl
admirably—ăd′-mĭr-à-blĭ, *not* ăd-mī′-rà-blĭ
adult—à-dŭlt′, *not* ăd′-ŭlt
advertisement—ăd-vẽr′-tĭz-ment or ăd-ver-tīz′-ment
alias—ā′-lĭ-ăs, *not* ăl-ī′-ăs
alma mater—ăl′-mà mā′-tẽr, *not* äl′-mä mä′-tẽr
alumnae—à-lŭm′-nē

105

alumni—a-lŭm′-nī
annex (n.)—ăn-nĕks′ or ăn′-nĕks
annex (vb.)—ăn-nĕks′
annihilate—ăn-nī′-hĭl-āt
applicable—ăp′-plĭk-à-bl, *not* ăp-plĭk′-ā-bl
appreciate—ăp-prē′-shĭ-āt, *not* ăp-prē′-sĭ-āt
apropos—ăp′-rō-pō or ăp-rō-pō′
aristocrat—à-rĭs′-tō-krăt or ăr′-ĭs-tō-krăt
ask—àsk, *not* ăsk
associate—ăs-sō′-shĭ-āt, *not* ăs-sō′-sĭ-āt
association—ăs-sō-sĭ-ā′-shŭn or ăs-sō-shĭ-ā′-shŭn
athlete—ăth′-lēt, *not* ăth′l-ēt or ăth′-a-lēte
avenue—ăv′-ĕn-yū, *not* ăv′-ē-no͞o
aviator—āv′-iātor
bade—băd, *not* bād
banquet—băng′-kwĕt, *not* băn′-kwĕt
bicycle—bī′-sĭk-l, *not* bī′-sī-kl
biography—bī-ŏg′-rà-fĭ
blatant—blā′-tănt, *not* blăt′-ănt
bouquet—bo͞o-kā′ or bo͞o′-kā, *not* bō-kā′
cello—chĕl′-ō
chaos—kā′-ŏs
chastisement—chăs′-tĭz-mĕnt, *not* chăs-tīz′-mĕnt
chiropodist—kī-rŏp′-ō-dĭst
clique—klēk, *not* klĭk
cognomen—kŏg-nō′-mĕn, *not* kŏḡ′-nō-mĕn
combatant—kŏm′-băt-ănt; kŭm′-băt-ănt
comparable—kŏm′-pà-rà-bl, *not* kŏm-pâr′-a-bl
complaisance—kŏm′-plā-zăns or kŏm-plā′-zăns
compromise—kŏm′-prō-mīz
comptroller—kŏn-trō′-lēr
condolence—kŏn-dō′-lĕns, *not* kŏn′-dō-lĕns
conscientious—kŏn-shĭ-ĕn′-shŭs, *not* kŏn-sĭ-ĕn′-shŭs
considerable—kŏn-sĭd′-ēr-à-bl, *not* kŏn-sĭd′-rà-bl
conspiracy—kŏn-spĭr′-à-sĭ, *not* kŏn-spī′-rà-sĭ
corps (military)—kōr; pl., kōrz
coupon—ko͞o′-pŏn
cowardice—kow′-ärd-ĭs, *not* kow′-ärd-īs
credence—krē′-dĕns, *not* krĕd′-ĕns
creek—krēk, *not* krĭk
crematory—krĕm′-à-tō-rĭ or krē′-mà-tō-rĭ
culinary—kū′-lĭn-ā-rĭ, *not* kŭl′-ĭn-ā-rĭ
data—dā′-tà, *not* dä′-tà

DICTION

datum—dā′-tŭm, *not* dä′-tŭm

deaf—dĕf

debris—dā-brē′

decade—dĕk′-ād, *not* dĕk-ād′

deficit—dĕf′-ĭs-ĭt, *not* dē-fĭs′-ĭt

detail (n.)—dē′-tāl or dē-tāl′

digest (n.)—dī′-jĕst

digest (vb.)—dĭ-jĕst′ or dī-jĕst′

digestion—dĭ-jĕs′-chŭn, *not* dī-jĕs′-chŭn

direct—dĭ-rĕkt′, *not* dī-rĕkt′

discourse—dis-kōrs′, *not* dĭs′-kōrs

economic—ē-kō-nŏm′-ĭk or ĕk-ō-nŏm′-ĭk

egotism—ē′-gō-tĭzm or ĕg′-ō-tĭzm

envelope—ĕn′-vĕl-ŏp or ĕn′-vĕl-ōp

epitome—ē-pĭt′-ō-mē, *not* ĕp′-ĭ-tōm

epoch—ĕp′-ŏk or ē′-pŏk

err—ēr

errata—ĕr-rā′-tȧ

exigency—ĕks′-ĭj-ĕn-sĭ

exit—ĕks′-ĭt, *not* ĕg̱z′-ĭt

exquisite—ĕks′-kwĭz-ĭt, *not* ĕks-kwĭz′-ĭt

extol—ĕks-tŏl′ or ĕks-tōl′

extraordinary—ĕks-trôr′-dĭn-ā-rĭ

faucet—fô′sĕt, *not* fȧs′-ĕt

fiat—fī′-ăt

finale—fē-nä′-lā, *not* fī-năl′-ē

finance—fĭn-ăns′, *not* fī′-năns

financial—fĭn-ăn′-shăl, *not* fī-năn′-shăl

financier—fĭ-năn-sēr′, *not* fī′năn-sēr

forbade—fôr-băd′, *not* fôr-bād′

forehead—fŏr′-ĕd or fōr′-hĕd

formidable—fôr′-mĭd-à-bl

forward—fôr′-wērd

fragile—frăj-ĭl, *not* frăj′-īl

frequent (adj.)—frē′kwĕnt

frequent (vb.)—frē-kwĕnt′

gala—gā′-lȧ, *not* găl′-ȧ

gamut—găm′-ŭt, *not* gā′-mŭt

genuine—jĕn-ū-ĭn, *not* jĕn-ū-īn

gigantic—jī-găn′-tĭk, *not* jĭg-ăn′-tĭk

gist—jĭst, *not* g̱ĭst

gondola—gŏn′-dō-lȧ, *not* gŏn-dō′-lȧ

gratis—grā′-tĭs, *not* grăt′-ĭs

107

Hades—hā'-dēz
harass—hăr'-ăs
hearth—härth, *not* hĕrth
height—hīt, *not* hītth
helm—hĕlm, *not* hĕl'-ŭm
herb—ērb or hērb
herculean—hēr-kū'-lē-ăn, *not* hēr-kū-lē'-ăn
humor—hū'-mēr or yū'-mēr
hypocrisy—hĭp-ŏk'-rĭs-ĭ
hysteria—hĭs-tē'-rĭ-à
illustrate—ĭl-lŭs'-trāt or ĭl'-lŭs-trāt
incomparable—ĭn-kŏm'-pà-rà-bl, *not* ĭn-kŏm-pâr'ā-bl
indict—ĭn-dīt'
indictment—ĭn-dīt'-mĕnt
indisputable—ĭn-dĭs'-pū-tà-bl or ĭn-dĭs-pū'-tà-bl
indissoluble—ĭn-dĭs'-ō-lū-bl or ĭn-dĭ-sŏl'-u-bl
industry—ĭn'-dŭs-trĭ, *not* ĭn-dŭs'-trĭ
inertia—ĭn-ēr'-shĭ-à, *not* ĭn-ēr'-shà
inexorable—ĭn-ĕks'-ō-rà-bl
inexplicable—ĭn-ĕks'-plĭk-à-bl
inextricable—ĭn-ĕks'-trĭk-à-bl
infamous—ĭn'-fà-mŭs
infantile—ĭn'-făn-tīl or ĭn'-făn-tĭl
inhospitable—ĭn-hŏs'-pĭt-à-bl, *not* ĭn-hŏs-pĭt'-à-bl
inquiry—ĭn-kwī'-rĭ, *not* ĭn'-kwĭ-rĭ
insatiable—ĭn-sā'-shà-bl or ĭn-sā'-shĭ-à-bl
interested—ĭn'-tēr-ĕst-ĕd, *not* ĭn-tēr-ĕst'-ĕd
interesting—ĭn'-tēr-ĕst-ĭng, *not* ĭn-tēr-ĕst'-ĭng
irreparable—ĭr-rĕp'-à-rà-bl, *not* ĭr-rē-păr'-à-bl
isolate—ĭs'ō-lāt, ĭz'-ō-lāt or ī'-sō-lāt
italic—ĭ-tăl'-ĭk, *not* ī-tăl'-ĭk
juvenile—jū'-vē-nĭl or jū'-vē-nīl
kept—kĕpt, *not* kĕp
length—lĕngth, *not* lĕnth
mischievous—mĭs'-chēv-ŭs, *not* mĭs-chē'-vŭs
municipal—mū-nĭs'-ĭp-ăl, *not* mū-nĭs-ĭp'-ăl
nauseate—nô'-shē-āt or nô'-sē-āt
nephew—nĕf'-ẏū or nĕv'-yū
often—ŏf'-n, *not* ŏf'-tĕn
oral—ō'-ràl
pageant—păj'-ent or pā'-jent
parquet—pär-kā' or pär-kĕt'
pertinacious—pēr-tĭn-ā'-shŭs, *not* pēr-tĭn-ăsh'-ŭs

DICTION

poem—pō´-ĕm, *not* pō´-ŭm
precedence—prē-sē´-dĕns, *not* prĕs´-ē-dĕns
precedency—prē-sē´-dĕn-sĭ, *not* prĕs´-ē-dĕn-sĭ
precedent (n.)—prĕs´-ē-dĕnt
precedent (adj.)—prē-sē´-dĕnt
premature—prē-mȧ-tūr´ or prē´-mȧ-tūr
promissory—prŏm´-ĭs-sō-rĭ
promulgate—prō-mŭl´-ḡāt
qualm—kwäm, *not* kwôm
radiator—rā´-dĭ-ā-tor
radio—rā´-dĭ-o
raillery—răl´-ēr-ĭ or rā´-lēr-ĭ
ratio—rā´-shĭ-ō or rā´-shō
recognize—rĕk´-ŏḡ-nīz
referable—rĕf´-ēr-ȧ-bl
retailer—rē-tā´-ler or rē´-tā-ler
revocable—rĕv´-ō-kȧ-bl, *not* rē-vō´kȧ-bl
revolt—rē-vōlt´ or rē-vŏlt´
rinse—rĭns, *not* rĕns
romance—rō-măns´ or rō-mȧns´
roof—rōōf, *not* rŏŏf
room—rōōm, *not* rŏŏm
root—rōōt, *not* rŏŏt
route—rōōt or rowt (*Century*)
salmon—săm´-ŭn, *not* sä´-mŭn
says—sĕz, *not* sāz
several—sĕv´-ēr-ăl, *not* sĕv´-răl
shone—shōn or shŏn
suggest—sŭḡ-jĕst´ or sŭj-jĕst´
suite—swēt, *not* sūt
superfluous—sū-pēr´-flū-ŭs
tedious—tē´-dĭ-ŭs or tēd´-yŭs, *not* tē´-jŭs
tepid—tĕp´-ĭd, *not* tē´-pĭd
tomato—tō-mā´-tō or tō-mä´-to
toward—tōrd, *not* tō-wôrd´
tribune—trĭb´-yūn
ultimatum—ŭl-tĭm-ā´-tŭm, *not* ŭl-tĭm-ä´-tŭm
usage—yū´-zāj or ū´-sāj
vagary—vȧ-ḡā´-rĭ, *not* vā´-ḡȧ-rĭ
vagrant—vā´-grănt, *not* văḡ´-rănt
vice versa—vī´-sē vēr´-sȧ, *not* vīs´-vēr-sȧ
wan—wŏn
yacht—yŏt

yolk—yōlk or yōk
yule—yūl
zealous—zĕl′-ŭs

Foreign Words and Phrases Commonly Used
(Selected from the Standard Dictionary)

LATIN WORDS AND PHRASES

annus mirabilis	Wonderful year
ante bellum	Before the war, especially before the Civil War
ante meridiem	Before the sun reaches the meridian, that is, before noon.
a priori	From what is before; from cause to effect
arbiter elegantiæ	A judge in matters of taste
bona fides	Good faith
carpe diem	Enjoy the present.
casus belli	A cause justifying war
causa sine qua non	An indispensable condition
cave canem	Beware the dog.
circa	About
conditio sine qua non	An indispensable condition
confer (cf)	Compare
consensus facit legem	Consent makes the law.
con spirito	With animation
copia verborum	Fluency of speech
cor unum, via una	One heart, one way
cui bono?	For whose advantage, to what end?
de gustibus non est disputandum	There is no disputing about tastes.
Dei gratia	By the grace of God
de mortuis nil nisi bonum	Concerning the dead say nothing but good.
Deo volente (D.V.)	God willing
Deus vobiscum	God be with you.
dis aliter visum	It seemed otherwise to the gods.
Dominus vobiscum	The Lord be with you.

dulce et decorum est pro patria mori	Sweet and seemly is it to die for one's country.
ecce homo	Behold the man.
ex cathedra	Officially, with authority
ex curia	Out of court
exempli gratia (e.g.)	By way of example
exeunt omnes	All go out (used as a stage direction).
ex more	According to custom
facile princeps	Easily the first
fide et amore	By faith and love
fidus Achates	Faithful Achates; trusty friend
fortuna favet fortibus	Fortune favors the brave.
gaudeamus igitur	Let us be joyful.
genius loci	The spirit of the place; guardian deity
gloria in excelsis	Glory to God in the highest.
hic et ubique	Here and everywhere
hic sepultus	Here lies buried
hinc illæ lacrimæ	Hence these tears
hoc anno	In this year
hoc loco	In this place
hoc tempore	At this time
hodie mihi, cras tibi	Mine today, yours tomorrow
homo sum; humani nihil a me alienum puto	I am a man; I count nothing human indifferent to me.
honores mutant mores	Honors change manners.
horribile dictu	Horrible to be told
humanum est errare	To err is human.
id est (i.e.)	That is
in curia	In court
in extremis	At the point of death
in hoc signo spes mea	In this sign is my hope.
in hoc signo vinces	By this sign you will conquer.
in hoc statu	In this state of things
in loco parentis	In the place of a parent
in medias res	In the midst of things; into the heart of the matter
in memoriam	In memory of
in nomine Domini	In the name of the Lord
in pace	In peace
in omnia paratus	Prepared for all things
in perpetuum	Forever

in personam	*Law.* Against the person instead of against specific things
in posse	In possibility; in potential existence
in propria persona	In one's own person
in re	In the matter of
in rem suam	*Civ. Law.* In his own affair; said of a certain power of attorney
in rerum natura	In the nature of things
in secula seculorum	To ages of ages; for ever and ever
in situ	In its place; in proper position
in statu quo	In the state in which it was before
in statu quo ante bellum	In the state in which it was before the war
in toto	Altogether; entirely
in transitu	In transit
in totidem verbis	In so many words
ipso jure	By the law itself
jure divino	By divine law
jus civile	Civil law
jus canonicum	Canon law
jus gentium	Law of nations
jus gladii	The law of the sword
justitia omnibus	Justice for all
laborare est orare	To work is to pray.
labor est etiam ipsa voluptas	Labor is pleasure itself.
labor ipse voluptas	Labor itself is pleasure.
labor omnia vincit	Labor conquers all things.
laesa majestas	Lese-majesty; treason
lapis philosophorum	The philosophers' stone
lares et penates	Household gods
laus Deo	Praise be to God.
legalis homo	A person in good standing before the law
lex loci	The law of the place
lex scripta	The written law
lex terræ	The law of the land
licentia vatum	Poetic license
lite pendente	During the trial

loco citato	In the place cited
locum tenens	One taking the place of another
locus in quo	Place in which
locus sigilli	The place of the seal
longe absit	Far be it
longo intervallo	At a long interval
loquitur	He (or she) speaks.
lux mundi	The light of the world
magna civitas, magna solitudo	A great city is a great solitude.
magni nominis umbra	The shadow of a great name
magnum bonum	A great good
malis avibus	Under bad auspices
malum in se	Evil in itself
maximus in minimis	Very great in little things
me judice	In my judgment
memento mori	Remember that you must die.
memoria in æterna	In everlasting remembrance
mens agitat molem	A mind keeps the mass in motion; mind animates matter.
mens legis	The spirit of the law
mens sana in corpore sano	A sound mind in a healthy body
meo periculo	At my own risk
meo voto	By my wish
merum sal	Pure salt; true good sense or wit
meum et tuum	Mine and thine
miles gloriosus	A braggart soldier
mirabile dictu	Wonderful to say
mirabile visu	Wonderful to be seen
mirabilia	Miracles
modus operandi	A mode of operating
modus vivendi	A mode of living
more majorum	According to the custom of our fathers
more meo	In my own way
more suo	In his own way
morituri te salutamus	We who are about to die salute thee.
motu proprio	Of one's own accord
multum in parvo	Much in little

mutatis mutandis	The necessary changes being made
mutato nomine	The name being changed
mutuus consensus	Mutual consent
natale solum	Native soil
natura abhorret a vacuo	Nature abhors a vacuum.
ne cede malis	Do not give way to misfortunes.
nemine contradicente	No one speaking in opposition
nemine dissentiente	No one dissenting
nemo me impune lacessit	No one attacks me with impunity.
nemo mortalium horis sapit	No one is wise at all times.
nihil ad rem	Nothing to the point
nihil quod tetigit non ornavit	He touched nothing without embellishing it.
nil admirari	To wonder at nothing
nil desperandum	Nothing to be despaired of
nil dicit	He says nothing.
nisi Dominus, frustra	Unless the Lord build the house, it is in vain (to build it).
nitor in adversum	I struggle against adversity.
nolens volens	Unwilling or willing
noli me tangere	Do not touch me.
non constat	It does not follow.
non libet	It does not please me.
non omnia possumus omnes	We cannot, all of us, do everything.
non possumus	We are not able.
non quis, sed quid	Not who but what
non quo, sed quomodo	Not whom but in what manner
nulla dies sine linea	Not a day without a line
nulli secundus	Second to none
nunc aut nunquam	Now or never
obiit	He or she has died.
omnia ad Dei gloriam	All things to the glory of God
omnia bona bonis	All things are good to the good.
omnia vincit amor	Love conquers all things.
operæ pretium est	It is worth while.

opere citato	In the volume cited.
opus artificem probat	The craftsman is proved by his work.
ora et labora	Worship and work
orator fit, poeta nascitur	The orator is made, the poet is born.
O tempora! O mores!	What times! What morals!
otium cum dignitate	Leisure with dignity
panem et circenses	Bread and circus; food and amusements
pari passu	With equal pace; at the same speed
particeps criminis	A sharer in the crime
pater patriæ	Father of his country
paucis verbis	In few words
pax vobiscum!	Peace be with you!
peccavi	I have sinned.
pendente lite	During the suit
per diem	Daily
periculum in mora	There's danger in delay.
per se	By itself
persona grata	An acceptable person
pleno jure	With full right
posse videor	I seem to myself to be able.
possunt quia posse videntur	They can because they think they can.
post meridiem	After the sun has reached the meridian, that is, after noon
primus inter pares	First among equals
principia, non homines	Principles, not men
probatum est	It has been proved.
pro bono publico	For the public good
pro Deo et ecclesia	For God and the church
pro et con	For and against
pro forma	As a matter of form
pro memoria	As a memorial
pro tempore	For the time, temporary
quantum libet	As much as you please
quantum meruit	As much as he deserved
quantum sufficit	As much as suffices
quantum vis	As much as you wish
qui docet discit	Who teaches, learns.

quid faciendum?	What is to be done?
quid pro quo	Something for something
quo animo?	With what intent?
quo Fata vocant	Whither the Fates call
quo jure?	With what right?
quo modo?	In what manner?
quo vadis?	Whither goest thou?
quod erat demonstrandum	Which was to be proved
quorum pars magna fui	Of which things I was a great part
re infecta	The business being unfinished
religio laici	The religion of a layman
requiescat in pace	Rest in peace.
sal Atticum	Attic salt; wit wisdom
scripsit	He or she wrote it.
sculpsit	He or she sculptured it.
secundum artem	According to art or custom
secundum naturam	According to nature
secundum usum	According to usage
semel pro semper	Once for all
semper eadem	Always the same
semper fidelis	Always faithful
semper paratus	Always prepared
sic passim	Thus everywhere
sic semper tyrannis	Thus ever to tyrants
sic transit gloria mundi	Thus passes the glory of the world.
si Deus vobiscum, quis contra nos	If God be with us, who can be against us?
si diis placet	If it pleases the gods
sine cura	Without care
sine die	Without a day being appointed definitely
sine dubio	Without doubt
sine mora	Without delay
sine qua non	Something indispensable
status quo	The state in which
sub judice	Under consideration
sub poena	Under a penalty
sub praetexto juris	Under the pretext of justice
sub rosa	Under the rose; in strict confidence

sui juris	In one's own right
summa summarum	Sum total
summum bonum	The supreme good
summum jus, summa injuria	The extreme of justice, the extreme of injustice
suo jure	In one's own right
suo loco	In its proper place
sursum corda!	Lift up your hearts!
suum cuique	To each one his own
tempora mutantur	Times change.
tempus fugit	Time flies.
tertium quid	A third something
timeo Danaos et dona ferentes	I fear the Greeks even when bearing gifts.
totum	The whole
ubi libertas, ibi patria	Where liberty is, there is my country.
ubique	Everywhere
ultimum vale	A last farewell
ultimus Romanorum	The last of the Romans
una voce	With one voice
usus loquendi	Usage in speaking
ut dictum	As said or directed
ut infra	As below
ut supra	As above
vade in pace	Go in peace.
vade mecum	Go with me; companion
væ victis	Woe to the conquered
vale	Farewell!
vera causa	A true cause or complaint
verbatim et literatim	Word for word and letter for letter
vide ut supra	See as above.
vincet amor patriæ	Love of country will conquer.
vita brevis, long ars	Life is short and art long.
vox populi, vox Dei	The voice of the people is the voice of God.

French Words and Phrases

à bon droit	With justice
à bon marché	At a good bargain
affaire de cœur	A love affair

à gauche	To the left
amende honorable	Public reparation; an apology
à propos de rien	Apropos of nothing
à tout prix	At any price
au fait	Skilled, expert
au fait	In fact
au revoir	Till we meet again
au rez-de-chaussée	On the ground floor
autre temps, autres mœurs	Other times, other manners
avec plaisir	With pleasure
beau monde	The fashionable world
bête noire	Black beast; object of abhorrence
bon ami	A good friend
bon jour	Good morning
bon soir	Good evening
bon voyage	A prosperous voyage to you!
catalogue raisonné	An illustrated or classified catalogue
cause célèbre	Celebrated case in law
cela va sans dire	That is a matter of course.
c'est-à-dire	That is to say
c'est une autre chose	That is a different thing.
chacun à son goût	Everyone to his own taste
chef de cuisine	Head cook
chemin de fer	Railway
cher ami, or (fem.) chère amie	Dear friend
cherchez la femme	Seek the woman.
chevalier d'industrie	Knight of industry; a swindler
communiqué	Official communication
compagnon de voyage	Traveling companion
compte rendu	An official report
conseil d'état	Council of state
coûte qui coûte	Cost what it may
dégagé	Free; unrestrained
de haut en bas	From top to bottom
dernier ressort	A last resource
de trop	Too much; too many
Dieu avec nous	God with us
Dieu défend le droit!	God defend the right!

DICTION

Dieu et mon droit	God and my right
distingué	Distinguished
distrait	Absent-minded
double entente	Double meaning
edition de luxe	An elaborate and costly edition, as of a book
embarras de richesses	Embarrassment of riches
en masse	In a body
en passant	In passing
en plein jour	Before the whole world
en rapport	In sympathetic relation
en règle	According to rule
entre nous	Between us
fait accompli	An accomplished fact
femme de chambre	A chamber-maid; a lady's maid
fête champêtre	An open-air festival
garde du corps	A body-guard
gardez bien	Take good care.
gardez la foi	Keep the faith.
grace à Dieu	Thanks to God
grand merci	Many thanks
grand monde	The world at large; refined society
homme d'affaires	Man of business
homme de lettres	Man of letters; literary man
homme d'esprit	Man of intellect; wit
honi soit qui mal y pense	Evil be to him who evil thinks.
honneur et patrie	Honor and fatherland
ici on parle français	French is spoken here.
il faut de l'argent	Money is necessary.
il n'y a rien à dire	There is nothing to be said.
il n'y a pas de quoi	There is no occasion; don't mention it.
je maintiendrai le droit	I will maintain the right.
je me fie en Dieu	I trust in God.
je ne sais quoi	I know not what.
je suis prêt	I am ready.
jeu de mots	Play on words.
jeu de'esprit	A play of wit or fancy.
j'y suis	I am here.

le bon temps viendra	There's a good time coming.
le jeu n'en vaut pas la chandelle	The game is not worth the candle.
le jour viendra	The day will come.
le roi est mort, vive le roi!	The king is dead! Long live the king!
le style est l'homme même	The style is the man himself.
le tout ensemble	The whole taken together
lettre de cachet	A sealed or secret letter, usually containing orders for the arrest or imprisonment of the person concerned
lettre de change	Bill of exchange
lettre de créance	Letter of credit
lettre de marque	Letter of marque
l'homme propose, et Dieu dispose	Man proposes and God disposes.
loyal en tout	Loyal in everything
ma foi	My faith
maître d'hôtel	A house-steward
mal de mer	Seasickness
mal du pays	Homesickness
mise en scène	Stage-setting; hence, visible surroundings, generally
mon ami	My friend
monde	World; society
moyen âge	The Middle Ages
n'est-ce pas?	Isn't that so?
ni l'un ni l'autre	Neither the one nor the other
n'importe	It does not matter.
nom de guerre	Literally, a war-name; any assumed name
nom de plume	A pen-name
n'oubliez pas	Do not forget.
objet d'art	A work of art
par accord	By agreement
pardonnez-moi	Pardon me.
pâté de foie gras	A paste of fat goose-livers
peu de chose	A small matter
pièce de résistance	A piece of resistance; the most substantial dish of a dinner
pied-à-terre	A temporary lodging

pis aller	To go worse; last shift; end of resources
place aux dames	Make way for the ladies.
poste restante	To remain at the post-office until called for; General Delivery
pour faire visite	To pay a visit
pour passer le temps	To pass the time
pour prendre congé (P.P.C.)	To take leave
procès verbal	A statement in writing
projet de loi	Bill (for legislation)
quand même	Notwithstanding
que voulez-vous?	What do you wish?
quelque chose	Something; a trifle
qui s'excuse, s'accuse	Who excuses himself accuses himself.
qui va là?	Who goes there?
raison d'état	Reason of state
raison d'être	Reason for being; an excuse for existing
répondez s'il vous plaît	Reply if you please. (R.S.V.P.)
salle à manger	Dining-hall
sans cérémonie	Without ceremony
sans Dieu rien	Nothing without God
sans doute	Without doubt
sans façon	Informally
sans gêne	Without embarrassment
sans pareil	Without equal
sans peine	Without difficulty
sans peur et sans reproche	Without fear and without reproach
sans souci	Without care
savoir-faire	The knowing how to do; tact
savoir-vivre	The knowing how to live
tant mieux	So much the better
tant pis	So much the worse
tour de force	A feat of strength or skill
tout à fait	Entirely
tout à l'heure	Instantly
voilà	There
vous l'avez voulu	You have wished it.

THE SECRETARY'S HANDBOOK

REFERENCE BOOKS

FOWLER, H. W. *A Dictionary of Modern English Usage*. The Clarendon Press, Oxford.

GREEVER and JONES. *The Century Handbook of Writing*. The Century Co.

OPDYCKE, JOHN B. *English of Commerce*. Charles Scribner's Sons.

PHYFE, W. H. P. *24,000 Words Often Mispronounced*. G. P. Putnam's Sons.

WESEEN, MAURICE H. *Crowell's Dictionary of English Grammar and Handbook of American Usage*. Thomas Y. Crowell Company.

ALLEN. *Synonyms and Antonyms*. Harper and Brothers.

Crabb's English Synonyms. Harper and Brothers.

FERNALD. *English Synonyms and Antonyms*. Funk and Wagnalls.

CHAPTER VIII

ABBREVIATIONS

Modern usage advocates, on account of appearance, the spelling out of most words. There are many cases, however, where abbreviations are sanctioned. The following illustrate abbreviations in common use:

Business Terms

The following abbreviations are frequently used in business terms:

acc., acct., or a/c	account
A. D.	In the year of our Lord
advt.	advertisement
A 1	first class
a.m. or A.M.	before noon
amt.	amount
anon.	anonymous
ans.	answer
asst.	assistant
avoir. or avdp.	avoirdupois
ave.	avenue
bal.	balance
bbl.	barrel
bds.	bound in boards
b.e. or b/e	bill of exchange
b.l. or b/l	bill of lading
bldg.	building
Bros.	Brothers
b. pay.	bills payable
b. rec.	bills receivable
c.a.f.	cost and freight
c.f.&i.	cost, freight, and insurance
cent.	(centum) one hundred

C. or Cent.	centigrade
cf. or cp.	compare
c/o	care of
C.O.D.	cash on delivery
C.P.A.	certified public accountant
cr.	creditor; credit; crate
ctge.	cartage
c.w.o.	cash with order
cwt.	hundredweight
dept. or dpt.	department
dis., disc., disct.	discount
do.	ditto
dr., Dr.	debtor; debit; doctor
ed.	editor
e.&o.e.	errors and omissions excepted
et al.	and others
etc.	and so forth
et seq.	what follows or the following
exch. or ex.	exchange
F. or Fahr.	Fahrenheit
f.a.s.	free alongside ship
fig.	figure
fl.	florins
f.o.b.	free on board
fol.	folio
ft.	foot
g.	gram
gal.	gallon
gs.	guineas
hdkf.	handkerchief
hhd.	hogshead
h.p.	horse power
hr.	hour
id. (*idem*)	the same
i.e. (*id est*)	that is
inc.	incorporated; increase
init. (*initio*)	at the beginning
in re	in regard to
ins.	insurance; inspector
I.O.U.	acknowledgment for money lent
inst. (*instant*)	in the present month
l. (*libra*)	left; lira; league

L. or l.	pound sterling
lb.	pound in weight
l.c.	lower case
l/c	letter of credit
lib. (*liber*)	book
loc. cit. (*loco citato*)	in the place quoted
ltd.	limited
m.	mark; mile; minute; meter
mdse.	merchandise
mem. or memo.	memorandum
mfd.	manufactured
mfg.	manufacturing
mfr.	manufacturer
mgr.	manager
misc.	miscellaneous
m.o.	money order
ms. *pl.* mss.	manuscript
mt.	mountain
n.b. (*nota bene*)	note carefully
nem. con. (*nemine contradicente*)	no one contradicting
non seq. (*non sequitur*)	it does not follow
n. d.	no date
ob. (*obiit*)	died
o.e.	omission excepted
o.p.	out of print
o.r.	owner's risk
p.c.	per cent
pfd.	preferred
p.&l.	profit and loss
P.M. or p.m.	afternoon
P.O.	post office, postal order
p.p.c. (pour prendre congé)	to take leave
pr.	pair
pref.	preface
pres.	president
pro tem. (*pro tempore*)	for the time
prox.	in the next month
P.S.	postscript
q. v. (*quod vide*)	which see
qr.	quarter
qt.	quart
qy.	query

re	regarding
rm.	ream
recd.	received
ref.	reference
reg.	registered
R.F.D.	rural free delivery
rom.	roman type
R.P.O.	railroad post office
R.R.	railroad
R.S.V.P. (*répondez s'il vous plaît*)	please answer
Ry.	railway
s. caps, s. c.	small capital letters
sect.	section
s. or sh.	shilling
soc.	society
Sr. or sr.	senior
ss. or SS.	steamship
str.	steamer
stet	let it stand
st.	street
supt.	superintendent
t. b.	trial balance
t. l.	total loss
tr.	transpose
treas.	treasurer
v. or vs.	versus
vol.	volume
u. c.	upper case
ult.	ultimo—in the last month
U.S.M.	United States Mail
vid. (*vide*)	see
viz. (*videlicet*)	namely
w.b.	way bill
w.f.	wrong font
wt.	weight
yr.	year
yd.	yard

ABBREVIATIONS

Geographical Names

1. Use the following official abbreviations for states and territories when necessary:

Ala.	Nebr.
Ariz.	Nev.
Ark.	N. C.
Calif.	N. Dak.
Colo.	N. J.
Conn.	N. H.
Del.	N. M.
D. C. (District of Columbia)	N. Y.
	Okla.
Fla.	Oreg.
Ga.	Pa.
Ill.	P. I. (Philippine Is.)
Ind.	P. R. (Porto Rico)
Kans.	R. I.
Ky.	S. C.
La.	S. Dak.
Mass.	Tenn.
Md.	Tex.
Me.	Vt.
Mich.	Va.
Minn.	Wash.
Miss.	W. Va.
Mo.	Wis.
Mont.	Wyo.

2. Do not abbreviate Alaska, Canal Zone, Guam, Hawaii, Idaho, Iowa, Ohio, Utah, Virgin Islands.   *Style Manual*

3. In general, do not abbreviate geographical names except to gain space in tabular matter: Fort William Henry, Port Jervis, Mount Vernon.

4. Always abbreviate *Saint* in the following:

St. John	St. Louis
St. Helena	Sault Ste. Marie

5. Use the abbreviated form *U. S.* for United States, when preceding the name of a Government vessel; also when used in footnotes, tables, or in names of departments, bureaus, commissions, and other services. (*Government Usage*)

U. S. Navy, U. S. Army.

But when used in ordinary text, United States should be spelled out.

Names of Firms and Corporations

6. In writing the words *Company, Brother, Brothers, Limited, Incorporated,* and *Corporation,* in firm or corporate names, follow the usage of the company:

> The Macmillan Company
> James McCreery & Co.
> Gimbel Brothers
> Brooklyn Edison Company
> Judd & Detweiler, Inc.
> C. F. Church, Mfg. Co.
> National City Company
> The Shelbourne Motor Company, Ltd.
> Trust Company of Larchmont
> Huguenot Trust Company

(1) It is better not to use & unless the firm's name consists of the names of persons. Many firms, however, do not follow this usage:

> American Bond & Mortgage Company
> The Mechanics & Metals Bank

(2) In footnotes and bibliographies use *Co., Bro.,* and & when they form part of the name of a firm.

(3) The character &, known as ampersand, should never be used to connect two names in text matter unless in connection with a firm name:

> Beaumont and Fletcher (Elizabethan dramatists whose names are closely associated)

Neilson and Thorndike (Joint authors of a history of English literature)

Lord & Taylor (firm name)

7. In writing given names of firms follow the usage of the writer or firm addressed:

Thos. Cook & Son (abbreviation of given name as used by firm)

Henry Clews & Co. (unabbreviated name as used by firm)

The H. W. Wilson & Co. (initials as used by firm)

TITLES

TITLES PRECEDING PERSONAL NAMES

8. Use the following abbreviations for titles preceding personal names:

Mr., Messrs., M. (Monsieur), MM. (Messieurs), Mme. (Madame), Mmes. (Mesdames), Mlle. (Mademoiselle), Mlles. (Mesdemoiselles), St. (Saint). (See p. 28.)

9. In formal usage such as invitations and announcements, it is better to spell out titles, such as *Honorable, Governor, Lieutenant-Governor, Reverend, Professor.*

The Honorable William E. Borah, Governor Alfred E. Smith, Professor John Dewey.

10. In writing salutations, titles should not be abbreviated except Mr., Mrs., and Dr.

Dear Professor Harris   Dear Mr. Bailey
Dear Colonel Brown   Dear Mrs. Luetscher
Dear Dr. Taylor   Dear Governor Roosevelt

11. In writing *doctor, general, professor,* and the like without the surname, no abbreviation should be used.

The doctor will be here tomorrow.
I hope, General, that you will accept the invitation.

12. The title of doctor is given to holders of high university degrees in any faculty. (*Doctor of Divinity, Music, Medicine, Literature, Law, Philosophy,* etc.)

The abbreviation *Dr.* should never be used together with *M.D.* or any other doctoral degree.

13. In the case of *Reverend* usage varies. The following are considered correct: (See pp. 3-4.)

> The Rev. Dr. Ramsay, or The Rev. Mr. Ramsay
> The Rev. Hugh Miller
> The Reverend President William Sloane Coffin
> The Right Reverend Bishop Manning
> The Reverend Harry Emerson Fosdick, D.D.
> The Reverend Professor Hugh Black

Reverend should never be used as follows:

> The Reverend Brown
> Reverend Brown

ABBREVIATIONS FOR TITLES FOLLOWING PERSONAL NAMES

14. Use the following abbreviations following personal names:

Esq. This title is written, according to the British usage, after a gentleman's name. In America, it follows most commonly names of lawyers, architects, and those of other professions. If used, it should not be written with any other title.

> Wallace Wolcott, Esq., *not* Mr. Wallace Wolcott, Esq.

Sr., Jr., and *3d* in personal names. Written of father and son with the same names. Usage differs as to the capitalization of these abbreviations.

The *Style Manual,* as well as several newspapers, uses *sr.* and *jr.; The New York Times* uses *Sr.* and *Jr.*

Usage differs also as to punctuation before such abbreviations. The following usages are employed by metropolitan newspapers: (See p. 50.)

The New York Times:	John Briggs Jr.
The New York Sun:	John Briggs, Jr.
The New York Herald Tribune:	John Briggs jr.

ABBREVIATIONS

15. ACADEMIC DEGREES

A.B. or B.A.	Bachelor of Arts
A.M. or M.A.	Master of Arts
A.R.A.	Associate of the Royal Academy of Arts
A.R.I.B.A.	Association of the Royal Institute of British Architects
B.Arch.	Bachelor of Architecture
B.C.E.	Bachelor of Civil Engineering
B.C.L.	Bachelor of Civil Law
B.D.	Bachelor of Divinity
B. L.	Bachelor of Law
B. Litt.	Bachelor of Literature or of Letters
B. Mus.	Bachelor of Music
B. S.	Bachelor of Science
C. E.	Civil Engineer
C.P.A.	Certified Public Accountant
D. C. L.	Doctor of Civil Law
D. D.	Doctor of Divinity
D.D.S.	Doctor of Dental Surgery
D.Litt. or Litt.D.	Doctor of Literature or Letters
D.Mus.	Doctor of Music
D.Sc.	Doctor of Science
E.E.	Electrical Engineer
F.B.A.	Fellow of the British Academy
F.R.A.S.	Fellow of the Royal Astronomical Society
F.R.C.P.	Fellow of the Royal College of Physicians
F.R.G.S.	Fellow of the Royal Geographic Society
F.R.C.S.	Fellow of the Royal College of Surgeons
F.R.I.B.A.	Fellow of the Royal Institute of British Architects
F.R.S.	Fellow of the Royal Society
F.S.A.	Fellow of the Society of Antiquaries
LL.B.	Bachelor of Laws
LL.D.	Doctor of Laws
M.D.	Doctor of Medicine
M.I.M.E.	Member of the Institute of Mining Engineers
Mus.B.	Bachelor of Music
Ph.B.	Bachelor of Philosophy
Ph.D.	Doctor of Philosophy
Ph.G.	Graduate in Pharmacy
R.N.	Registered Nurse
S.T.B.	Bachelor of Sacred Theology

MILITARY TITLES AND DIVISIONS

16. Use the following abbreviations for military titles and divisions:

Adjt.	Adjutant
A.E.F.	American Expeditionary Forces
Capt.	Captain
Brig. Gen.	Brigadier General
Col.	Colonel
F.M.	Field Marshal
F.G.	Foot Guards (British)
G.A.R.	Grand Army of the Republic
Gen.	General
G.H.Q.	General Headquarters
H.G.	Horse Guards
Lt.	Lieutenant
Lieut. Col.	Lieutenant Colonel
Lieut. Gen.	Lieutenant General
Lieut. Gov.	Lieutenant Governor
Lieut. Com.	Lieutenant Commander
Maj.	Major
Maj. Gen.	Major General
N.	Navy
N.G.	National Guard
N.C.O.	Non-commissioned officer
O.T.C.	Officers' Training Corps
R.A.F.	Royal Air Force (British)
R.F.C.	Royal Flying Corps (British)
R.N.R.	Royal Naval Reserve (British)
R.O.T.C.	Reserve Officers' Training Corps
Sergt.	Sergeant
Sergt. Maj.	Sergeant Major
Surg. Gen.	Surgeon General

MILITARY AND OTHER HONORS

17. The following abbreviations are often used to designate military and other public honors:

C.S.C.	Conspicuous Service Cross
D.S.C.	Distinguished Service Cross
D.S.M.	Distinguished Service Medal
D.S.O.	Distinguished Service Order (British Army and Navy)
G.C.B.	Grand Cross of the Bath (British)
G.C.I.E.	Grand Cross of the Indian Empire (British)
G.C.L.H.	Grand Cross of the Legion of Honor (French)
G.C.M.G.	Grand Cross of the Order of St. Michael and St. George (British)
G.C.S.I.	Grand Cross of the Star of India (British)
G.C.V.O.	Grand Cross of the Victorian Order (British)
I.E.	Order of the Indian Empire (British)
K.B.	King's Bench; Knight of the Bath (British)
K.C.	King's Counsel (British)
K.C.B.	Knight Commander of the Bath (British)
K.C.I.E.	Knight Commander of the Indian Empire (British)
K.C.M.G.	Knight Commander of the Order of St. Michael and St. George (British)
K.C.S.I.	Knight Commander of the Star of India (British)
K.C.V.O.	Knight Commander of the Victorian Order (British)
K.G.	Knight of the Garter (British)
K.L.H.	Knight of the Legion of Honor (French)
K.T.	Knight Templar; Knight of the Thistle (British)
M.C.	Military Cross (British)
O.M.	Order of Merit (British)
V.C.	Victoria Cross (British honor for conspicuous bravery in army or navy)
V.O.	Victoria Order (British honor for personal service to sovereign)
Q.C.	Queen's Counsel (British)

Titles of British Officials

18. The following abbreviations are frequently used for titles of British officials and members of the nobility:

C.J.	Chief Justice
H.I.H.	His or Her Imperial Highness
H.I.M.	His or Her Imperial Majesty
H.M.	His or Her Majesty
H.R.H.	His or Her Royal Highness
Hon.	Honorable
Hon.Sec.	Honorable Secretary
Kt.	Knight
M.P.	Member of Parliament
Q.C.	Queen's Counsel
R.	Regina (queen); Rex (king)
R. et I.	Rex et Imperator (King and Emperor); Regina et Imperatrix (Queen and Empress)
G.R.	Georgius Rex (King George)
H.B.M.	His or Her Britannic Majesty
H.E.	His Excellency
V.A.	Vice-Admiral
V.C.	Vice-Chancellor

Associations and Societies

LEARNED AND PROFESSIONAL SOCIETIES

19. Use the following abbreviations for various learned, professional and scientific associations:

A.L.A.	American Library Association
A.S.C.E.	American Society of Civil Engineers
A.S.M.E.	American Society of Mechanical Engineers
M.L.A.	Modern Language Association
N.A.D.	National Academy of Design
N.E.A.	National Educational Association
R.G.S.	Royal Geographical Society
R.A.	Royal Academy
R.A.M.	Royal Academy of Music
S.P.E.	Society for Pure English

ABBREVIATIONS

Organizations of Social and Religious Nature

20. The following abbreviations are often used in place of the names of social and religious organizations:

A.F. of L.	American Federation of Labor
Bapt.	Baptist
B.P.O.E.	Benevolent Protective Order of Elks
C.E.	Church of England
C.S.	Christian Science
Cong.	Congregational
D.A.R.	Daughters of the American Revolution
D.R.	Daughters of the Revolution
F. & A.M.	Free and Accepted Masons
I.O.F.	Independent Orders of Foresters
I.O.O.F.	Independent Order of Odd Fellows
I.W.W.	Industrial Workers of the World
K. of C.	Knights of Columbus
K. P.	Knights of Pythias
M. E.	Methodist Episcopal
P. E.	Protestant Episcopal
R. C.	Roman Catholic
S.A.R.	Sons of the American Revolution
S.R.	Sons of the Revolution
S.P.C.A.	Society for the Prevention of Cruelty to Animals
S.P.C.C.	Society for the Prevention of Cruelty to Children
W.C.T.U.	Women's Christian Temperance Union
Y.M.C.A.	Young Men's Christian Association
Y.W.C.A.	Young Women's Christian Association
Y.M.H.A.	Young Men's Hebrew Association
Y.W.H.A.	Young Women's Hebrew Association
Y.P.S.C.E.	Young People's Society of Christian Endeavor

Months

21. Do not abbreviate the names of the months except when necessary; especially is it better, in accordance with modern usage, to spell out the names of the months in the heading of a letter.

The forms *st, d, th, rd, nd,* written after the date, are no longer considered necessary in the heading, but are still used in the body of a letter, as, the 20th of April, 4th of July (calendar day), *Fourth of July* (holiday). In letters it is not considered good form to abbreviate the date as follows: 1/5/24. When necessary on account of space to use abbreviations, write the names of months as follows: Jan., Feb., Mar., Apr., Aug., Sept., Oct., Nov., Dec. Do not abbreviate May, June, and July.

22. The Dewey System of abbreviations recommends the following for tabular matter, particularly for library use:

Ja.	My.	S.
F.	Je.	O.
Mr.	Jy.	N.
Ap.	Ag.	D.

DAYS OF THE WEEK

23. The names of the days of the week should usually be written in full, but when space makes abbreviations necessary, use the following:

Sun.	Thurs.
Mon.	Fri.
Tues.	Sat.
Wed.	

COMPASS DIRECTIONS

24. For compass directions use the following letters with a period:

N.	E.	N.E.	S.E.	N.N.W.
S.	W.	N.W.	S.W.	N.N.E., etc.

SIZES OF BOOKS

25. Use the following without a period to denote the sizes of books where abbreviations are desirable:

4to quarto	24mo twenty-four-mo
8vo octavo	32mo thirty-two-mo
12mo duodecimo	36mo thirty-six-mo
16mo sextodecimo	48mo forty-eight-mo
18mo octodecimo	64mo sixty-four-mo

ABBREVIATIONS

The Books of the Bible and Principal Versions

26. Abbreviations for the books of the Bible and for names of translations and versions may be found in the following lists.

The Books of the Old Testament

Gen.	I and II Chron.	Isa.	Jonah
Exod.	Ezra	Jer.	Mic.
Lev.	Neh.	Lam.	Nah.
Num.	Esther	Ezek.	Hab.
Deut.	Job	Dan.	Zeph.
Josh.	Ps. (Pss.)	Hos.	Hag.
Judg.	Prov.	Joel	Zech.
Ruth	Eccles.	Amos	Mal.
I and II Sam.	Song of Sol.	Obad.	
I and II Kings			

The Books of the New Testament

Matt.	Gal.	Philem.
Mark	Eph.	Heb.
Luke	Phil.	Jas.
John	Col.	I and II Pet.
Acts	I and II Thess.	I, II and III John
Rom.	I and II Tim.	Jude
I and II Cor.	Titus	Rev.

Principal Versions of the Bible

A.V.	Authorized Version
R.V.	Revised Version
A.R.V.	American Standard Revised Version
E.R.V.	English Revised Version
E.V.	English Version(s) of the Bible
Vulg.	Vulgate
LXX (See p. 17.)	Septuagint

References to books or chapters of the Bible are not usually abbreviated in text matter:

The story of the Creation is found in Genesis, chapter I.

REFERENCES TO PARTS OF BOOKS

27. Write out references to chapters, pages, verses, and notes occurring in the text; but in parentheses, footnotes, cut-in notes, side notes, and tables, abbreviate as follows:

art. (arts.)	article	pl. (pls.)	plate
ch. (chs.)	chapter	pt. (pts.)	part
fig. (figs.)	figure	sec. (secs.)	section
p. (pp.)	page	vol. (vols.)	volume

Note that the Roman numeral with capital letter is used with these abbreviations except in the case of *p.* or *pp.*

REFERENCE BOOKS

Dictionaries.

Burke's Peerage, Baronetage and Knightage.
Whitaker's Peerage, Baronetage, Knightage and Companionage.

CHAPTER IX

POINTS OF GRAMMAR

Suggestions for Correct Usage

NOUNS

Case

1. A noun modifying a gerund must be in the possessive case.

> I had not heard of John's (not John) going away.

2. Possession should not be attributed to inanimate objects.

> The streets of the town (not the town's streets) were carefully laid out.

Exceptions: Certain idiomatic uses of this type do not show possession. (See *College Handbook of Composition,* Woolley and Scott, p. 217.)

a day's vacation	a month's notice
a week's work	a year's interest
a dollar's worth	three years' salary

Number

3. A verb should agree with its subject in person and number.

(1) Two or more nouns connected by *and* take a plural verb.

> Weather and unemployment *are* (not *is*) cited as causes of the decline in trade.
> The secretary and the treasurer *were* (not *was*) absent from the meeting when their names were called.

(2) Do not mistake the form of the plurals of foreign nouns for the singular. (See p. 142.)

> The data *are* (not *is*) ready for the expert.
> The errata *are* (not *is*) placed in the front of the book.
> The phenomena of the Northern Lights *are* (not *is*) striking.

(3) Collective nouns may be regarded as singular or plural: singular, if the word denotes a group acting as an individual; plural, if the word denotes the individuals that make up the group.

> The jury *has* (not *have*) agreed upon the verdict.
> The jury *have* (not *has*) disagreed as to their verdict.
> The company *has* (not *have*) decided to give *its* (not *their*) employees a bonus at Christmas.
> The Brown, Penton, Robinson Company *has* issued bonds for sale.
> Smith, Porter and Company *is* going into bankruptcy.

With such words as *number, remainder,* and *rest,* use a singular or a plural verb according as they refer to a whole or to the several members of a group.

> The number of students in economics *has* increased rapidly.
> A number of students in economics *have* signified their intention to take advanced work.
> The remainder of the hour *was* spent in discussion.
> The rest of the votes *were* lost.

(4) A verb should agree with its subject rather than with a noun placed between the verb and its subject.

> The joint meeting between the American and British engineers *is* one of the most amazing examples of the development of the radio.
> A group of seven communities south of Springfield *is* served by the company.

But with fractions, the verb agrees with the noun in the prepositional phrase.

> Half of the chairs *were* painted red.
> Half of the chair *was* painted red.

POINTS OF GRAMMAR

(5) Expressions introduced by such phrases as *as well as, together with, in addition to,* are not part of the subject and, therefore, do not affect the number of the verb.

The book, together with the newspapers and magazines, *was* destroyed.

(6) Certain words are used with the plural only; as, *goods, thanks, scissors, wages.*

(7) Certain words may be used either as singular or as plural.

Athletics (that is, *athletic training*) *has become* popular.
Athletics (that is, *sports*) *are indulged* in by many students.

(8) Singular subjects connected by *or* or *nor* always take a singular verb.

The letter or the report *was* lost.
Either the secretary or the treasurer *is* always present at the monthly meeting.
Neither America nor England *fears* the outcome.

(9) When two subjects differing in number are connected by *or* or *nor,* the verb agrees with the subject nearest it.

Neither his sisters nor his mother *was* present.
Neither the garage nor the houses *were* burned.

(10) When the verb precedes the subject, care should be taken to have it agree with its subject in person and number.

In this catalogue *are* (not *is*) the requirements of admission, the courses, and the fees.
There *are* ten on the executive committee.
There *are* a filing cabinet and a typewriter in the office.

Formation of Plurals of Nouns

1. Most nouns form the plural by adding *s* to the singular: *banks, letters, desks.*

2. Nouns ending in *s, sh, ch, x,* and *z* form their plurals by adding *es* to the singular: *kisses, bushes, branches, boxes, waltzes.*

3. Nouns ending in *f* or *fe* change *f* to *v* before adding *es*: *thieves, halves, shelves, wives*.

But the following nouns in *f* add *s* to form the plural:

beliefs	proofs
chiefs	scarfs (sometimes
dwarfs	*scarves*)
handkerchiefs	serfs
hoofs	

4. Nouns ending in *y*.

(a) Nouns ending in *y* preceded by a consonant, and those ending in *quy*, form their plurals by changing *y* to *i* and adding *es*: *cities, colloquies*.

(b) Nouns ending in *y* preceded by a vowel form the plural in the usual way by adding *s* to the singular: *valleys, alleys*.

5. Nouns ending in *o* preceded by a vowel add *s* to form the plural: *cameos, portfolios, studios*.

6. Nouns ending in *o* preceded by a consonant form the plural by adding *es*: *mulattoes, tomatoes*.

Some of the most common exceptions to this rule are the following: *pianos, solos, sopranos, cantos*.

Several words ending in *o* form their plurals in both ways: *cargoes, cargos; mottoes, mottos*.

7. Nouns that retain in English their foreign endings form their plurals in the following ways: those ending in *a* to *ae*; *us* to *i*; *um* to *a*; *on* to *a*; *is* to *es*.

Note the plurals of the following nouns which retain their foreign forms and in some cases have also an English plural:

a to ae	alumna-alumnae (f)
	formula-formulae-formulas
	minutia-minutiae
	vertebra-vertebrae
us to i	alumnus-alumni (m)
	genius-genii; geniuses
	terminus-termini

um to a	bacterium-bacteria
	curriculum-curricula
	datum-data
	erratum-errata
	memorandum-memoranda-memorandums
on to a	criterion-criteria
	phenomenon-phenomena
is to es	analysis-analyses
	axis-axes
	crisis-crises
	oasis-oases
	parenthesis-parentheses
	synopsis-synopses
	thesis-theses

The following nouns also retain their foreign forms and in some cases have also an English plural:

beau	beaux, beaus
chateau	chateaux, chateaus
cherub	cherubim, cherubs
genus	genera
index	indices, indexes
madame	mesdames
monsieur	messieurs
seraph	seraphim, seraphs
tableau	tableaux, tableaus

8. Some nouns are plural in form but singular in meaning. They, therefore, take a singular verb:

acoustics	mumps
aims	civics
mathematics	news
means (in the sense of	politics
way to an end)	statistics
measles	tactics
molasses	

9. Proper nouns form their plurals in the usual way by adding *s*: *Helens, Franks, Kellers.*

Those ending in a sibilant form their plurals by adding *es*: *Joneses, Adamses.*

10. Some nouns form their plurals by the change of an internal vowel: *men, women, geese, mice.*

11. Some nouns have the same form in the plural as in the singular: *deer, salmon, sheep, trout.*

12. Most compound nouns form the plural by adding the sign of the plural to the fundamental part of the word: *courts-martial, aides-de-camp, sons-in-law, poets-laureate.*

When the words are written solid, the sign of the plural is always at the end: *handfuls, spoonfuls.*

13. Some nouns form their plurals by adding an additional syllable: *oxen, children.*

14. Letters and figures form their plural by adding *'s*: *A's, 8's.* (See p. 50.)

15. Some nouns have two plurals differing in meaning: *dies, dice; pennies, pence; brothers, brethren.*

PRONOUNS

Case

1. The object of a verb should be in the objective case.

Whom (not *who*) did you wish to see?
He was one *whom* (not *who*) you could trust.

2. The object of a preposition should be in the objective case.

The task was to be divided between *you* and *me* (not *you* and *I*).
The result depended upon us (not we) younger men.
The book was left for *you* and *him* (not *you* and *he*).

3. The subject of an infinitive is in the objective case.

They told *him* and *me* (not *he* and *I*) to report to the office.
Let *her* and *me* (not *she* and *I*) finish the proofreading.

4. The verb *to be* takes the same case after, as before it.

> It is *I* (not *me*).
> They took it to be *him* (not *he*).
> I am often taken to be *she* (not *her*).

5. A pronoun modifying a gerund must be in the possessive case.

> The success of the meeting depends on *his* (not *him*) being present.
> Father would not hear of *my* (not *me*) taking the case.

6. A pronoun must agree with its antecedent in person, number, and gender, but not in case.

> He who is ready may go.
> I, who am stronger, can bear it.
> Many a person has asked himself this question.

7. Such words as *each, every, everyone, everybody, anybody, either, neither, no one, nobody,* are singular in number.

> 1. Each of the girls was (not were) present.
> 2. Every book and every magazine was eagerly read.
> 3. Everybody should pay *his* (not *their*) share.
> 4. Neither of the students *was* (not *were*) accepted.

8. None may be singular or plural according to the meaning.

(See *College Handbook of Composition,* Woolley and Scott, p. 169.)

> 1. None of the directors wishes to cast his vote for the appropriation.
> 2. None were willing to sign the petition.
> 3. None of the jewels were found.

9. A relative pronoun must agree with its antecedent in person and number. It is often incorrectly made to agree with a word which is not its antecedent; therefore, carefully determine what word is the antecedent.

> This is the only *one* of my brothers *who* likes to travel.
> He is one of the best *governors that* have ever served the State.

10. Note that there is no apostrophe in possessive pronouns. The correct forms are *its, hers, ours, yours, theirs.*

Note that *whose,* the pronoun, must not be confused with *who's* meaning *who is.*

> Whose book is that?
> Who's going to the theater with me next Thursday?

VERBS

Tense

1. The present tense should be used to express action or being of the present time.

(1) The present tense should not be used in telling of a past event.

> Mary *said* (not *says*) to me, "The tire was punctured on the way from Newton."

(2) The present tense should not be used to express time begun in the past and still continuing.

> I have *been* (not *am*) in New York for ten years.

(3) The present tense should be used to express a present fact or an unchangeable truth.

> The guide explained that Grant's Tomb *is* (not *was*) at 122d Street and Riverside Drive.
> He said that Europe *is* (not *was*) separated from America by the Atlantic Ocean.

2. The past tense should be used in speaking of a definite past event or action.

> I *heard* Dr. Cadman speak when I *was* in New York.

3. The present perfect tense denotes "something happening repeatedly, continuously, or at a time not specifically mentioned." *James Melvin Lee.*

> I *have heard* John Masefield speak many times.
> Helen *hasn't arrived* yet.

146

4. The past perfect tense denotes that the action of the verb was completed at some definite point in past time.

> Before my visit to New York I *had* never *heard* him speak. If he *had* (not *would have*) *waited,* he would have won the prize.

Note the correct use of tense in the following sentences:

> He didn't ring the bell.
> He hasn't rung the bell yet.
> He hadn't rung the bell when I entered the room.
> I have visited most of the capitals of Europe.
> I have been in America ten years.
> He always has paid and always will pay the bill.
> *Not:* He always has and always will pay the bill.

5. The tense of the infinitive is always relative to the time of the main verb.

(1) The present infinitive denotes the same time or future time in relation to the action of the main verb. Notice that in the following sentences the present infinitive is used with verbs denoting present or past time. The time denoted by the infinitive is the same as that of the principal verb or later than that denoted by the principal verb.

> I intend *to go* tomorrow.
> I intended *to go* Thursday.
> For several days I have been intending *to write.*
> I should have liked *to do* it (not *to have done* it).
> Jim would have liked *to go* with his brother last week (not *to have gone*).
>
> I had intended *to write* the letter before breakfast (not *to have written*).

(2) The perfect infinitive denotes action that is complete at the time of the principal verb.

> The Zeppelin was reported *to have been sighted* off Bermuda at noon.

6. Note the difference in meaning implied by the present and perfect infinitives in the following sentences:

His men believed Washington to be a great general.

We believe Washington to have been a great general.

The Milan Cathedral is said *to be* one of the largest in the world.

The Parthenon is said *to have been* erected in the Age of Pericles.

Principal Parts

7. The principal parts of verbs consist of the present and the past indicative, and the past or perfect participle.

The following table shows the principal parts of many troublesome verbs, most of which are irregular.

Present	Past	Perfect Participle
am or be	was	been
arise	arose	arisen
awake	awoke	awaked
bear	bore	borne
beat	beat	beaten
begin	began	begun
bend	bent	bent
beseech	besought	besought
bid (to order)	bid	bid
bid (to greet)	bade	bidden
bleed	bled	bled
blow	blew	blown
break	broke	broken
bring	brought	brought
burst	burst	burst
catch	caught	caught
choose	chose	chosen
climb	climbed	climbed
cling	clung	clung
come	came	come
dive	dived	dived
do	did	done
draw	drew	drawn
drink	drank	drunk
drive	drove	driven
fall	fell	fallen
fight	fought	fought

Present	*Past*	*Perfect Participle*
flee	fled	fled
fly	flew	flown
flow	flowed	flowed
forbid	forbade	forbidden
forget	forgot	forgotten
forsake	forsook	forsaken
freeze	froze	frozen
get	got	got
go	went	gone
grow	grew	grown
hang (of a picture)	hung	hung
hang (of a person)	hanged	hanged
hide	hid	hidden
hurt	hurt	hurt
lay (to cause to lie)	laid	laid
lie (to recline)	lay	lain
lie (to tell a falsehood)	lied	lied
lead	led	led
leap	leaped	leaped
loose	loosed	loosed
lose	lost	lost
pay	paid	paid
plead	pleaded	pleaded
prove	proved	proved (not *proven*)
ring	rang	rung
rise	rose	risen
run	ran	run
say	said	said
see	saw	seen
seek	sought	sought
set (to place)	set	set
shake	shook	shaken
shine	shone	shone
shrink	shrank	shrunk
sing	sang	sung
sink	sank	sunk
sit (to sit down)	sat	sat
show	showed	shown
speak	spoke	spoken
slay	slew	slain

Present	Past	Perfect Participle
sleep	slept	slept
stay	stayed (staid)	stayed (staid)
steal	stole	stolen
stick	stuck	stuck
stop	stopped	stopped
sting	stung	stung
strive	strove	striven
swear	swore	sworn
swim	swam	swum
swing	swung	swung
take	took	taken
teach	taught	taught
tear	tore	torn
throw	threw	thrown
tread	trod	trodden or trod
wake	woke (waked)	waked
wear	wore	worn
weave	wove	woven
win	won	won
wring	wrung	wrung
write	wrote	written

8. ILLUSTRATIONS OF THE CORRECT USAGE OF VERBS.

Perry *began* (not *begun*) his speech early in the evening.
Anna *did* (not *done*) her work well.
Charles *drank* (not *drunk*) a glass of milk.
Father *has gone* (not *has went*) to Florida.
The criminal *was hanged* (not *hung*) at twelve.
He *knelt* (not *kneeled*) before the altar.
She *lay* (not *laid*) on the beach every afternoon.
Mother *has lain* (not *laid*) down for her afternoon nap.
Helen was *lying* (not *laying*) down when I called her.
He told the dog to *lie* (not *lay*) still.
Lie (not *lay*) down, Fido.
He was *lying* (not *lieing*) to you about the accident.
The patient *paid* (not *payed*) his bill promptly.
His lawyer has *proved* (not *proven*) his point.
The bell *rang* (not *rung*) at ten o'clock.
He *ran* (not *run*) to meet his mother.
I *saw* (not *seen*) Mr. Brown yesterday.
The secretary has *shown* (not *has showed*) me his report.

ADJECTIVES AND ADVERBS

1. Adverbs, not adjectives, are used to modify verbs.

He behaved *perfectly* (not *perfect*) even in that trying situation.

Will you do this for me? *Surely* (not *sure*).

Note that when the condition of the subject is described, an adjective is used.

The vegetables boiled *soft*.

But when the action of the verb is explained, an adverb is used.

The vegetables boiled *softly*.

2. The following words have the same form whether they are used as adjectives or as adverbs: *fast, first, ill, loud.*

3. Note that both *quick* and *quickly*, *slow* and *slowly* are adverbial forms.

> *Correct*
> He drives slow.
> He drives slowly.
> Come quick.
> Come quickly.

4. A few adjectives end in *ly*, such as *cowardly, gentlemanly, leisurely, lonely, orderly.*

5. Verbs of the senses, such as *look, sound, smell, taste, feel*, and copulative verbs, such as *be, appear, seem*, take an adjective to denote a quality or condition of the subject.

Hazel looked *pretty* (not *prettily*) in her new hat.
Bells sound *clear* (not *clearly*) at dusk.
Violets smell *sweet* (not *sweetly*).
The pudding tastes *delicious* (not *deliciously*).
Robert feels *unhappy* (not *unhappily*) about his Latin.

Note that usage is divided in regard to *He feels bad* and *He feels badly*.

6. Note that the modifier should be an adjective if it denotes the condition of the object, but an adverb if it explains the action of the verb.

> He kept it *firm* (not *firmly*).
> She held the wheel *tight* (not *tightly*).
> He looked *quietly* around.
> He spoke *clearly* over the telephone.

7. *Well* may be an adjective or an adverb.

> How did you sleep? *Well,* thank you.
> The work was *well* done.

Note that *good* is not used of physical well-being.
> I feel *well* (not good).

Comparison

8. The comparative degree is used in comparing two persons or things. The superlative degree is used in comparing more than two persons or things.

> Webster is the *more* (not *most*) reliable of the two authorities.
> In our club Alfred Noyes is the *most popular* poet read.

9. Adjectives of one syllable and most adjectives of two syllables form their comparative by adding *er,* and their superlative by adding *est,* to the positive.

> Susie's manner was *gayer* (not *more gay*) than her sister's.
> Elmer seems *wittier* (not *more witty*) than his brother.
> Shakespeare is the *greatest* British dramatist.

Many adjectives of two syllables and most adjectives of more than two syllables form their comparative by adding *more* or *less,* and their superlative by adding *most* or *least.*

> The recent news of the Zeppelin seemed *more hopeful.*
> As a business man he became *most successful.*

10. Some adjectives, and adverbs derived from them, are incapable of comparison because they express a quality complete or perfect; as, *universal, unique, perfect, infinite, preferable.*

11. In comparing two things exclude the thing compared; as, Chicago is *larger* than any *other* city in Illinois.

12. In comparing more than two objects include the thing compared; as, Chicago is the *largest* city in Illinois.

Note that a double comparison, although once in good use, is now considered incorrect.

> The flood was the *gravest* (not *most gravest*) in the history of the country.

Negatives

13. Two negatives make an affirmative.

> There aren't *any* (not *no*) books on the shelf.
> He doesn't want *any* (not *no*) help.

The words *hardly, scarcely, but,* and *only* are negative in meaning and should not be used with another negative.

> He *can hardly* (not *can't hardly*) hear what you say.
> There was scarcely *any* (not *no*) water in the jar.
> John had *but one* (not *hadn't but one*) sheet of paper.
> They *had* (not *hadn't*) only one report of the meeting.

Repetition of the Article

14. The article should be repeated in referring to two separate persons or objects.

> We engaged a typist and a stenographer (two persons).
> We engaged a typist and stenographer (one person).
>
> She has a maple and a mahogany bureau (two bureaus).
> She has a maple and mahogany bureau (one bureau).

But when two or more nouns refer to the same person, the article should not be repeated.

> Cæsar was a general, writer, and statesman (not *a general, a* writer, and *a* statesman).

Position of "Only"

15. The adverb *only* should be placed as near as possible to the word it modifies.

> The bookkeeper made *only* one error (not *only made*).
> He only nominated the president (he didn't vote for him).
> He nominated only the president (he did not nominate anyone else).
> Only he voted for Jones (no one else voted for him).

Agreement of Adjective and Noun

16. *This* and *that* are singular and must be used to modify singular nouns. *These* and *those* are plural and must be used to modify plural nouns.

> *This* kind (not *these* kind) of books is instructive.
> *These* kinds (not *these* kind) of books are instructive.
> *That* sort (not *those* sort) of answer carries little weight.
> *Those* sorts (not *those* sort) of answers carry little weight.

Note that *kind of* (not that *kind of a*) and *sort of* (not *sort of a*) are permissible although colloquial.

> That kind of (not that *kind of a*) boy ranks high.
> That sort of (not that *sort of a*) position is what I want.

Unnecessary Adverbs

17. Unnecessary adverbs should be avoided.

Each sheet of paper should be carefully numbered (not numbered *throughout*).

> Repeat it (not repeat it *again*).
> They returned (not returned *back*) to the hotel.
> Let us cooperate (not cooperate *together*).
> Finish the business (not finish *up* the business).
> They expect to divide (not divide *up*) the proceeds.

PREPOSITIONS

Care must be taken in the use of prepositions. A dictionary should always be consulted in case of doubt as to correct usage. The following illustrations may be helpful:

among, between
(Use *among* with more than two; *between* with two.)

The flowers were divided *among* (not *between*) the patients of the ward.

The flowers were divided *between* (not *among*) the two patients.

at, with
(*with* a person, *at* a thing)

Jane was angry *with* (not *at*) me.

The minority was angry *at* (not *with*) the resolution passed.

The lawyer was displeased *with* (not *at*) the witness.

beside, besides
(at the side of, in addition to)

George walked *beside* (not *besides*) Mary.

Besides (not *beside*) the large doors, there are several smaller ones.

back of, behind
They ran *behind* (not *back of* or *in back of*) the garage.

of, for
The family is in need *of* (not *for*) funds.

of, on
The company has a monopoly *of* (not *on*) sugar.

The preposition *of* should not be used in such verb phrases as *could of, may of, must of.*

on, onto
(*onto* is usually avoided by careful writers.)

They stepped *on* (not *onto*) the grass.

IDIOMATIC PREPOSITIONAL PHRASES

adapted for	The apartment is adapted for housekeeping.
adapted to	Helen soon adapted herself to her changed circumstances.
	The tone of a letter should be adapted to the reader.
adapted from	The story is adapted from the French.
agree on	The faculty agreed on limiting the number of students.
agree to	Do you agree to this proposition?
agree with	He agrees with me on the matter.

155

apply for	Mary may apply for the position.
apply to	She must apply to the president.
argue about	Do not argue about the question.
argue for	They argued for the abolition of child labor.
argue with	He argued with me about prohibition.
confide in	May I confide in you?
confide to	She confided her troubles to me.
consist in	Success does not always consist in achieving wealth.
consist of	The play consists of five acts.
denounce as	Arnold was denounced as a traitor.
denounce for	The thief was denounced for his crime.
die from	They died from exposure.
die of	She died of pneumonia.
differ about	We differ about the success of coeducation.
differ from	Mary differs from her sister in appearance.
differ in	Mother and Father differ in their opinions about our summer vacation.
differ on	They usually differ on religious questions.
differ with	I differ with you in regard to the discipline of the school.
disappointed of	Bad weather often disappoints the farmers of their harvest.
disappointed in	Farmers are often disappointed in their yearly income.
enter at	Enter at the front gate.
	He entered his son at Harvard.
enter for	John has entered for the championship.
enter in	He has entered the bill in his accounts.
enter into	The Faculty entered into an agreement with the townspeople.
enter upon	He entered upon his new work with enthusiasm.
impatient at	The superintendent was impatient at the delay.
impatient with	Mother was impatient with the boys.

| live at | He lives at the Hotel Astor. |
| live in | Helen lives in Florida. |

| prejudice against | No one is prejudiced against you. |

| reconcile to | He was reconciled to his father. |
| reconcile with | These opinions can be reconciled with hers. |

NECESSARY PREPOSITIONS

Prepositions should not be omitted when they are needed to make the meaning clear. In the following sentences note the need of the italicized prepositions.

It is *of* no use to object.
Barbara will be *at* home tomorrow.
The tree was a foot *in* diameter.
Will you refrain *from* reading aloud?
His remark is unworthy *of* your notice.
They are going either to France or *to* Italy.
On this side of the river is a group of houses.
An appointment with the dentist prevented Rose *from* going to the concert.
You will find reading a comfort in youth as well as *in* later life.
The states of the East and *of* the West stood together on the question.
I had no faith *in*, or hope *for*, the movement.

UNNECESSARY PREPOSITIONS

Prepositions should be omitted when they are not needed to make the meaning clear. In the following illustrations note the unnecessary prepositions:

The girls in the school were all *about* (not *of about*) sixteen.
No one can help observing (not *from* observing) her.
Let us examine (not examine *into*) the room.
The class entered (not entered *into*) the room.
They are going home (not *to* home).
The tree is *near* (not *near to*) the garage.
The child fell *off* (not *off of*) the chair.

They sail *about* (not *on about*) the thirteenth of June.
The club disbanded *about* (not *at about*) ten.
Where has John been (not *been at*)?
Where shall we go (not *go to*)?
She does not remember (not *remember of*) any such happening.

CONJUNCTIONS

The correct use of conjunctions is sometimes confusing. Note the following suggestions which illustrate good usage:

as, as if

Do *as* (not *like*) the manager suggests.
I feel *as if* (not *like*) I need a change.

but, and

The manager believed in auditing the report, *but* (not *and*) the vice-president did not consider it necessary.

unless

Do not do it *unless* (not *without*) he gives you directions.
I cannot write a story *unless* (not *without*) I am in the proper mood.

COORDINATE CONJUNCTIONS

Correlative conjunctions, that is, conjunctions used in pairs, should be placed next to the words they connect. These words or expressions should be in the same construction.

The most common correlatives are *either–or, neither–nor, not only–but also, both–and, and–therefore, whether–or.*

They have read neither the book nor the magazine.
Not: They have neither read the book nor the magazine.
The work gave me both pleasure and experience.
Not: The work both gave me pleasure and experience.
Not: We visited not only London, but also Paris, Nice, and Rome.
Not: We not only visited London, but also Paris, Nice, and Rome.

With coordinate conjunctions such as *and* and *but,* ideas must be expressed in similar construction.

158

He was strong in body and in mind.

Or: He was strong physically and mentally.

Not: He was strong in body and also mentally.

SUBORDINATE CONJUNCTIONS

When one idea in a sentence is dependent upon another, a subordinate conjunction is used to connect the dependent with the main thought.

Do not use *as, because, how, where* for *that* or *whether*.

He doesn't see *that* (not *as*) he ought to do it.

I don't know *whether* (not *as*) I can go.

The reason for his absence was *that* (not *because*) he felt ill.

He told them *that* (not *how*) he expected to go to South America.

I saw in the advertisement *that* (not *where*) cars were to be sold much cheaper this year.

REFERENCE BOOKS

BALL, FRANCIS K. *Constructive English, A Handbook of Speaking and Writing*. Ginn and Company, 1923.

CANBY and OPDYCKE. *Good English*. The Macmillan Company, 1925.

GREEVER and JONES. *Century Handbook of Writing*. The Century Company, 1922.

HOTCHKISS and KILDUFF. *Handbook of Business English*. Harper and Brothers, 1920.

KITTREDGE and FARLEY. *Advanced English Grammar*. Ginn and Company, 1913.

MACCRACKEN and SANDISON. *Manual of Good English*. The Macmillan Company, 1917.

NESFIELD, J. C. *Modern English Grammar*. The Macmillan Company, 1920.

OPDYCKE, JOHN B. *The English of Commerce*. Charles Scribner's Sons, 1926.

SMART, WALTER KAY. *Handbook of Effective Writing*. Harper and Brothers, 1922.

WESEEN, MAURICE H. *Crowell's Dictionary of English Grammar and Handbook of American Usage*. Thomas Y. Crowell Company, 1928.

WOOLLEY, EDWIN C. *The Mechanics of Writing*. D. C. Heath and Company, 1909.

WOOLLEY and SCOTT. *College Handbook of Composition*. D. C. Heath and Company, 1928.

PART II

CHAPTER I

LETTER-WRITING AND ANNOUNCEMENTS

Letter-writing has become important, particularly in relation to business. It forms the main subject of so many texts on Business English that there is no need for extended discussion here.

As correspondence fills a large part of the secretary's day, he should know the principles of letter-writing, for to write a good letter is a real accomplishment. Modern letters, whether coming from a great public organization or from a private individual, are personal and individual. Like those of the great letter-writers, they reveal personality. They show due regard for the viewpoint of the reader. They are planned with care. Their language is informal but dignified; and their tone courteous and well-bred.

The cheap cordiality of some letters, particularly of the sales type, that strains to compel the reader by a too familiar colloquial tone, suggests poor taste, insincerity of purpose, and tawdriness of material. Better firms season friendliness with dignity, for they know that their clientele resents being addressed by the "hail-fellow-well-met" attitude, all too common in American business correspondence.

Dignity, however, does not mean such senseless formality as that produced by stereotyped phrases. Many expressions such as those that follow, once considered necessary to give a business-like tone to correspondence, are fortunately disappearing from modern letters.

Yours of the 13th inst. received
We have your esteemed favor of March 20

In reply to yours of the tenth, would say
Answering yours of June 10th, would say
Under separate cover
The favor of an answer is requested
This is to acknowledge receipt of your valued order
Awaiting your further commands
We beg to announce
We beg to call your attention
Your letter has come to hand
Enclosed you will find
Your letter of recent date
Inst., ult., prox.
Replying to your letter of the 5th wish to say we have duly noted the contents
Replying to your telegram relative to, etc.
Hoping to hear from you soon, I remain
And oblige, Yours truly
Trusting to hear from you soon
Believing these considerations to be of interest, and assuring you that we shall appreciate a word in reply from you, we are, etc.

Assuring you that your past favors have been highly appreciated and anticipating a continuance of your valued patronage, we remain

Anticipating the courtesy of your favored patronage and thanking you in advance for same, I remain

Words, too new or too old, as well as trite expressions, must be guarded against. If the dictionary does not vouch for the good standing of a word, the secretary should not include it in his vocabulary. The following are a few objectionable words, often unthinkingly used by even experienced secretaries:

enthuse	*for*	to be enthusiastic
humans	*for*	persons
recommend	*for*	recommendation
gotten	*for*	got
have got	*for*	have
proven	*for*	proved
educating	*for*	educational
anxious	*for*	desirous or eager
fulfill	*for*	fill
partake	*for*	participate

New York
247 Park Avenue
46TH TO 47TH STREETS
Boston
247 Berkeley Street
NEAR COMMONWEALTH AVE.
Providence
155 Angell Street
CHURCHILL HOUSE

Katharine Gibbs School
of Secretarial and Executive Training
for Educated Women

K.W.C. GRAND, GENERAL AGENT
FOR THE UNITED STATES AND CANADA

TELEPHONE VANDERBILT 1830
CABLE ADDRESS "PADDINGTON" NEW YORK

GREAT WESTERN RAILWAY OF ENGLAND
505 FIFTH AVENUE
NEW YORK

HARPER & BROTHERS
PUBLISHERS
NEW YORK AND LONDON

ESTABLISHED
1817

Columbia University
in the City of New York

THE ENGLISH GRADUATE UNION

COLUMBIA UNIVERSITY
IN THE CITY OF NEW YORK

HALL OF PHILOSOPHY

HERBERT K.TWITCHELL, President
GEORGE F. CRANE, Vice President
HENRY R. TAYLOR, Vice President
WILLISTON H. BENEDICT, Secretary

RALPH H. STEVER, Cashier
FREDERICK A. CUMMINGS, Treasurer
ELMER RAND JACOBS, Asst. Treasurer
THORNTON C. THAYER, Asst. Cashier

THE SEAMEN'S BANK FOR SAVINGS
IN THE CITY OF NEW YORK
56 WALL STREET
NEW YORK

FORMS FOR HEADINGS

On paper containing letterheads, the typist inserts the date directly under the letterhead, or in the more conservative style to form the marginal line on the right. In some modern letters the date is placed at the lower left-hand corner, written either as May 1, 1929, or as May First, Nineteen Hundred and Twenty-nine.

The following forms illustrate correct arrangement:

May 1, 1929	April 25	15th
	1 9 3 0	April
		1931

July the Fourth
Nineteen Hundred Thirty

November	October	M A Y
fifteenth	20	Fourth
1 9 3 2	1930	1 9 2 8

On paper that does not contain letterheads, the headings should be written according to the following order: street address, name of city or town, name of state, date.

414 West 121 Street,	41 West 76 Street
New York City,	New York, New York
June 30, 1929.	July 18, 1929
McMinnville, Oregon	Lima, New York
January 1, 1930	August 1, 1932

INSIDE ADDRESS

In a business letter the inside address, containing the name and the address of the receiver, precedes the salutation; in an official letter it is usually placed beneath the letter at the lower left-hand; in a friendly letter it is omitted.

Indented style with closed punctuation:

> Mrs. George McClelland,
> 121 Harmon Drive,
> Larchmont,
> New York.

Block style with open punctuation:

George Fulton, Esq.
317 Madison Avenue
New York, New York

SALUTATION

Correct forms for business letters:

Dear Sir: (Dear Sirs seldom used in America)
Dear Madam:
Gentlemen:
Mesdames or *Ladies:*
My dear Mrs. Bryan: (formal American usage)
Dear Mr. Bryan: (informal American usage)

When open punctuation is used in the heading and in the inside address, either closed or open punctuation may be used after the salutation; but when closed punctuation is used in the heading, it should also be used after the salutation. (See p. 41.)

When the writer wishes to bring his letter to the attention of a certain official, he should write on the same line as the salutation or beneath it to the right, *Attention of Mr.* ....

The Macmillan Company
  60 Fifth Avenue
    New York, N. Y.
Gentlemen: Attention of Dr. J. F. Brown

COMPLIMENTARY CLOSE

Correct forms for business letters:

Very truly yours,   Cordially yours,
Yours truly,   Faithfully yours,
Respectfully yours,   Sincerely yours,

The complimentary close should not be preceded by a participial phrase, as, *Hoping to hear from you soon*. Punctuation following a complimentary close depends on punctuation following the salutation. If punctuation is omitted there, it should also be omitted after the complimentary close.

ADDITIONAL DATA

Additional data, such as the initials of the dictator of the letter with those of the typist, are usually placed at the lower left hand. They may be written thus:

KM S A T	FCS:RG	CB
MLK/ECC	PGB,ABR	HEA

When enclosures are made in the letter, that fact should be noted in the lower left-hand corner, as, *Encl.* or *Enclosures*.

SIGNATURES

Placement of signatures should correspond to the style of the heading or of the inside address.

CORRECT FORMS FOR THE INDIVIDUAL

John F. Brown
John Francis Brown
J. F. Brown

Such titles as Dr., Rev., Prof., should not precede signatures nor should such degrees as B.A., M.D., LL.D., follow them.

An unmarried woman should not sign herself as *Miss* Elizabeth Jones, but should place *Miss* in parenthesis before her name if she thinks it necessary.

A married woman must sign her own name, as, *Vera C. Martini*. This may be preceded by *Mrs.* in parenthesis or by her married name written in parenthesis below the signature.

(Mrs.) Vera C. Martini
or Vera C. Martini
(Mrs. Herbert Martini)

When the secretary signs his chief's name to a letter, he may add his own initials or he may sign his own name adding below it *For* with the chief's name.

CORRECT SIGNATURES FOR LETTERS SIGNED BY OFFICIALS

Very truly yours,

[signature]

President.

H.K.T.
MV

M a y
Fourth
1 9 2 8

Very Sincerely yours

[signature: Leon Wieder]

Vice-President

Sincerely yours

[signature: Katharine C. Reiley]

Katharine C. Reiley
Associate Director

KOR:C

FRED F. FRENCH COMPANIES

[signature: Fred F. French]

CHAIRMAN OF THE
BOARDS OF DIRECTORS

Sincerely yours,

[signature: Cameron Beck]

CB
HEA

Personnel Director

Sincerely yours,

[signature: Molly Blumenthal]

Secretary to Mrs. Oakley.

Very truly yours,

[signature: A. Swoboda]

A. SWOBODA.
TRAVEL DEPARTMENT

AS/HK.

167

ILLUSTRATIONS OF VARIOUS TYPES OF LETTERS

An Order Letter

394 Maple Street
Woodsville, N. H.
December 18, 19—

Mark Cross
145 Tremont Street
Boston, Mass.

Gentlemen:

Will you please send me by parcel post the articles listed below. As the merchandise is for Christmas presents, I shall appreciate your prompt attention to my order.

1 brown envelope purse of antelope in modernistic design with satin trimming, moire lining, and handle at back	$19.70
1 sewing bag, collapsible style in "peacock" calf, yellow, with flowered silk lining, 7 in. diameter	12.75
1 bridge set in tan pigskin leather case	8.75
	$41.20

You will find enclosed my check for $41.20.

Yours truly,
Mildred K. Bentley

Letters of Acknowledgment

(1)

We acknowledge with thanks your request for the following articles:

1 pr. rubber boots, size 6, price $4.35	$4.35
2 khaki cotton shirts, size 34, price $1.00	2.00
2 prs. grey worsted socks, size 9, price $1.20	2.40
	$8.75

We shall attend to this order, making sure that it will reach you before May sixteenth. We notice, however, that you have omitted to say whether you require knee length or full length rubber boots. We have both kinds at $4.35 a pair, and we are desirous not to make a mistake in filling your order. If you will let us know at once which kind you wish to purchase, we shall forward the articles to you without delay.

(2)

The Community Center acknowledges with genuine appreciation the receipt of your contribution of Three Dollars to the work of the organization for the year 1928.

(3)

Thank you for your order of May 2. We are sending out the goods as you instructed and hope they will reach you safely.

If we can serve you further, we shall be glad to do so.

(4)

We thank you for your order of May 4th. We have already made shipment by parcel post, C.O.D., of the following, which is our order No. 8235:

1 dozen best quality ladies' plain white linen handkerchiefs	$5.00
6 pairs Gordon chiffon silk hose, gunmetal, square heels, size 8½	12.00
1 dozen spools Coats' white, No. 6, linen thread	1.50
	$18.50

We hope that these goods will so please you in every detail that we shall continue to receive your orders and that we may number you among our thousands of steadily satisfied customers. We assure you of our constant personal attention and of our steadfast desire to please you.

(5)

Miss Marie Haines,
Harmon Drive,
Larchmont, New York.

Dear Madam:

Thank you for your check for $500. which we received from Miss Hathaway and which we have put to work immediately in a guaranteed first mortgage certificate maturing January 1, 1930.

As we explained to Miss Hathaway and your sister, we do not happen to have today any $500. certificate of an earlier maturity and so I have followed their suggestion in sending you this one. We firmly believe that the interest rate will drop and are recommending to all of our clients that they take as long maturities as possible, in order that they may take advantage of the present 5½% guaranteed rate.

Our interest checks will be mailed to you and the certificate will be forwarded to you within ten days.

We are glad of this opportunity of investing for you. We know you will be greatly pleased with your investment and hope to have the pleasure of serving you again soon.

Yours very truly,
Florence Tyler

Letters Offering Charge Accounts

(1)

We've just finished the greatest year in the history of this business . . . established more than a century ago . . . greatest not only in volume of sales but greatest in the number of new friends we have made—customers who have come to know our high standard of Values and Service.

In the conduct of this business, it will be our earnest endeavor to surpass our former achievements, both in Values and Service and in timely offerings of dependable merchandise and styles.

We believe this is your kind of store and that you will enjoy shopping here. We offer "More than 100 years of Service" not as an appeal to sentiment but as proof of integrity and stability.

We should like to feel that you are going to become a regular patron of our Store and, to make your shopping easier, desire to extend to you the convenience of a Charge Account. A signature card is enclosed for your convenience.

(2)

Appreciation of the many conveniences of a charge account has grown with the years, and it is to increase the pleasure of your shopping that we offer you a charge account in our establishment.

In your case, we will dispense with the usual formalities—just say "Charge it" when sending your next purchase home, and an account will be opened in your name. This will apply whether you purchase in person, by mail, or by phone.

(3)

It is our endeavor to understand the desires of our customers, and to keep up with important style centres at home and abroad. From the knowledge these studies give, we try to offer at fair prices appropriate assortments of carefully chosen merchandise. We should like very much to have you visit our store often because we believe we can take good care of most of your wants.

Many of our friends feel so much at home that they frequently give us helpful criticism about the goods we offer and the service we render. Often they suggest new lines of merchandise and new methods of presenting them. If you would take such interest in us, we believe it would make the task of shopping a real pleasure.

You may regard a charge account as a matter of convenience. If so, we shall be glad to open one. No formality is required. When you make purchases, simply tell the salesperson to charge them, and they will be delivered to you without any further formality. We should appreciate the return of the enclosed card.

LETTERS REFUSING CHARGE ACCOUNTS

(1)

We are sorry to say that the data at our command are not sufficient to justify us in opening the account you wish.

It is sometimes difficult to determine just what measure of financial responsibility our friends have, and when such is the case, we are obliged to appeal to them for additional information.

If you will be good enough to call or drop us a line, we shall be glad to go into the matter further.

(2)

To our regret, we do not see our way clear, at the present time, to open a charge account for you in compliance with your recent request. We shall be very happy, however, to offer you our facilities, in the way of store service, in other directions as usual.

We appreciate your kind interest in making this inquiry.

(3)

We are sorry not to be able to pass favorably upon your application for an account.

You will doubtless appreciate that a fair knowledge must be had of a customer's responsibility and bill-paying habits, and unfortunately the data of this nature at our command are very limited.

Although we cannot be of service with a charge account, we shall always take pleasure in serving you and hope to have your permission to send your recent purchases on our regular cash terms.

(4)

In answer to your recent application for a charge account, we are sorry to say that we have been unable to secure from the usual business sources the information necessary for the establishment of an account.

We, therefore, regret that we shall be unable to comply with your request at this time, unless additional business or bank references are submitted, in which case we shall be pleased to give the matter further consideration.

LETTERS CONCERNING UNUSED CHARGE ACCOUNTS

(1)

As you know, your name was placed on our list of charge customers some time ago. Yet we have no record of your having used your account.

Are we to blame in any way?

We'd appreciate a frank reply and are enclosing a stamped envelope for your convenience.

Meanwhile you may be interested in glancing through the enclosed announcement of the new spring stocks now in our stores.

(2)

We have had no answer to the letter we sent you two weeks ago asking what we could do to renew your patronage with us.

As the letter has not been returned to us, we assume it has reached you.

We should like to make good whatever is wrong and hope that you will let us know how we can do so either by dropping us a line or, better still, by coming in and talking it over with us.

(3)

We like to keep in close touch with our charge customers. We notice that we have not had the pleasure of serving you for some time.

Your good-will and patronage are very highly valued, and if our service or merchandise has fallen short of the high standards we try to maintain, we shall appreciate your bringing it to our attention.

We shall be very grateful for any criticism that you may have to make.

(4)

For over a hundred years we have enjoyed the patronage of the people of New York and many other places. As we grow older we appreciate more and more the importance of keeping old friends. So I am sure you will forgive any anxiety we may feel over the fact that your account is not so active as it once was.

Even if you do not care to buy, we should like you to visit us. Throughout the store, we think you will see the results of more careful preparation in larger and better stocks, and very generally we think you will find our people courteous, hospitable, and desirous to understand. We believe you would enjoy a visit to our eighth floor where we offer antique furniture and decorative pieces of various kinds. The sixth and seventh floors are devoted to home furnishings, but there also are points of interest all through the store which we think would appeal to you.

Criticisms of past performance and suggestions that would show us how to render better service in the future are always appreciated, and I am presuming to enclose a stamped envelope in the hope that if you cannot come, you will find it convenient to write us a letter.

CLAIM LETTERS

LETTER OF CLAIM WRITTEN BY A SECRETARY

(1)

17 East Main Street
Rochester, N. Y.
April 25, 19—

The Brown Paper Company
154 West 14th Street
New York City

Gentlemen

On Friday, April 22, Mr. Glendenning received from your firm ten dozen boxes of Grade A paper which are being returned immediately, as the quality is far below the Brown standard that we have learned to expect.

There are two noticeable errors in the engraving, which I have checked on the sheet enclosed for your inspection. One of these is the spelling of Mr. Glendenning's name.

Will you please send us a correct shipment as soon as possible? The previous order was as follows:

10 dozen boxes Grade A paper, size, 8 x 10.

Very truly yours
Pearl J. Russell
Secretary to Mr. Glendenning

(2)

411 West 116 Street
New York City
May 6, 19—

Claim Department
Pennsylvania Railroad Company
Pittsburgh, Pa.

Gentlemen:

I wish to present a claim for one hundred and fifty dollars to cover the loss of a suitcase checked on a passenger ticket from Pittsburgh to New York on May the first.

I surrendered the suitcase in the baggage room of the Pennsylvania Station at Pittsburgh about 11:00 p.m. on May 1st to be checked to New York. I left on train No. 6 at 11:45 the same evening.

When I arrived in New York the following morning and presented myself at the baggage room, my suitcase was missing. I was told that it might come on a later train, but since that time, five days ago, I have made a daily call at the baggage room of the New York station, but have not yet obtained my bag. The check number which I hold is 8543A.

The contents of the suitcase are valued as follows:

2 silk dresses	$80.00
1 pair of slippers	10.00
2 pairs of hose	2.00
Lingerie	20.00
1 silk negligee	10.00
Toilet articles	6.00
1 pair of gloves	2.00
2 books	5.00
1 traveling clock	15.00
	$150.00

I shall gladly give you any additional information which you may need to establish the authenticity of my claim or to help you in tracing the lost baggage. If it cannot be found within a few days, I shall expect a settlement in full for my claim.

Very truly yours,
Rose Wolcott

ADJUSTMENT LETTERS

(1)

REFUSAL OF A CLAIM

We are very sorry indeed that you are not pleased with the dress we made for you, and we can well appreciate your disappointment.

It sometimes happens that a made-to-order garment does not look the same made up as it does in a picture, and that the goods does not appear as it did in the piece. The same thing might happen, however, if you had a dress made in your own home by a dressmaker.

Since you yourself chose the material and style of the garment and have no complaint to make about the fit and work-manship, we must regretfuily say that we cannot take back the dress. When you ordered it, we were careful to tell you that we never take back made-to-order clothing. When a garment is made to fit one person, we cannot sell it to any one else, and thus your dress would be a total loss to us.

You will understand our position and realize we regret to make this decision.

(2)

A FAVORABLE ADJUSTMENT

We are sorry to know from your letter of May 1st that the radio which you ordered as a birthday gift for your husband arrived with the cabinet so badly marred that you cannot accept it.

As the Long Island Railroad Company gave us a receipt acknowledging that the desk was satisfactorily crated and in good condition when it was received, it must have been damaged in transit. Although the responsibility is really now up to the railroad company, we realize what must have been your disappointment when you found that the gift you purchased for your husband was not in good condition for his birthday. We are, therefore, sending you at once another cabinet exactly like the one you originally ordered.

If you will ask the express company to make a special delivery as soon as the cabinet arrives at the station, we hope that you may still receive it in time for your husband's birthday.

Please leave the damaged cabinet with the railroad company, and we shall ourselves enter a claim for it. You will then have no further trouble.

We thank you for notifying us promptly. We want you to know our first desire is that you should receive your order promptly in perfect condition.

LETTERS OF APPRECIATION FOR ADJUSTMENTS MADE

(1)

Thank you for your corrected bill for the month of September. Your explanation of the error, caused by a similarity in the names of the accounts, makes it entirely excusable.

The promptness with which you rectified this matter is

indeed appreciated; and now, that it has been adjusted to my entire satisfaction, I am enclosing my check for $141.50, the amount due.

(2)

I wish to thank you for your courtesy in replacing the chiffon hose which I recently returned to you.

This is particularly generous of you, as there is no guarantee given with chiffon hose. It was hardly to be expected, however, that hose of this quality should go to pieces during the first wearing. I hope I shall be more fortunate with the second pair.

In the meanwhile, please accept my grateful acknowledgment for your fairness and promptness in answering my complaint. The incident leaves me more convinced than ever of the expediency of trading with a firm that always stands back of its goods.

(3)

I wish to thank you for the courteous and prompt adjustment you made last week for the necklace I purchased and found imperfect.

It is pleasant to receive such considerate attention, which naturally tends to strengthen my confidence in your establishment. In the future, there will be no doubt in my mind as to the reliability and justice of your shop.

COLLECTION LETTERS

(1)

May we remind you of your account for $985.25.

This amount is somewhat past due, so won't you oblige us with a check?

(2)

Did you overlook our recent reminder of your account? The amount past due for your purchases is $985.25. Your check at this time will be appreciated.

(3)

We must again remind you of the balance $985.25 open on your account.

It is very much past due, and your check at this time would be appreciated.

(4)

Previous communications having brought no response, we must again remind you of your account for $985.25.

As this amount has been outstanding for some time, may we respectfully call attention to our terms of sale, bills due when rendered—the first of each month.

LETTERS OF APPLICATION

(1)

332 East 67 Street
New York City
April 19, 19—

The College of the City of New York
139th Street and Amsterdam Avenue
New York City
Gentlemen

I should like to apply for the position of stenographer, advertised in the *Times*. In answer to your requirements, I can offer the following qualifications:

Age	twenty-four years
Education	I have recently completed the two-year Secretarial Course at Columbia University and, consequently, have received thorough stenographic training.
Experience	Last summer I held a position as typist with the Indemnity Insurance Company of North America and also did some stenographic work.
Special Assets	I have studied stenography, typewriting, bookkeeping, accounting, economics, secretarial correspondence, French, and Spanish. In all of these, I have received marks of A or B. Mathematics has always been my best subject.
References	Mr. N. K. Bryant, Broadway and 116th St., New York City.
	Mr. David Grant, Indemnity Insurance Co. of North America, 122 William Street, New York City.
	Rev. Frank W. Crowder, 865 Madison Avenue, New York City.

I shall be glad to call at your office for a personal interview at any time that is convenient to you.

Very truly yours
Evelyn Gillis

(2)

Your advertisement in the *Times* appeals to me strongly, and I should like to apply for the position. As my experience has included work in the sales division of a manufacturing company and as I am a college graduate, I believe you will be interested in my application.

I am twenty-six years old, single, and a graduate of Barnard College.

The various positions I have filled have made me an expert stenographer and an intelligent correspondent; they have required an understanding of office routine and the ability to assume responsibility and work on my own initiative. My experience, extending over a period of five years, has been as follows:

> Secretary to a Department Manager in the Columbia Graphophone Company
> Secretary to an executive in the Queens Chamber of Commerce
> Secretary to an organization engaged in building and financing a church edifice
> Secretary to a Vice-President and Sales Manager of Pathex, Inc.

In my present position with Pathex, Inc., which I have held for the past fifteen months, I compose many of my own letters, supervise the keeping of sales records and the work of an office force.

To the position you wish to fill I can bring resourcefulness, the use of good judgment in matters for which I am responsible, the ability to meet people intelligently and to relieve you of details, as well as the desire to understand and be loyal to your interests.

I can furnish excellent personal and business references from those who know my work and who will be glad to tell you about it.

May I come to see you to explain my qualifications in greater detail?

(3)

Dear Sir:

Mr. J. A. Northcott, Associate Director of University Extension, writes me that Dr. Knox and you are looking for a secretary. Please consider me an applicant for the position.

My education has been obtained in private schools in Canada Park School, London, Ontario, and Westbourne School, Toronto. Near the close of my last year of high school work my health became impaired, and I was obliged to give up my studies for some months. Afterwards my education was continued along general cultural lines—languages, music, nature, travel—rather than academic ones. The only degree I hold is that of Associate of the Canadian Guild of Organists.

The desire for a useful and busy life rather than an empty social one, coupled with a natural aptitude for practical things, led me to take a two-year course in English and French, bookkeeping, filing, typography, and secretarial correspondence.

As to my religious affiliations, I am a Presbyterian. I have had a little experience in social service work.

To me the prime requisite is not salary but congenial work in a cultural environment—such work as will interest me and to which I can bend all my energies.

I enclose a list of references.

If you desire any further information, I shall be pleased to furnish it.

May I hear from you?

> Very truly yours,
> Margaret E. Young

(4)

Gentlemen:

Miss Callan of the University Employment Bureau has referred me to you in the hope that you might have an opening in secretarial work. I am especially desirous of obtaining a position connected with a social service organization.

I am a graduate of Smith College from which I received my A.B. degree in June 1927. My course there consisted of a liberal arts program—English Composition and Literature, and Sociology as my main subjects. Sociology gave me excellent theoretical knowledge. I am now taking at Columbia University the one-year secretarial course, which I shall complete this June. This course has given me a firm foundation for secretarial work. Among my subjects are typewriting, shorthand, secretarial correspondence, vocational psychology, and bookkeeping, all of which provide good practical knowledge.

Although I have not had much actual secretarial work, I am familiar with business. My father is the proprietor of a large store, where I have worked for two summers as a clerk. This experience, I believe, has given me some knowledge of business principles and management helpful in any secretarial position.

The training I have received has provided a good background for the type of work I desire. Since the subject would be familiar to me and much of the business of "learning the ropes" would be done away with, I should need less supervision than the ordinary stenographer and could take up matters of an executive nature.

I am very much interested in social welfare, and I also enjoy secretarial work. I do not think I go too far in saying that you would find me willing and adaptable.

For references, I offer the following:

> Professor H. E. Barnes
> Smith College
> Northampton, Mass.

> Miss Z. Macdonald
> Columbia University
> New York City

I hope that I shall receive a favorable reply.

> Yours sincerely,
> Harriet Cohen

(5)

I wish to apply for the secretarial position which you advertise in the April 30th issue of the *Times*.

I am twenty-six years old and have had seven years of business experience. I am a graduate of Sharpsville High School, Sharpsville, Pa., and of Sharon College of Commerce, Sharon, Pa. I am at the present time taking the two-year secretarial course at Columbia University and expect to receive the Secretarial Certificate next August. I have had wide and varied office experience and am thoroughly familiar with business methods and routine. The details of my training and experience follow.

From April, 1920, until September, 1922, I acted as stenographer in a real estate and lumber office, the Charles S. Flower Lumber Company of Sharon, Pa. My work there included switchboard operating and assistant bookkeeping. While in this position I was also active as stenographic and clerical assistant when my employer organized the Dollar Title and Trust Company. I attended stockholders' meetings, took minutes, and wrote reports. In September, 1922, I left this position for one paying a higher salary at the freight office of the Erie Railroad Company at Farrell, Pa. There, my work consisted mainly of stenography and abstract typing.

In June, 1924, I was employed in the office of the National Malleable and Steel Castings Company at Sharon, where I was trained in the work of all departments so that I was ready to step instantly into the routine work of any absent clerk or stenographer and keep the wheels of his department running smoothly. I also did private secretarial and statistical work of a confidential nature for the treasurer, and clerical work in the payroll department.

The winter of 1926-27 I spent in the West. While there, I did secretarial and clerical work for the Ionaco Company of Denver, Colorado, and some sales work selling their product, an electro-therapeutic device. Not wishing to remain permanently in the West, I obtained a position in the spring of 1927 as private secretary to the sales manager of the Elf Motor Company at Cleveland, Ohio, distributors for Marmon automobiles for the State of Ohio.

As I had always regretted my lack of college training, I left my position in Cleveland and came to New York for the two year secretarial course at Columbia University. Because of my previous training and experience, I am able to shorten the course somewhat and expect to receive the Secretarial Certificate of Columbia University next August. Some of my studies at Columbia are: English composition, business administration, economics, bookkeeping, secretarial correspondence, and Spanish.

Each change in position that I have made has represented a distinct advance. The variety of my work has given me a splendid background of valuable experience such as could never be obtained in the routine of one company.

I am eager to secure a permanent position in New York City, where I expect to continue studying in special night courses along the lines of whatever work I enter. I am looking for a position that offers a real future, and I welcome responsibility.

It is difficult to state a suitable salary with slight knowledge of the requirements and demands of the position. My last salary, however, was .... a month, and I believe that my training at

Columbia warrants a considerable increase. I believe that I should receive a beginning salary of .... a month.

I should be glad to have you consult any of my former employers regarding my qualifications. I am enclosing a list of the names and addresses of the men under whom I have worked.

May I have the favor of a personal interview at your convenience?

LETTERS ADDRESSED TO REFERENCE

(1)

Miss Ida Hailparn of 1121 East Seventh Street, Brooklyn, New York, has applied to this organization for the position of private secretary and stenographer. She has given us your name as a reference, having worked with you for two years.

We should greatly appreciate a prompt reply to the following questions:

1. Is she capable in her duties as a stenographer and private secretary?
2. Is she honest and dependable?
3. What was the reason for her leaving your employ?

We are sorry to trouble you for this information, but are sure that you realize the necessity for our obtaining it.

(2)

Miss Mary E. Griffen has just applied for the stenographic position now open in our office, and has given us your name as a reference.

We should very much appreciate it, therefore, if you would send us a letter giving us your opinion in regard to her ability as a stenographer while in your employ.

(3)

Miss Janette Curlenjik, a student of your Secretarial Course last year, has given me your name for reference.

I should appreciate it greatly if you would write me, giving me your opinion of her personality and business qualifications. From my short talk with her, she seems to be a very capable young woman.

LETTERS OF RECOMMENDATION

(1)

I can sincerely recommend Miss Harriet Blake as a business secretary.

During the two years she was with me I found her work careful and accurate. In fact, I can truthfully say she is one of the best secretaries I have employed. She has a good knowledge of shorthand and typewriting, and an excellent general background, which makes her all the more valuable in an executive position. She is enthusiastic about whatever task she is performing and willing to devote as much time and energy as is necessary to have things done to perfection.

I think you will find Miss Blake a valuable helper. I myself am very sorry to lose her, but, as she wished to enter a broader field, she gave up her position with me.

If I can supply any further information, I shall be glad to do so.

(2)

TO WHOM IT MAY CONCERN:

Miss Jean Johnson was a student in my English class at C— College from February to June 1927. During that time she impressed me as a student of ability interested in doing well whatever she had to do. Miss Johnson was not afraid of hard work, nor was she content to have merely a passing mark. She showed herself to be careful, painstaking, and accurate, producing always a work of fine quality. When given an unusual assignment, she proved that she had read widely and appreciatively and possessed keen judgment and critical understanding.

Whatever Miss Johnson decides to do, she will, in my opinion, bring to that work ability, character, and discrimination.

I am pleased to recommend her unqualifiedly.

A. B. Butler
Instructor in English

Brooklyn, N. Y.
January 8, 1928

(3)

It affords me a welcome avenue for expressing my appreciation to say regarding Miss Theresa Callan that I have found her a remarkably capable secretary. She combines the qualities which one most desires of technical training and practical efficiency, good judgment, accuracy in word and action, reserve, sympathy and quick understanding, and adaptability in all contacts.

Miss Callan is rarely gifted as a writer and her pure diction and delightful facility of expression made the correspondence which she attended to for me an eminently satisfactory service.

She is a cultured young woman with the highest standards of honor and conduct.

(4)

It is a pleasure to say a word of recommendation in behalf of Miss Mary Burns, who has been my secretary until ill health made it impossible to continue the active interests which made such assistance necessary.

Miss Burns is, besides being a most efficient secretary of unusual mental and social qualities, a young woman of high character and honor, tireless and unselfish in the execution of her employer's interests, thoroughly trustworthy in her work and judgment; always tactful, able and sympathetic as an executive.

During long absences from home, I have felt the utmost confidence and satisfaction in leaving to Miss Burns not only the manipulation of my large correspondence, accounts, etc., but also the entire oversight and direction of our household, including a large staff of servants. When I have been away, she has directed all the housekeeping for my home-keeping family and their visitors. I must stress that she has a perfect balance of knowing when to be on hand and when to withdraw, and she is never obtrusive. I think this is what one so much desires in a resident secretary.

I am always glad to give any information about one who has been a most valued secretary and friend to me.

(5)

Miss Louise Hepburn has been an invaluable secretary-housekeeper to me. She is not only thoroughly trained and experienced but she has, with these, natural gifts which particularly fit her to be of service to a busy woman with a large household who needs a sympathetic and experienced woman at her side.

She is loyal and trustworthy in every way, diligent, patient and sweet-tempered, reserved, sympathetic under all circumstances, adapts herself with absolute satisfaction to the entire household. She is an excellent shopper, and on occasions when she has tutored or chaperoned for me, she has been most acceptable. Few women can fill a resident secretaryship as well as Miss Hepburn (so few that I never found anyone else who was really satisfactory) and I can think of no household, however complicated, where she would not be valued in this capacity. Her leaving me to go to New York was a matter of great regret to me.

BUSINESS LETTERS OF INTRODUCTION

(1)

605 West 115th Street
New York City
April 29, 19—

Mr. Samuel M. Jones
President, Arnold Print Works
North Adams, Mass.

Dear Mr. Jones:

This letter will introduce to you Miss Lois Littlepage, who is visiting your factory with the idea of gathering material for a survey of industrial relations that she is making. I believe that it would be very much to her advantage to meet you personally to learn your opinion on several subjects connected with this report.

I shall appreciate whatever assistance you give her.

Sincerely yours,
Dorothy Briggs

(2)

This will introduce to you Miss Mary E. Murray, a friend of mine, who is particularly eager to apply for the stenographic position now open in your office.

I hope that you will be able to spare a few moments of your already busy day to extend to Miss Murray the privilege of an interview.

LETTER-WRITING AND ANNOUNCEMENTS

(1)

Theodore Roosevelt
Oyster Bay, Long Island

May 18, 1927

My dear Mr. Ambassador:

This will introduce to you Captain Charles A. Lindbergh, who is a real sportsman. I sincerely hope he is successful in his flight and delivers this to you after having landed in Paris.

Like the best type of sportsman, Captain Lindbergh is modest. He won't ask you to do anything for him. If I were you, however, I would insist on seeing something of him, for I know you will like him. Anyway, if you are able to help him I will deeply appreciate it.

With kind regards,
(sgd) Theodore Roosevelt

The Honorable Myron T. Herrick,
Embassy of the United States of America,
Paris, France.

TR/meh

(2)

Theodore Roosevelt
Oyster Bay, Long Island

May 18, 1927.

My dear Mr. Ambassador:

This letter will introduce to you Captain Charles A. Lindbergh, who is a thorough-going sportsman. I hope he will present it to you at the successful conclusion of a transatlantic flight.

I am sure you will like him. Anything you can do to help him I will deeply appreciate.

With best wishes to Mrs. Houghton, and also to the bride and groom,

(sgd) Theodore Roosevelt

The Honorable A. B. Houghton,
Embassy of the United States of America,
London, England.

TR/meh

[1] Reprinted by permission of Colonel Theodore Roosevelt. These letters of introduction were carried by Captain Charles A. Lindbergh in the *Spirit of St. Louis*, on his famous New York-to-Paris flight, May 20-21, 1927.

A Card of Introduction

FACE OF CARD

Mr. Norman McAllister
Introducing
Mr. Henry Winkelman
to
Mr. Roger Brown Peel

REVERSE OF CARD

Dear Mr. Peel:

Mr. Winkelman, like yourself, is interested in first editions. May he have the pleasure of seeing yours?

Yours sincerely,
Norman McAllister

April 15

FACE OF CARD

Introducing Mr. Leonard Grant
to
Dr. Burton Masters

Mr. Richard Kennedy

Mr. Grant wishes to consult you professionally. I have assured him that you will be interested in his case.

R. K.

A Letter of Reminder

Dear Mr. Mitchell,

I have received your letter telling me that the convention has been extended until June fifth. May I remind you that you have a week-end engagement at Miss Smith's beginning June fourth. In case you decide to stay until the end of the convention, please let me know what word to send Miss Smith canceling the engagement.

Yours sincerely,
Catherine Rossbach, Secretary

A Letter of Confirmation

562 West 11 Street
New York City
May 10, 19—

Mr. Norman Walker
620 West 67 Street
New York City

Dear Sir

In regard to our conversation of yesterday afternoon, I want to make a statement, in writing, of the impression I received from it. I understood you to say that you would guarantee a rise of five per cent in the net profits from my factory if I would make a contract with your company. I understand that the service can be completed in six months at a cost of $900.00 a month.

Please reply telling me if I have the proposition correctly stated.

Yours very truly
Kathleen Wall

.. A Letter Confirming a Telephone Conversation

This is to confirm my telephone conversation with you on May 1, in regard to the second mortgage which you desire to have placed on your house located at 411 St. Clair Avenue, Buffalo.

The terms agreed upon are as follows: a mortgage of $3000, payable $150 semi-annually, with interest at six per cent.

Will you please call at this office as soon as possible so that Attorney Sloane may proceed to search the title and draw up the mortgage deed.

A Letter Making a Hotel Reservation

Hotel Benjamin Franklin
    Philadelphia, Pa.

Gentlemen:

Please reserve for Mr. R. M. Williams a moderately priced room with bath at your hotel for January sixth to February twelfth, and inform him what the rate will be.

Yours very truly,
Anne E. Burden, Secretary

A Letter Making a Steamship Reservation

The Cunard Steamship Company
    25 Broadway
        New York City

Gentlemen:

Please reserve for Mr. and Mrs. Nathan Keith an outside room with bath on Deck C, first cabin, on the *Aquitania* sailing September 12 for Cherbourg.

Yours truly,
Ellen A. Stevenson
Secretary to Mr. Keith

LETTER-WRITING AND ANNOUNCEMENTS

A Letter Asking for an Appointment

Chadwick Place,
Biddeford, Maine,
June 1, 19—.

Dear Miss Clark,

Mrs. Marcia P. Leslie wishes me to ask whether it would be possible for you to see her at your apartment Tuesday, June twelfth, at three o'clock, to discuss with you an article she is writing on Tea Room Management.

Yours sincerely,
Annie Perkins
Secretary to Mrs. Leslie

Miss Grace Clark,
1 Fifth Avenue,
New York City.

A Letter Canceling an Appointment

Dear Mr. Johnson:

As Mr. Roberts has suddenly been called out of town, he has asked me to inform you that he will have to postpone the conference with you at three o'clock. On his return he will be glad to make another appointment with you at your convenience.

Yours very truly,
Josephine Gold
Secretary to Mr. J. L. Roberts

A Letter of Suggestion

I enjoyed so much two or three chapters in your *Training for Secretarial Practice,* particularly the admirable specimens of letters, that I venture to record one difference of opinion with regard to the drafting of resolutions as outlined on pages 266 and 267.

Is it not possible to be formal without being perfunctory, and to have at least a spice of originality? To this end it is not a bad plan to avoid the conventional form with its "whereas's" and "be it resolved."

Can you not warn drafters of resolutions to avoid conventional phrases and to be sparing of adjectives?

Pray do something to improve the quality of resolutions, which are often so trite as to be almost a mockery.

191

A Letter of Inquiry

Willard Street
Newton, Mass.
May 26, 19—

Institute of Politics
Williamstown
Massachusetts

Gentlemen:

I have read a great deal about the Institute of Politics which is held in Williamstown every summer. As I shall be nearby in Stockbridge this summer, I am interested to know if I may attend the conferences while I am there.

I should like to ask:

1. What are the requisites of membership in the Institute?
2. What is the essential difference between Associate and Regular Membership?
3. Are Associate Members allowed to attend the Round Table Conferences?
4. Do you provide lodging for members in case I should decide to stay in Williamstown?

I shall appreciate it if you will also send me such printed material as you have on hand.

Very truly yours,
Blanche Greenberg

Letters of Information

(1)

Rothesay Collegiate School
Rothesay, N. B.

June 12, 19—

My dear Miss McKean,

We are all delighted to hear that you are planning to include New Brunswick in your summer wanderings. We shall certainly be very glad to see you again, and hope you will spend as much time with us as you can spare on your way home.

As you are in Quebec, the simplest way for you to enter New Brunswick would be to come through Grand Falls and Edmundston. You could spend the night at Edmundston where there is an excellent hotel, the *Madawaska Inn*. If you leave by nine the next morning, you can easily reach Fredericton by late afternoon or early evening, as the distance is only about two hundred miles over very good roads. There are several good hotels in Fredericton. You would find either the *Queen* or the *Windsor* very comfortable. If you leave for St. John by ten the next morning, you should be able to arrive about three o'clock.

There are two roads down from Fredericton, the Old Broad Road and the River Road. The River Road will give you a beautiful view of the St. John River all the way down, but it is some thirty-five miles longer than the other.

Unless you have a special fondness for your own fishing tackle, don't bother to bring any, as I have enough for us both. I thought we might make a canoe trip up the Washedamoak, and, if you are able to stay until the fifteenth, we may get a little shooting. Try to tuck your golf-bag somewhere in the car, and *don't* forget a bathing suit. I am looking forward to introducing you to—or should it be *into*—the Bay of Fundy with its fifty degrees Fahrenheit.

I am enclosing a guide book that will give you explicit directions as to roads and mileage, and I know you will have no trouble in getting here.

> Affectionately yours,
> Emily E.

(2)

American University
Washington, D. C.
COLLEGE OF LIBERAL ARTS

Office of the Dean, Hurst Hall, American University Campus

June 22, 1927.

Miss Florence Allen,
1014 Vermont Avenue,
Temple, Texas.

My dear Miss Allen:

I am very glad to answer your letter of June 21 inquiring about the college of Liberal Arts of American University.

As you probably know, next year will mark the third year of the College. We have set up a very strong course of study under the direction of the best teachers we can possibly secure. We are all very proud of our faculty, and people outside have said that it ranks with any college faculty in the country. I have every confidence that this point of view is valid.

We are making a special effort to build a strong Department of English, and we believe that a young woman who majors in English in this College will be admirably equipped for graduate study in that department if she should so desire.

One other point I should like to mention. We intend to keep our registration low enough so we may maintain small classes. We want our students to be thoroughly trained, and we want all the students to come into intimate contact with the faculty. We expect about two hundred students next year; there will be twenty-five members of the faculty.

In accordance with your request, I have sent you a copy of our recent catalog. This will give you complete information about the work which is to be offered next year, together with general information pertaining to the life and activities of the College during the present academic year.

I need not stress, I am sure, the advantages of taking a college course in Washington. We have a most delightful location in one of the highest and most beautiful sections of the District. Three new buildings have recently been completed—the Women's Residence Hall, the Library, and the Gymnasium.

If there is further information that you desire at any time in regard to the College, I shall be glad to have you write me.

Sincerely yours,
Maenette Olsen
Registrar

LETTERS OF APPRECIATION

(1)

411 West 116 Street,
New York, New York,
May 8, 1928.

To the Mother Superior,
    St. Francis Hospital,
        Hartford, Connecticut.

Reverend Mother:

I feel that it is my duty to convey to you an expression of appreciation and thanks for the unusually kind treatment which was given to me while I was a patient, not so long ago, at St. Francis Hospital.

The friendliness and cheerfulness of the nurses and the gentle and maternal care and attention of the nuns were a great aid in helping me to recover from my serious operation. I really believe that it was through their kindness and encouragement that I was given the spirit to struggle through those awful weeks in which I was so critically ill.

Won't you please let them know how deeply indebted I feel to them for all that they did for me? I also want to thank you, too, Mother Superior, for the interest which you showed in my welfare.

Sincerely yours,

Mary E. Griffen

(2)

Iola Sanatorium
Rochester, New York

September 29, 1926

Mr. Bruce Johnson
Granite Building
Rochester, N. Y.

My dear Mr. Johnson:

Through Mr. Robert Mac Murray we have just learned that you were one of the contributors to a fund which he collected for the benefit of our occupational therapy department. It is a pleasure to acknowledge your contribution and to tell you that you have done something that is of great value.

For some time Mrs. Munchow, the worker in charge of the occupational therapy department, has been asking me for material to be used by the patients in making the different articles at their bedside or in the shop. To each request I have replied, "Sometime I will be able to secure the aid you need." This time has arrived, and the money is in the bank. A conference with Mrs. Munchow has just been concluded in which I was the recipient of great thanks. These thanks I transfer to you.

Sincerely yours,
Ezra Bridge
Medical Director

SOCIAL NOTES

INFORMAL INVITATION

45 West 119th Street,
July the fifth.

My dear Mrs. Holmes,

Will you and Mr. Holmes give us the pleasure of dining with us on Friday, July the twelfth, at seven o'clock? We shall be very glad if you are able to come.

Cordially yours,
Mary R. Fox

INFORMAL REGRET

(1)

My dear Mrs. Fox,

We are sorry that we are unable to accept your very delightful invitation for dinner on Friday, July the twelfth, as unfortunately we have another engagement for that evening.

Sincerely yours,
Elizabeth Holmes

52 West 13th Street,
July the tenth

(2)

52 West 13th Street,
New York City,
July 10, 19—.

Dear Mrs. Fox,

Mr. Holmes and I regret exceedingly that we shall be unable to dine with you on Friday the twelfth, as unfortunately we have accepted another invitation for that evening.

Yours sincerely,
Elizabeth Holmes

Mrs. Alexander Fox,
45 West 119th Street,
New York City.

Informal Acceptance

(1)

My dear Mrs. Fox,

Mr. Holmes and I are delighted to accept your very kind invitation to dine with you on Friday, June the twelfth, at seven o'clock, and are looking forward to that evening with great pleasure.

Cordially yours,
Elizabeth Holmes

52 West Thirteenth Street
June fifth

(2)

My dear Mrs. Fox,

There is nothing we should like to do more on Friday the twelfth than to dine with you and Mr. Fox at the Ritz at seven-thirty and attend the play with you later. We are delighted to accept your very kind invitation.

Cordially yours,
Elizabeth Holmes

52 West Thirteenth Street
June Fifth

Informal Regret for an At Home

27th November 1928

Dear Mrs. Garrett,

I am so sorry that pressure of engagements will prevent my being present at your At Home on Thursday afternoon next, but if you will allow me I will take another opportunity of calling upon you.

With kindest regards, believe me,

Yours sincerely,
James Martin

Mrs. Alexander Garrett,
  7, King's Bench Walk,
    Temple, E.C.4.

197

A Formal at Home Invitation

Mr. and Mrs. Henry McIntyre
At Home
Wednesday afternoon, February twenty-first
from four to six
Forty East Seventieth Street

It is unnecessary to answer an *At Home* invitation unless requested. If one cannot attend, it is customary to send one's card by mail so that it will arrive on the day of the reception. A husband and wife send one card each if the invitation has been extended in the name of the hostess only; if it has been given in the name of the hostess and her daughter, two cards each. Women who do not attend the reception send cards, one for each woman whose name appears on the invitation. Men send cards to each woman and one for the husband.

Formal Invitation for a Reception Given in Some One's Honor

To meet
Mrs. Edward Howard

Mrs. John Richard Thornton
requests the pleasure of your company
On Friday afternoon, the twelfth of April
from four until seven o'clock
at 7 Lenox Drive

Invitation for a Reception at Which a Daughter Is Introduced

Mrs. John Richard Thornton
Miss Helen Louise Thornton
will be at home
on Wednesday afternoon, the fifth of April
from four until seven o'clock
at 7 Lenox Drive

INFORMAL INVITATION WRITTEN ON A VISITING CARD FOR AN AT HOME GIVEN IN SOME ONE'S HONOR

To meet Mrs. Edward Howard

Mrs. John Richard Thornton

Four to seven o'clock
Tuesday, November the twelfth

INVITATION FOR A DANCE

Mr. and Mrs. John Richard Thornton
Miss Helen Louise Thornton
Mr. Harold Thornton
request the pleasure of your company
at a dance
on Wednesday evening, the tenth of February
at ten o'clock
at 7 Lenox Drive

The favor of a reply is requested.

INVITATION TO A DANCE AT WHICH A DAUGHTER IS TO BE INTRODUCED

Mr. and Mrs. John Richard Thornton
request the pleasure of your company
at a dance in honor of their daughter
Miss Helen Louise Thornton
on Thursday evening, the fifteenth of March
at half after ten o'clock
at The Riverside Country Club

199

INVITATION TO A SUBSCRIPTION DANCE

The pleasure of your company
is requested at the
Second Annual Subscription Dance
on Thursday evening, the tenth of October
at half after ten o'clock
at the Susquehanna Valley Hunt Club

Subscription Tickets, $5.
Please respond to
Mrs. Frank Stevenson
410 College Road

INVITATION TO A LUNCHEON GIVEN IN HONOR OF SOME ONE

Mrs. Thomson would be glad if Miss Varney would take luncheon with her quite informally, at half after twelve o'clock, on Saturday, January fifteenth, at the City Club, 55 West 44th Street, to meet Miss Monteith.

Philosophy Hall
January 9, 19—

ACCEPTANCE

Miss Varney accepts with pleasure Mrs. Thomson's kind invitation to meet Miss Monteith at luncheon at half after twelve o'clock, on Saturday, January fifteenth, at the City Club.

Larchmont Gardens
January 10, 19—

ANNOUNCEMENT OF AN ENGAGEMENT

Mr. and Mrs. Max Mueller
have the honor of announcing
the engagement of their daughter
Ilse
to
Mr. Donald Burton Caryl
June, Nineteen hundred and twenty-six
in the City of New York

Wedding Invitation

Mr. and Mrs. M. H. Bigelow
request the honour of your presence
at the marriage of their daughter
Dorothy Bristol
to
Mr. Thaddeus Ely Baer
on Friday evening, the ninth of April
nineteen hundred and twenty-six
at six o'clock
at 140 South Bartram Place
Atlantic City, New Jersey

Wedding Announcements

1

Mr. and Mrs. Ira Glidden Whittier
announce the marriage of their daughter
Amy Constance
to
Mr. Philip Edward Starrett
on Friday, the first of January
One thousand nine hundred and twenty-six
Edgewood, Rhode Island

2

Mrs. William Joseph Wilson
announces the marriage of her daughter
Margaret Mary
to
Mr. Frank Randall Dunham
on Monday, September the sixth
nineteen hundred and twenty-six
St. Paul the Apostle Church
New York City

3

Mr. and Mrs. Martin George Olsen
announce the marriage of their daughter
Maenette
to
Perry Kenneth Jeanes
Ensign, United States Navy
on Saturday, the eleventh of August
nineteen hundred and twenty-eight
U.S.S. Idaho
Seattle, Washington

UNIVERSITY RECEPTION

The President of ——— University
and Mrs. ———
At Home
on Thursday, the 25th of October
from 4 until 7 o'clock

President's House
70 College Circle

INVITATION FOR A DEDICATION CEREMONY

The Joint Administrative Board
on behalf of

Columbia University	The Sloane Hospital for
The Neurological Institute	Women
The Babies' Hospital	The Vanderbilt Clinic
The Presbyterian Hospital	

invites you to be present at the
Dedication of the Medical Center
on
Friday afternoon, October 12, 1928
at three o'clock
at 180 Fort Washington Avenue
New York

R.S.V.P.
620 West 168th Street

A Club At Home

The Women's Faculty Club
of Columbia University
At Home
on Monday, the ninth of February
One thousand, nine hundred and twenty-five
from four to six and eight to ten o'clock
at the Club Rooms in Johnson Hall
Four hundred and ten West One Hundred and Seventeenth
Street
New York City
Afternoon, from four to six, Open House
Greetings   Miss Gunther
Lighting the hearthfire   Miss Nutting
Reminiscences   Miss Goodsell, Miss Carney
Music   Mrs. Cowl, piano, Mr. Rosanoff, cello
Evening, from eight to ten, Reception
Honorary Guests

President and Mrs. Butler   Dean and Mrs. Russell
Dean Gildersleeve   Trustees

Address at nine o'clock, President Butler
Music   Mr. Erskine

REFERENCE BOOKS

CROWTHER, MARY OWENS. *The Book of Letters*. Doubleday, Page and Company, 1922.

DOLCH, EDWARD WILLIAM. *Business Letter Writing*. Ronald Press Company, 1922.

HERZBERG, MAX J. *New Style-Book of Business English*. Isaac Pitman & Sons, 1928.

HOTCHKISS and KILDUFF. *Advanced Business Correspondence*. Harper and Brothers, 1921.

TOCKLEY, LAWRENCE C. *Principles of Effective Letter Writing*. McGraw-Hill Book Company, Inc.

MANLY and RICKERT. *The Writing of English*. Henry Holt and Company, 1923.

MEYERS, ELIZABETH. *The Social Letter*. Brentano's, 1918.

NAETHER, CARL A. *The Business Letter*. D. Appleton and Company.

———. *Problems in Business Corespondence*. McGraw-Hill Book Company, Inc., 1927.

THE SECRETARY'S HANDBOOK

OPDYCKE, JOHN B. *Business Letter Practice*. Isaac Pitman & Sons, 1922.

POST, EMILY. *Book of Etiquette*. Doubleday, Page and Company.

RAYMOND, CHARLES HAWLY. *Modern Business Writing*. The Century Company, 1921.

TAINTOR, SARAH AUGUSTA. *Training for Secretarial Practice*. McGraw-Hill Book Company, Inc., 1926.

COLLECTIONS OF LETTERS

A Letter Book, compiled and edited by George Saintsbury. London, George Bell and Sons, 1922.

Letters from Many Pens, edited by Margaret Coult. New York, The Macmillan Company.

Nineteenth Century Letters, edited by Byron Johnson Rees. New York, Charles Scribner's Sons, 1919.

Selected Letters, compiled and edited by Stella S. Center. New York, Charles F. Merrill Co., 1915.

The Gentlest Art, edited by E. V. Lucas. New York, The Macmillan Company, 1913.

The Great English Letter Writers, compiled and edited by W. J. and Coningsby Dawson. New York, Harper and Brothers, 1909.

The Literature of Letters, compiled and edited by John B. Opdycke. Chicago, Lyons and Carnahan, 1925.

The Second Post, compiled by E. V. Lucas. New York, The Macmillan Company, 1910.

LETTERS BY INDIVIDUAL AUTHORS

BELL, GERTRUDE.
   The Letters of Gertrude Bell; selected and edited by Lady Bell. London, 1927.

BROOKS, PHILLIPS.
   Letters of Travel, edited by M. F. B. The Macmillan Company. New York, Dutton and Company, 1915.

BROWNING, ELIZABETH BARRETT.
   The Letters of Elizabeth Barrett Browning, edited with biographical additions, by Frederic G. Kenyon. Macmillan, 1897.

BROWNING, ELIZABETH and ROBERT.
   Letters of Robert and Elizabeth Barrett Browning. New York, The Macmillan Company, 1897.

CARLYLE, JANE WELSH.
   Letters to her Family, edited by Leonard Huxley. Garden City, N. Y., Doubleday, Page and Company, 1924.

CARLYLE, JANE WELSH.
   Letters and Memorials, annotated by Thomas Carlyle and edited by Alexander Carlyle. London, J. Lane, 1903.

LETTER-WRITING AND ANNOUNCEMENTS

CONRAD, JOSEPH.
Conrad to a Friend: 150 selected letters from Joseph Conrad to Richard Curle, edited with an introduction and notes by Richard Curle. Garden City, N. Y., Doubleday Doran, 1927.

CLEMENS, SAMUEL LANGHORNE (Mark Twain).
Mark Twain's Letters, edited by A. Bigelow Paine. New York, Harper and Brothers, 1917.

COWPER, WILLIAM.
Letters of William Cowper, edited by the Rev. W. Benham. New York, The Macmillan Company, 1914.

DICKENS, CHARLES.
Letters of Charles Dickens, edited by his sister-in-law and his eldest daughter. London, Chapman, 1882.

DODGSON, CHARLES LUTWIDGE (Lewis Carroll)
Life and Letters of Lewis Carroll, by Stuart Dodgson Collingwood. New York, The Century Company, 1899.

FITZGERALD, EDWARD
Letters of Edward Fitzgerald, edited by William Aldis Wright. New York, The Macmillan Company, 1894.

GRAY, THOMAS.
Letters of Thomas Gray, edited by D. C. Tovey. London, George Bell and Sons, 1912.

HEARN, LAFCADIO.
Life and Letters of Lafcadio Hearn, by Elizabeth Bisland. Boston, Houghton Mifflin Company, 1906.
——, *The Japanese Letters of Lafcadio Hearn,* edited with notes by Elizabeth Bisland. Boston, Houghton Mifflin Company, 1911.

JAMES, WILLIAM.
Letters of William James, edited by his son, Harry James. Boston, Little Brown and Company, 1926.

LAMB, CHARLES.
Letters of Charles Lamb, newly arranged with additions, edited with Introduction and notes by Alfred Ainger. New York, The Macmillan Company, 1888.

LANE, FRANKLIN K.
Letters, Personal and Political. Boston, Houghton Mifflin Company, 1922.

LOWELL, JAMES RUSSELL.
Letters of James Russell Lowell. New York, Harper and Brothers, 1894.

MONTAGU, LADY MARY WORTLEY.
Letters from 1709 to 1762. London, J. M. Dent and Company, 1906.

PAGE, WALTER HINES.
Life and Letters of Walter Hines Page, edited by Burton J. Hendricks. Garden City, New York, Doubleday, Page and Company, 1922.

ROOSEVELT, THEODORE.
> Letters from Theodore Roosevelt to Anna Roosevelt Cowles, from 1870 to 1918. New York, Charles Scribner's Sons.

SÉVIGNÉ, MADAME DE.
> Letters of Madame de Sévigné to her Daughter and her Friends, edited and annotated by J. A. Harrison, selected with an introductory essay by Richard Aldington. New York, Brentano's, 1927.

STEVENSON, ROBERT LOUIS.
> Letters of Robert Louis Stevenson, edited by Sir Sidney Colvin. New York, Charles Scribner's Sons, 1925.

THACKERAY, WILLIAM MAKEPEACE.
> A Collection of Letters by William Makepeace Thackeray. New York, Charles Scribner's Sons, 1890.

WALPOLE, HORACE.
> Letters of Horace Walpole, edited by Mrs. Paget Toynbee. Oxford, Clarendon Press, 1903-1905.

WILSON, WOODROW.
> Life and Letters of Woodrow Wilson, edited by Ray Stannard Baker. Garden City, N. Y., Doubleday, Page and Company, 1927.

CHAPTER II

CORRECT USAGE IN LETTER PARTS

Official Usage

The President of the United States

Address:	The President,
	The White House.
	or
	The President,
	Washington, D. C.
Salutation:	Sir:
	or
	To the President:
	or
	My dear Mr. President:
Complimentary Close:	Respectfully submitted,
	or
	Yours respectfully,
	or
	Faithfully yours, (informal)

The Vice President of the United States.

Address:	The Vice President,
	The United States Senate.
	or
	The Honorable
	The Vice President of the United
	States,
	Washington, D. C.

Salutation: Sir:

or

My dear Mr. Vice President:

Complimentary Close: Yours respectfully,

or

Very truly yours,

Speaker of the House of Representatives.

Address: The Honorable
> The Speaker of the House of Rep-
> resentatives,

or

> The Speaker of the House of Rep-
> resentatives,
> Washington, D. C.

Salutation: Sir:

or

My dear Mr. Speaker:

Complimentary Close: Very truly yours,

Cabinet Officers.

Address: The Honorable
> The Secretary of State,
> Washington, D. C.

or

The Honorable Henry L. Stimson,
> Secretary of State,
> Washington, D. C.

Salutation: Sir:
                                   or
                               Dear Sir:
                                   or
                               My dear Mr. Secretary:

Complimentary Close: Very truly yours,

Address: The Honorable
                                   The Attorney General of the
                                       United States,
                                   Washington, D. C.
                                       or
                               The Honorable Henry S. Mitchell,
                                   The Attorney General

Salutation: Sir:
                                   or
                               Dear Sir:
                                   or
                               My dear Mr. Attorney General:

Complimentary Close: Very truly yours,

Undersecretary of State.

Address: The Undersecretary of State,
                                   Washington, D. C.
                                       or
                               The Honorable Robert E. Olds,
                                   Undersecretary of State,
                                   Washington, D. C.

Salutation: Sir:
                                   or
                               Dear Sir:
                                   or
                               My dear Mr. Undersecretary:
                                   or
                               Dear Mr. Olds: (informal)

Complimentary Close: Very truly yours,

Assistant Secretary of War.

Address:	The Assistant Secretary of the War Department, Washington, D. C.
	or
	The Honorable Hanford MacNider Assistant Secretary of the War Department, Washington, D. C.
Salutation:	Sir:
	or
	My dear Mr. MacNider: (informal)
Complimentary Close:	Very truly yours,

Senator.

Address:	The Honorable William E. Borah, The United States Senate, Washington, D. C.
Salutation:	Dear Sir:
	or
	My dear Senator:
	or
	My dear Senator Borah:
Complimentary Close:	Very truly yours,

Representative.

Address:	The Honorable Ogden L. Mills, The House of Representatives, Washington, D. C.
Salutation:	Sir:
	or
	Dear Sir:
	or
	My dear Mr. Mills:
Complimentary Close:	Very truly yours,

210

Commissioner.

Address: The Honorable —— — ——,
            Commissioner of the Bureau of
            Education,
            Washington, D. C.

Salutation: Sir:
               or
               My dear Mr. ——.

Complimentary Close: Very truly yours,

Chief Justice of the Supreme Court.

Address: The Chief Justice of the United
            States,
            Washington, D. C.
            or
            The Chief Justice,
            Washington, D. C.

Salutation: Sir:
               or
               My dear Mr. Chief Justice.

Complimentary Close: Very truly yours,

Associate Justice of the Supreme Court.

Address: Mr. Justice Holmes,
            Washington, D. C.

Salutation: My dear Mr. Justice:
               or
               My dear Justice Holmes: (informal)

Complimentary Close: Very truly yours,

District Judge.

Address:	The Honorable George B. Adams, United States District Judge, Southern District of New York, New York, N. Y.
Salutation:	Dear Sir:
	or
	My dear Judge Adams:
Complimentary Close:	Very truly yours,

Judge of State Courts.

Address:	The Honorable Benjamin Cardozo, Chief Judge of the Court of Appeals, Albany, New York.
Salutation:	Dear Sir:
	or
	My dear Judge Cardozo:
Complimentary Close:	Very truly yours,

Governor.

Address:	The Honorable The Governor of New York, Albany, New York.
	or
	The Honorable Franklin D. Roosevelt, Governor of New York.
Salutation:	Sir:
	or
	Dear Sir:
	or
	My dear Governor Roosevelt: (informal)
Complimentary Close:	Very truly yours,

Lieutenant Governor.

Address:

The Honorable Herbert H. Lehman,
Lieutenant Governor of New
York,
Albany, New York.

Salutation:

Sir:
or
Dear Sir:

Complimentary Close:

Very truly yours,

State Senator.

Address:

The Honorable Bernard Downing,
The State Senate,
Albany, New York.
or
Senator Downing,
The State Capitol,
Albany, New York.

Salutation:

Sir:
or
Dear Sir:
or
My dear Senator Downing: (informal)

Complimentary Close:

Very truly yours,

Member of Assembly.

Address:

The Honorable A. G. Stockweather,
Member of Assembly,
Albany, N. Y.
or
Assemblyman Stockweather,
The State Capitol,
Albany, New York.

Salutation:

Dear Sir:
or
My dear Mr. Stockweather:
(informal)

Complimentary Close:

Very truly yours,

Mayor.

Address: The Honorable James J. Walker,
                      Mayor of the City of New York,
                      City Hall, New York.
                              or
                  The Mayor of the City of New York,
                      City Hall, New York.

Salutation: Sir:
                          or
                  My dear Mr. Mayor:
                          or
                  My dear Mayor Walker: (informal)

Complimentary Close: Yours respectfully,
                                or
                       Very truly yours,

Foreign Ambassador.

Address: His Excellency,
                  The Ambassador of the French Re-
                      public,
                      Washington, D. C.

Salutation: Excellency:
                          or
                  Your Excellency:
                          or
                  Sir:

Complimentary Close: Accept, Excellency, the renewed as-
                          surance of my highest con-
                          sideration,
                                or
                       Yours respectfully,

British Ambassador.

Address: His Excellency,
                  The Ambassador of Great Britain,
                      Washington, D. C.

Salutation: Excellency:
or
Sir:

Complimentary Close: I have the honor to be,
    With the highest consideration,
        Your Excellency's most obedi-
          ent servant,
or
Yours respectfully,

Ministers from Foreign Countries.

Address: The Honorable ....
    Minister of ....
or
Envoy Extraordinary and
    Minister Plenipotentiary from
    ....
or
Mr. .... (followed by the of-
    ficial title)

Salutation: Sir:
or
My dear Mr. Minister:

Complimentary Close: Same as Ambassador's

American Ambassador.

Address: His Excellency,
    The American Ambassador,
        London.
or
The Honorable Charles G. Dawes,
    American Ambassador,
        London,
          England.

Salutation: My dear Mr. Ambassador:
or
Your Excellency:
or
Sir:

Complimentary Close: I have the honor to be, Sir,
                     Your obedient servant, (old form)
or
            Respectfully yours,
or
            Very truly yours,

Chargé d'Affaires.

Address: Baron Raymond de Waha,
            Chargé d'Affaires,
            Luxemburg.

Salutation: Dear Sir:
or
            Sir:

Complimentary Close: Accept, Sir, the renewed assurance
                     of my high consideration,
or
            Respectfully yours,
or
            Very truly yours,

Consul.

Address: To the American Consul at......
            ......, *or*
            ...., Esq.,
                American Consul at..........,

Salutation: Dear Sir:

Complimentary Close: Very truly yours,

DIPLOMATIC CORRESPONDENCE

In diplomatic notes and reports to the President, the address should appear at the lower left-hand corner of the page. In instructions and miscellaneous letters, the address should precede the salutation on the left-hand margin.

CORRECT USAGE IN LETTER PARTS

HONORABLE

The title *Honorable* should be used in addressing the following: Governors, Cabinet officers, Senators, Congressmen, American Ambassadors, American Ministers, The Secretary to the President, Assistant Secretaries of the Executive Departments, Judges (not of the Supreme Court), Heads of the Independent Boards of Commissioners.

ESQUIRE

The title *Esquire* is used with the following government officials: Chief clerks and chiefs of Bureaus of the Executive Department, Commissioners of the District of Columbia, Mayors of cities, American diplomatic officers below the grade of ministers, American consular officers, Clients of the Supreme Court of the United States.

CORRECT USAGE IN ADDRESSING INVITATIONS TO GOVERNMENT OFFICIALS

The President
    and Mrs. ————
        The White House

The Vice President
    and Mrs. ————

The Secretary of State
    and Mrs. ————

Senator and Mrs. ————

Congressman and Mrs. ————, *or*
    Mr. and Mrs. ————

His Excellency
    The Ambassador of the French Republic
        and Madame ————

The Minister of Costa Rica
    and Madame ————

The Chargé d'Affaires of Luxemburg
    and Madame ————

The following titles are used in addressing officials of the diplomatic corps:

Minister of Albania
Ambassador of the Argentine Republic
Minister of Austria
Belgian Ambassador
Minister of Bolivia
Ambassador of Brazil
Minister of Bulgaria
Minister of Canada
Ambassador of Chile
Chinese Minister
Minister of Colombia
Minister of Costa Rica
Ambassador of Cuba
Minister of Czechoslovakia
Minister of Denmark
Minister of the Dominican Republic
Minister of Ecuador
Minister of Egypt
Consul General of Estonia
Minister of El Salvador
Minister of Finland
Ambassador of the French Republic
Ambassador of Germany
Ambassador of Great Britain
Minister of Greece
Minister of Guatemala
Minister of Haiti
Minister of Honduras

Minister of Hungary
Minister of the Irish Free State
Ambassador of Italy
Japanese Ambassador
Consul General of Latvia
Lithuanian Minister
Chargé d'Affaires of Luxemburg
Ambassador of Mexico
Minister of the Netherlands
Minister of Nicaragua
Minister of Norway
Minister of Panama
Minister of Paraguay
Minister of Persia
Ambassador of Peru
Ambassador of Poland
Minister of Portugal
Minister of Rumania
Siamese Minister
Ambassador of Spain
Minister of Sweden
Minister of Switzerland
Ambassador of Turkey
Minister of the Union of South Africa
Minister of Uruguay
Minister of Venezuela
Minister of Yugoslavia

King.

Address:	The King's Most Excellent [or Gracious] Majesty,
Salutation:	Sire:
	or
	May it please your Majesty:
Complimentary Close:	I have the honor to remain
	Your Majesty's most obedient servant,

Queen.

Address:	The Queen's Most Excellent [or Gracious] Majesty,
Salutation:	Madam:
	or
	May it please your Majesty:
Complimentary Close:	Same as King's

Prince.

Address:	His Royal Highness the Prince of Wales,
	His Royal Highness Prince George,
Salutation:	Sir:
	or
	May it please your Royal Highness:
Complimentary Close:	I remain, Sir, with the greatest respect
	Your Royal Highness's most dutiful and obedient servant,

Princess.

Address:	Her Royal Highness the Princess Mary,
Salutation:	Madam:
Complimentary Close:	Similar to Prince's

219

Royal Duke.

Address:	His Royal Highness the Duke of York,
Salutation:	Sir:
	or
	May it please your Royal Highness:
Complimentary Close:	I have the honour to be, My Lord Duke,
	Your Grace's most obedient and humble servant,

Royal Duchess.

Address:	Her Royal Highness the Duchess of York,
Salutation:	Madam:
	or
	May it please your Royal Highness:
Complimentary Close:	Similar to Duke's

Duke.

Address:	The Most Noble the Duke of————,
	or
	His Grace the Duke of————,
	or
	The Duke of————, (informal)
Salutation:	My Lord Duke: (formal) *or,*
	Your Grace: (formal)
	Dear Duke of————: (informal)
Complimentary Close:	I have the honour to remain
	Your Grace's most obedient servant,
	or
	Believe me, my dear Duke,
	Yours very sincerely, (informal)

Duchess.

Address:	The Most Noble the Duchess of ————, (formal) *or,*
	Her Grace the Duchess of————,
	or
	The Duchess of————, (informal)

Salutation:	Madam: (formal)
	Your Grace:
	Dear Duchess of————, (informal)
Complimentary Close:	Similar to Duke's.

Duke's Eldest Son.

Takes the title of Marquess (Marquis) or Earl by courtesy. (See Marquess and Earl)

Duke's Daughters and Younger Sons

Address:	The Right Honorable Lord John ————,
	The Right Honorable Lady Mary ————,
	The Lord John————,(family name)
	The Lady Mary————,(family name)
Salutation:	My Lord: (formal)
	My Lady: (formal)
	Dear Lord John: (informal)
	Dear Lady Mary: (informal)

Wives of Younger Sons.

The Lady John Smith (not Lady Smith)

Marquess.

Address:	The Most Honourable the Marquess (Marquis) ————, or,
	The Marquess of ————,
Salutation:	My Lord Marquess: or, My Lord: (formal), or
	Dear Lord ————: (informal)
Complimentary Close:	I have the honour to be, My Lord Marquess,
	Your Lordship's obedient and humble servant,

Marchioness.

Address:	The Most Honourable the Marchioness of ————,
Salutation:	My Lady Marchioness: (formal) or,
	Madam: or,
	Dear Lady ————: (informal)

Complimentary Close: Similar to Marquess's

Daughters and Younger Sons of a Marquess.

Address: Lord Frederick———,(family name)

    Lady Helen———,(family name)

Earl.

Address: The Right Honourable the Earl of
———,

Salutation: My Lord: (formal)

    Dear Lord ———: (informal)

Complimentary Close: Believe me, my dear Lord ———,
sincerely yours,

Countess.

Address: The Right Honourable the Coun-
tess of ———,

Salutation: Madam: (formal)

    Dear Lady———, (informal)

Complimentary Close: Similar to Earl's

Earl's Eldest Son.

See Viscount

Earl's Younger Son.

Address: The Honourable William ———,

Salutation: Sir: (formal)

    Dear Mr. ———, (informal)

Complimentary Close: I have the honour to remain
Your obedient servant, (formal)

Earl's Daughter.

Address: The Lady Mary———,(family name)

Salutation: Madam: (formal)

    Dear Lady (Christian name): (in-
formal)

Complimentary Close: I have the honour to remain
Your obedient servant, (formal)

Viscount.

Address: The Right Honourable the Viscount
————,
or
The Right Honourable Lord ————,
The Viscount ————,

Salutation: My Lord Viscount ————: (formal)
Dear Lord ————: (informal)

Complimentary Close: Believe me, my dear Lord ————,
sincerely yours,

Viscountess.

Address: The Right Honourable the Viscountess ————,
or
The Right Honourable Lady ————,
or
The Viscountess ————,

Salutation: Madam: (formal)
Dear Lady ————: (informal)

Son and Daughter of Viscount.

Address: The Honourable Robert ————,
The Honourable Mary ————,

Salutation: Sir: [Madam:] (formal)
Dear Mr. ————:
Dear Miss ————: (informal)

Complimentary Close: Believe me, sincerely yours,

Baron.

Address: The   Right   Honourable   Lord
————, (formal)
or
The Lord ————, (informal)

Salutation: My Lord: (formal)
Your Lordship:
Dear Lord ————: (informal)

Complimentary Close: Believe me, my dear Lord ————,
sincerely yours,

Baroness.

Address:	The Right Honourable Lady ———, (formal)
	or
	The Lady ———, (informal)
Salutation:	Madam: (formal)
	Dear Lady ———: (informal)
Complimentary Close:	Similar to Baron's

Baroness in Her Own Right.

Address:	The Right Honourable Baroness ———,
	or
	The Baroness ———, (informal)
Salutation:	Madam:
	Dear Lady ———:
Complimentary Close:	Believe me, my dear Lady ———, sincerely yours,

Baron's Son.

Address:	The Honourable Arthur ———,
	Wife: The Honourable Mrs. ———,
Salutation:	Sir: (formal)
	Dear Mr. ———:
	Dear Mrs. ———: (informal)
Complimentary Close:	I have the honour to remain your obedient servant, (formal)
	Believe me, Mr. or Mrs. ———, sincerely yours, (informal)

Baron's Daughter.

Address:	The Honourable Mary ———,
Salutation:	Madam: (formal)
	Dear Miss ———, (informal)
Married Name:	The Honourable Mrs. ———, *or* The Honourable Lady ———,
Complimentary Close:	Believe me, sincerely yours,

Baronet.

Address: Sir George Robinson, Bt. or Bart.,

Salutation: Sir: (formal)
Dear Sir George: (informal)

Complimentary Close: Believe me, dear Sir George,
            faithfully yours,

Wife of Baronet.

Address: Lady Robinson:

Salutation: Madam: (formal)
Dear Lady Robinson: (informal)

Complimentary Close: Similar to Baronet's

Knight.

Address: Sir William ———, K.C.M.G.,

Salutation: Sir: (formal)
Dear Sir William: (informal)

Complimentary Close: Believe me, dear Sir William, faith-
            fully yours,

Knight's Wife.

Address: Lady ———, (family name)

Salutation: Madam: (formal)
Dear Lady Mary: (informal)

Complimentary Close: Similar to Knight's

CORRECT ECCLESIASTICAL USAGE FOR OFFICIALS OF THE ANGLICAN CHURCH

Archbishop.

Address: The Most Reverend His Grace
        The Lord Archbishop of ———,

Salutation: My Lord Archbishop: (formal)
My dear Archbishop: (informal)

Complimentary Close: I have the honor to be, my Lord
    Archbishop,
    Your Grace's most obedient and
    humble servant,

Archbishop's Wife.

Address: Mrs. ————, (unless she has a
    title of her own)

Salutation: Dear Mrs. ————:

Complimentary Close: Sincerely yours,

Bishop.

Address: The Right Reverend the Lord
    Bishop of ————,
    or
    The Lord Bishop of ————,

Salutation: My Lord:
    or
    My Lord Bishop: (formal)
    or
    Dear Bishop: (informal)

Complimentary Close: I have the honour to remain your
    Lordship's obedient ser-
    vant, (formal)
    I have the honour to remain, my
    dear Lord Bishop, faith-
    fully yours, (informal)

Dean.

Address: The Very Reverend the Dean of
    ————,

Salutation: Very Reverend Sir: (formal)
    Dear Dean ————, (informal)

Complimentary Close: Faithfully yours,

Archdeacon.

Address: The Venerable the Archdeacon of
    ————,

Salutation:	Venerable Sir: (formal)
	Dear Archdeacon ————: (informal)
Complimentary Close:	Faithfully yours,
	or
	Respectfully yours,

Canon.

Address:	The Reverend Canon ————,
Salutation:	Reverend Sir:
	or
	Dear Canon, (informal)
Complimentary Close:	Yours faithfully,
	Yours respectfully,

Right Honourable.

The title *Right Honourable* is given to all Privy Councillors and precedes all other titles.

Commoner.

The Right Hon. Arthur ————

Knight.

The Right Hon. Sir John ————

Baronet.

The Right Hon. Sir Arthur ————, Bart.

Younger Son of a Duke or Marquess.

The Right Hon. Lord ———— ————

Honourable.

The title *Honourable* is given to children of peers, maids of honour, and judges of the High Court of Justice.

Lady.

The title *Lady* is held by all Peeresses under the rank of a Duchess, by all daughters of the three highest ranks of the peerage, and by the wives of Baronets and Knights.

ARMIGER'S *Titles*

Correct Ecclesiastical Usage for Officials of the Catholic Church

The Pope.

Address:	His Holiness, Pope Pius X,
	or
	His Holiness, the Pope,
Salutation:	Your Holiness:
	or
	Most Holy Father:
Complimentary Close:	Your dutiful son or daughter,
	or
	Respectfully yours,

Cardinal.

Address:	His Eminence Cardinal ————,
Salutation:	Your Eminence:
Complimentary Close:	Respectfully yours,

If also an Archbishop.

	His Eminence the Cardinal Archbishop ————,
	or
	His Eminence Cardinal ————, Archbishop of ————,

Archbishop.

Address:	His Excellency, the Archbishop of ————,
	or
	The Most Reverend Archbishop of ————,
Salutation:	Your Excellency:
	or
	Most Reverend Archbishop:
	or
	Dear Archbishop ————: (informal)
Complimentary Close:	Respectfully yours,

228

Bishop.

Address:	His Excellency, Bishop of ———,
	The Right Reverend ———, D.D.
	or
	The Right Reverend Bishop ———,
Salutation:	Your Excellency:
	Dear Bishop ———: (informal)
Complimentary Close:	Respectfully yours,
	Sincerely yours,

Member of the Papal Household.

Monsignor:

Address:	The Very Reverend Monsignor ———,
Salutation:	Dear Monsignor:
Complimentary Close:	Respectfully yours,

Priest.

Address:	The Rev. Father Brown,
	or
	The Rev. J. B. Brown,
Salutation:	Dear Father Brown:
	or
	Dear Reverend Father:
	or
	Dear Father:
Complimentary Close:	Respectfully yours,
	or
	Sincerely yours,

CORRECT ECCLESIASTICAL USAGE FOR PROTESTANT AND JEWISH
CLERGY IN AMERICA

Protestant Episcopal Bishop.

Address:	To the Right Reverend William T. Manning,
	Bishop of New York,
Salutation:	Right Reverend and Dear Sir: (formal)
	or
	Dear Bishop Manning: (informal)
	or
	My dear Bishop ———:
Complimentary Close:	Sincerely yours,

Dean.

Address:	Dean ———— ————,
	or
	The Very Rev. Dean ————,
Salutation:	Very Reverend Sir: (formal)
	Dear Dean ————: (informal)
Complimentary Close:	Yours respectfully,
	or
	Sincerely yours,
	or
	Cordially yours, (informal)

Methodist Bishop.

Address:	The Reverend Bishop ————,
Salutation:	Dear Bishop ————,
	or
	My dear Bishop ————,
	or
	Dear Sir:
Complimentary Close:	Sincerely yours,
	or
	Respectfully yours,

Other Clergymen.

Address:	The Reverend William D. Robinson,
	or
	The Rev. Dr. W. D. Robinson (if entitled to a degree)
	or
	The Rev. W. D. Robinson, D.D. (See p. 232.)
Salutation:	Dear Sir: *or* My dear Sir:
	or
	Dear Mr. Robinson: (informal)
	or
	Dear Dr. Robinson: (if entitled to a degree)

Complimentary Close: Yours respectfully,
or
Yours sincerely,

Jewish Rabbi.

Address: Rabbi Stephen Wise,
or
The Rev. Stephen Wise,

Salutation: Dear Sir:
or
Dear Dr. Wise:

Complimentary Close: Yours respectfully,

CORRECT USAGE FOR MEMBERS OF RELIGIOUS INSTITUTES

Superior of a Sisterhood.

Address: Reverend Mother (followed by initials designating order, if desired)
or
Reverend Mother Superior (without initials of order)

Salutation: Reverend Mother:
or
Dear Reverend Mother: (informal)
or
My dear Reverend Mother: (name added if desired)

Complimentary Close: Yours respectfully,

Member of a Sisterhood.

Address: Sister Mary Angela, (followed by initials of order, if desired)
or
Sister Mary Angela, O. S. D. (Order of St. Dominic)

Salutation: Dear Sister, or My dear Sister:
or
Dear Sister Angela:
or
My dear Sister Angela:

Complimentary Close: Yours sincerely,

Superior of a Brotherhood.

Address:	Rev. Brother ———,
Salutation:	Dear Brother ———,
Complimentary Close:	Respectfully yours,

Member of a Brotherhood.

Address:	Brother ———,
Salutation:	Dear Brother ———,
Complimentary Close:	Sincerely yours,

or

Respectfully yours,

CORRECT USAGE FOR OFFICIALS IN UNIVERSITIES AND COLLEGES

President of a Theological Seminary.

Address: The Rev. President Henry Sloane Coffin,

Salutation: Dear President Coffin:

or

Dear Dr. Coffin: (if preferred)

Complimentary Close: Yours respectfully,

or

Yours sincerely,

Professor in a Theological Seminary.

Address: The Reverend Professor Hugh Black,

or

The Rev. Hugh Black, D.D.

or

Professor Hugh Black,

Salutation: Dear Professor Black:

or

Dear Dr. Black:

Complimentary Close: Yours respectfully,

or

Yours sincerely,

President of a University.

Address: Nicholas Murray Butler, LL.D. President of Columbia University,

or

President Nicholas Murray Butler, Columbia University, New York

Salutation:	Dear Sir: Dear President Butler:
Complimentary Close:	Sincerely yours, Very truly yours,

College or University Professor.

Address:	Professor John M. Manly,
	    University of Chicago, Chicago.
	or
	John M. Manly, Ph.D.,
	    Professor of English

Salutation:	Dear Sir: Dear Professor Manly: (informal)
Complimentary Close:	Sincerely yours, Very truly yours,

Dean of a Woman's College.

Address:	Dean Jane Louise Mesick,
	    Simmons College, Boston.
	Dean Gildersleeve,
	    Barnard College, New York.

Salutation:	Dear Dean Mesick: Dear Dr. Mesick: Dear Miss Mesick: (informal)
Complimentary Close:	Sincerely yours, Very truly yours,

College or University Instructor.

Address:	Murray Pollins, Esq.: *or* Murray Pollins, Ph.D.: (if entitled to the degree) *or* Dr. Murray Pollins:
Salutation:	Dear Mr. or Dr. Pollins:
Complimentary Close:	Sincerely yours,

French Usage

Gentleman.

Address:	Monsieur ———— ————,
Salutation:	Monsieur:
Complimentary Close:	Agréez, monsieur, mes meilleurs voeux,

Married Woman.

Address:	Madame ———— ————,
Salutation:	Madame:
Complimentary Close:	Recevez, madame, l'assurance de mes meilleurs sentiments,

Unmarried Woman.

Address:	Mademoiselle ———— ————,
Salutation:	Madame: (formal) Mademoiselle: (informal)
Complimentary Close:	Veuillez agréer, chère madame, l'expression de ma considération distinguée,

Spanish Usage

Firm or Organization.

Address:	Señores (Sres.) Gonzáles Hermaños,
Salutation:	Muy señores nuestros:
Complimentary Close:	Muy attos. y as. ss.,

Gentleman.

Address:	Señor (Sr.) Gonzáles or Señor (Sr.) Rafael Gonzáles,
Salutation:	Muy señor mío:
Complimentary Close:	Muy atentamente.

Married Woman.

Address:	Señora (Sra.) de Gonzáles or
	Señora (Sra.) Doña (Da.) María de González,
Salutation:	Muy estimada señora:
Complimentary Close:	Soy de Vd. s.s.,

Unmarried Woman.

Address:	Señorita (Srta.) or
	Señorita (Srta.) Doña (Da.) María González,
Salutation:	Muy distinguida señorita:
Complimentary Close:	De Vd. afma. amiga,

GERMAN USAGE

Firm or Organization.

Address:	Name, ——— ———,
Salutation:	Geehrte Herren:
Complimentary Close:	Ihrer gefälligen Antwort entgegensehend, zeichnen wir, Hochachtungsvoll,

Gentleman.

Address:	Herrn ——— ———,
Salutation:	Sehr geehrter Herr: (formal)
Complimentary Close:	Ihnen bestens dankend verbleibe ich, Hochachtungsvoll,

Married Woman.

Address:	Frau ——— ———,
Salutation:	Meine liebe Frau ———: (semiformal)
Complimentary Close:	In Erwartung Ihrer freundlichen Antwort bin ich, Ihre Ergebenste.

Unmarried Woman.

Address:	Fräulein ————— —————,
Salutation:	Mein liebes Fräulein, (cordial)
Complimentary Close:	Mit Grüssen an Sie und Ihre Freundin,

ITALIAN USAGE

Firm Name or Organization.

Address:	Spettabile Ditta —————,
Salutation:	Spettabile Ditta:
Complimentary Close:	Di voi Obbligatissimo, (*also:* Con rispettosa osservanza)

Gentleman.

Address:	Gentilissimo Signore —————,
Salutation:	Gentilissimo Signore:
Complimentary Close:	Cordialmente suo, (*also:* Distintamente suo)

Married Woman.

Address:	Distinta Signora —————,
Salutation:	Distinta Signora:
Complimentary Close:	Di Lei devotissimo,

Unmarried Woman.

Address:	Esimia Signorina ————— —————,
Salutation:	Esimia Signorina:
Complimentary Close:	Devotamente suo,

Prince.

Address:	Principe Reale, (*also:* Sua Altezza Reale), (*also:* Altezza)
Salutation:	Altezza:
Complimentary Close:	Di Lei obbligatissimo e devotissimo, (*also:* Con i sensi della piu' profonda devozione)

Count.

Address:	Nobiluomo ———, *(also:* Pregiatissimo Signore)
Salutation:	Pregiatissimo Signore:
Complimentary Close:	Di Lei devotissimo,

Countess.

Address:	Nobildonna ———,
Salutation:	Nobildonna:
Complimentary Close:	Con i sensi della piu' profonda stima *(also:* Di Lei devotissimo)

REFERENCE BOOKS

ARMIGER: *Titles. A Guide to the Right Use of British Titles and Honours.* A. & C. Black, Ltd.

Burke's Peerage, Baronetage, Knightage.

Catholic Encyclopedia, Vol. I.

Kelly's Handbook to the Titled, Landed, and Official Classes, 1928.

MAWSON, C. O. SYLVESTER: *Style-Book for Writers and Editors.* Thomas Y. Crowell Company, New York.

POST, EMILY: *The Book of Etiquette.* Doubleday, Doran & Company, Inc.

SQUIRE, ANNE: *Social Washington.*

Whitaker's Almanack for 1928.

Whitaker's Peerage, Baronetage, Knightage and Companionage.

Century Dictionary.

Standard Dictionary.

CHAPTER III

TELEGRAMS, CABLEGRAMS, AND RADIOGRAMS

TELEGRAMS

Telegrams are classed as follows:

1. Telegrams
2. Day letters
3. Night messages
4. Night letters

1. Telegrams are regular day messages sent at full rate for expedited service. The rate on such messages is based on ten words. Code language may be used.

2. Day letters are messages deferred in service at lower rates than those of regular day telegrams. Code may not be used.

3. Night messages are sent at reduced rates to be delivered the following day. Code may not be used.

4. Night letters which contain not more than fifty words are accepted up to 2 A.M. for delivery the following day. Rates are less than those for night messages. Code language may not be used.

Telegrams should be clear, concise, and brief. Omit all unnecessary words. The parts of speech most often used in telegrams are nouns, verbs, adjectives, and adverbs. If possible, do without pronouns, prepositions, articles, and copulative verbs. Use simple sentences, rather than complex or compound. If more than one sentence is needed, use the same form or the same order of words. Insert the word *stop,* if necessary for clearness, to indicate the end of a sentence.

Note that the following classes of words, figures, and letters are counted as one word:

1. All dictionary words.
2. Abbreviations.
3. Surnames.
4. Punctuation marks within sentences.
5. Foreign names with preceding particles.
6. Figures.
7. Initials.
8. Common weights and measures.

Certain abbreviations are counted as one word:

A. M., P. M., COD, FOB, OK., etc.

Figures are estimated according to the number of digits, decimal points, and commas used. Often it is better to write out a group of figures in words; for example, 3,000,000 would count as nine words; three million as two; and 224.14 as six.

Fractions are computed as follows:

1/2 three words
12 1/2 five words

Telegrams, that is, fast day-messages, may be written in the United States in the following languages other than English: French, German, Spanish, Portuguese, Latin, Dutch, Italian.

In the United States there is no charge for date, address, or signature. In Great Britain and on the Continent, every word including date, address, and signature is counted. The rate is, however, lower than in America.

CABLEGRAMS

Cablegrams are classed as follows:

1. Full-rate Cablegrams.
2. Deferred Cablegrams.

1. Full-rate cablegrams are used for expedited service in messages requiring quick delivery. As the cost of transmitting a cablegram is high, code language is often used. Code language is made up of coined or condensed words that are pronounceable and formed according to established dictionary usage. They may be written in English, French, German, Italian, Dutch, Portuguese, Spanish, or Latin. Code addresses may be used.

Separate initials, abbreviations like *d, rd, st, th,* used with figures, and the dollar sign are counted as single words, and cost computed accordingly. Hyphenated or compound words are counted as single words. In cablegrams, written in plain language, each word of fifteen letters or less is counted as a single word.

2. Deferred cablegrams are designed for messages of unimportant matter not requiring immediate transmission. The rate is lower than that of the regular cablegram. A deferred cablegram must be written in the language of the country from which it is sent or to which it is going, or in French which is considered a universal language.

Code addresses and signatures may be used. Each word of fifteen letters or less is counted, as in ordinary cablegrams, as one word.

The following code-words, taken from the code-book of the American Express Company, illustrate words invented to represent various meanings:

RESERVATIONS

Lojob	Have reserved stateroom on .... sailing ....
Lojug	Reserve double room (at) ....
Lokan	Reserve double room with bath (at)..........
Lokes	Reserve first class seat (s) ....
Lokma	Reserve hotel accommodations for .... persons.
Lokoc	Reserve one double room and bath for me at first class hotel. Am due to arrive ....
Lokre	Reserve one double room for me at first class hotel. Am due to arrive ....

Radiograms may be written in any of the languages used in cablegrams.

They are classed as follows:

1. Full or Ordinary Rate
2. Deferred Rate
3. Urgent Rate

1. Full or Ordinary Rate applies to all messages requiring prompt transmission which rank after radiograms sent at Urgent or Partly Urgent Rates.

2. Deferred, half-rate service, is provided for messages of a less urgent nature. Such radiograms must be written in plain language of either the country of origin, country of destination or in French.

The first word in the address should be one of the following:

(1) LCO (Language Country of Origin)
(2) LCD (Language Country of Destination)
(3) LCF (Language Country of France)

according to the language used, and is a chargeable factor.

3. Urgent Rate Service Radiograms are given priority over all ·other commercial messages. The word *Urgent* must be written as the first word of the address and is charged for as one word.

Partly Urgent Rate provides for preferred service on the radio and Urgent Service on the foreign telegraph systems. The indicator PU should be written as the first word of the address and is charged for as one word.

In Radioletters and Week-End Radioletters, especially adapted for social and business correspondence admitting of some deferment, RLT or WLT must be written as the first word and is charged for as one word.

CHAPTER IV

THE FRAMING OF PETITIONS

The writing of petitions should be characterized by clearness of expression, by an orderly marshaling of ideas, by forceful presentation of material, and by dignified, respectful tone.

Petitions are usually expressed in a conventional form based on one of the following plans:

1. The reasons arranged in order of their importance followed by the request, each reason being preceded by *In view of the fact that* or by *Inasmuch as*.

2. The explanation of who is making the request, as, *We, the Members of the New Rochelle Woman's Club,* or *We, the Undersigned Citizens of* ...., or *We, the Residents of* ...., followed by the request itself and the reasons for such a request.

The following forms of petition illustrate those used in city offices concerning local improvements:

New York,   192 .

To (Name of Borough President)
President of the Borough of

 The subscribers, whose names are written underneath, respectfully petition you and the Local Board of the
District for a certain local improvement, to wit:

   Regulate, reregulate, grade, regrade, curb, recurb,
  lay or relay sidewalk and pave with a permanent (type
  of pavement—granite, sheet asphalt, etc.) on a concrete
  foundation   avenue from   street
  to   street, together with all work incidental
  thereto

and they hereby request that you appoint a time for a meeting
of the said Local Board, and that you submit this petition to

said Board and do all such other acts as may be required of you by law, in order that the local improvement above described may be initiated and obtained or constructed:

Names   Addresses   Description of
                property owned:

New York City,......................192 .

HON. HENRY BRUCKNER,
  President of the Borough of The Bronx,
   and Chairman of the Local Board,
    of............................District.

DEAR SIR:

The subscribers whose names are written underneath, being owners of property directly affected respectfully petition you and the Local Board of....................................
for the laying out on the map of The City of New York......
....
....
in accordance with accompanying sketch.

And we hereby request that you appoint a time for a meeting of the said Local Board, and that you submit this petition to said Board, and do all such other acts as may be required of you by law in order that the above described lay-out may be obtained and become a part of the map of The City of New York.

NAME OF OWNER	ADDRESS	Frontage on Improvement	Lot Number	BLOCK NUMBER

Reprinted by permission.

A PETITION IN LETTER FORM TO A CITY COMMISSION

THE BRONX BOARD OF TRADE
In The City of New York

March 19, 19—

Hon. John F. Gilchrist, Chairman,
Transit Commission,
New York, N. Y.

Dear Mr. Chairman:

Within a few months the new Theodore Roosevelt High School, on the south side of East Fordham Road, east of Third Avenue, is scheduled to be opened. This new high school will have a register of at least five thousand pupils. It is expected that approximately 50% of the pupils will use the Third Avenue "L" to and from the school.

If these pupils have to cross Fordham Road in order to reach the "L," they will do so at considerable risk of accident. Fordham Road is a very busy thoroughfare, and the volume of traffic thereon is constantly increasing.

In order to reduce the possibility of accident to these children and others, The Bronx Board of Trade urges that the Transit Commission take steps to bring about the construction of an additional stairway leading to the southeast corner of Third Avenue and Fordham Road.

This will involve additional station facilities on the south side of Fordham Road, or the erection of a passageway across Fordham Road similar to that which now crosses East 149th Street.

In case additional station facilities are not provided, we feel it will be necessary to install more turnstiles at the present station to reduce congestion, especially in the morning when the youngsters on their way to school will be proceeding in a direction opposite to that of the general public.

Attention also is called to the lack of protection on the present narrow station platforms. We believe that steps should be taken to provide for the erection of guard-rails on each side of these platforms, to prevent anyone's being pushed off onto the tracks in case of overcrowding such as may occur just before and after school hours.

We shall appreciate it if the Transit Commission will make an intensive study of conditions at this station in the light of the prospective high school opening, and take steps to have necessary changes in facilities made prior to the opening, if possible.

Very truly yours,
Charles E. Reid
Executive Secretary

A Petition for Extension of a Bus Line

Hon. James J. Walker
Board of Aldermen
Board of Estimate and Apportionment
Board of Transportation
Of the City of New York

Gentlemen:

We, the residents of the district including and adjacent to Morningside Drive from 110th Street to 123rd Street, respectfully petition you to grant to the Fifth Avenue Coach Company, a license to operate a bus line from some point between Washington Square and Forty-second Street to Morningside Drive and 110th Street, along Morningside Drive to 120th Street, and then along 120th Street to Riverside Drive, in order to meet transportation needs of this section.

Signed:

Reprinted by permission.

CHAPTER V

THE WRITING OF MINUTES

Minutes are records of meetings and of the action taken in them. They should, therefore, be written accurately, clearly, and concisely, for they are often referred to in confirmation of an action, as a source of information, or as records.

The language is formal and follows traditional lines. Generally, definite forms are used which are to be observed strictly. Minutes often conform to the following order:

(*a*) Name of Company or Organization
(*b*) Name of body holding meeting
(*c*) Date and number of meeting
(*d*) Hour of meeting and location
(*e*) Names of those present and those absent
(*f*) Reading of previous minutes
(*g*) Unfinished business and reports of committees of investigation
(*h*) Action taken on unfinished business; digest of business pending
(*i*) New business
(*j*) Informal discussion
(*k*) Date of next meeting
(*l*) Adjournment and time of adjournment
(*m*) Approval and signature of minutes

The following minutes of an academic organization illustrate the form and phraseology often used in writing reports of meetings:

MINUTES

Of the first meeting of the English Graduate Union

At the first meeting of the English Graduate Union, some eighty charter members being present, the association was called to order by Ernest Hunter Wright, who acted as temporary Chairman and who requested Mildred Loxton de Barritt to serve as temporary Secretary.

For the information of the members, the Chairman spoke at some length of the purposes and prospects of the Union. In record of the state of the association as of March 1, he reported a membership of 186, of whom 121 were resident members and 65 non-resident; and of whom 40 were life-members, 28 being resident and 12 non-resident. He further reported subscriptions already pledged to the Endowment as totalling $1719.00, and to current expenses as totalling $188.00.

In behalf of the Committee of Organization, the Chairman then read a copy of the Constitution for the Union as drawn and offered with a view to the proximate incorporation of the association under the laws of the State of New York. Upon motion of Dudley Howe Miles, seconded by William Haller, the Constitution was unanimously adopted, and ordered printed and distributed to members.

As a first act under the Constitution, Charles Sears Baldwin, in behalf of the Committee of Organization who had so far acted as the Council of the Union, moved the election to honorary membership of Brander Matthews, Emeritus Professor of Dramatic Literature, and of William Peterfield Trent, Emeritus Professor of English Literature. The motion was seconded in a speech of reminiscence by Arthur H. Nason, and was carried by a rising vote.

The next business under the Constitution was the election of officers for the remainder of the current year. The following nominations were made by Dorothy McSparran Arnold:

President: ERNEST HUNTER WRIGHT	*Members of the Council:*
	Harry Morgan Ayres
Secretary: Mildred Loxton de Barritt	Arthur E. Christy
Treasurer: Hoxie Neale Fairchild	Dwight L. Durling
	Ruth Mohl

247

Members of the Committee of Admissions:

Rose Mary Davis
Raymond A. Houk
Anna E. Lincoln
Louie M. Miner

George Nobbe
Frank Allen Patterson
Ralph L. Rusk

Custodians of the Endowment:

Ashley H. Thorndike
William T. Brewster
Arnold Whitridge

At the request of the Chairman, Mr. Nason took the chair. After a call for further nominations, it was moved by William A. S. Dollard that the Secretary cast one ballot for the officers nominated. The motion was seconded and carried, and the officers were declared elected.

After brief congratulations, in prose and verse respectively, by Blanche Colton Williams and by Harry Morgan Ayres, the Union adjourned.

MILDRED LOXTON DE BARRITT
Secretary

MINUTES OF THE HIGH SCHOOL TEACHERS ASSOCIATION, MAY 16, 1925, AT 2:15 P. M., HOTEL MCALPIN

The meeting was called to order by the President. The minutes of the previous meeting were read and approved. The Treasurer presented his annual report, and showed that in the last two years the Association has more than doubled in membership.

Mr. Stebbins reported for the Committee on Sub-Normal Pupils, that the committee had discussed types of pupils, and principles to be observed in planning their course of study, and had formulated recommendations for organizing these pupils as a separate unit in a different building from other pupils, and for their course of study in the first year, with selected and correlated subjects. After some discussion of the report, it was moved by Miss Fahey that the committee be continued, and that the report be printed and circulated among the teachers. The motion was carried.

The report of the Pension Committee recommends that new blanks for Option No. 1 be filled out each term. The principals can now get blanks and keep a supply. It was stated that by the five year pension law there would be no increased rates for present teachers. For new entrants there would be a slightly higher rate, which would be optional.

Under old business came the question of withdrawal from the Federation of Teachers' Associations which had been referred to this meeting by the Board of Representatives. Mr. Chamberlain moved that the High School Teachers Association hereby withdraw from the Federation. This motion was carried unanimously.

Mr. Guiness brought up the subject of education for peace, and reminded the Association that a committee had been authorized to call a meeting of teachers from all schools for this purpose, but that such meeting had not been called. After some discussion of the difficulties involved in this question, it was moved and carried that a committee be appointed to take the matter under advisement.

The subject announced for discussion was: "Plans for a Larger and More Efficient High School Teachers Association." Various plans, including a tentative suggestion of a paid executive secretary, were brought forward.

Mr. Chamberlain moved that the H. S. T. A. send the President to the meeting of the National Education Association, which was carried. A motion was made and passed that a committee be appointed to get in touch with associations and administrative officials dealing with problems of secondary education in large cities, and to report to this Association what might be done toward furthering an exchange of experience on matters of secondary education.

The Nominating Committee reported the following names as candidates for office in the Association for the coming year:

For President .... William R. Lasher
For Vice-President .... Grace Helene Miller
For Secretary .... Harriet F. Hale
For Treasurer .... Loring B. Mullen

(Additional Members of Executive Committee)
Francis H. J. Paul

Alexander L. Pugh   Fred C. White
Ernest D. Lewis   Lolabel Hall

As there were no further nominations, these nominees were each in turn declared elected by unanimous choice, and a single ballot cast.

A vote of appreciation of the work of the President and officers for the past year was moved and carried.

Upon motion the meeting adjourned.

Respectfully submited,

HARRIET L. HALE, Secretary

The following illustrate minutes of business organizations:

At the annual meeting of the ...., held at .... on ...., the President called for the report of the tellers. The report as read by the Chairman, ..., stated that the following officers had been duly elected for the year 1928:

President ....
First Vice President ....
Second Vice President ....
Third Vice President ....
Recording Secretary ....
Corresponding Secretary..........
Treasurer ....

Extract from minutes of the Executive Board of the........ .... held at the ....,
on ....

The Treasurer be authorized to open an account with the .... Trust Company, ..., and that said account shall not be removed from the ....
Trust Company unless authorized by the Executive Board.

....
Secretary

1928

THE —————— CLUB

Extract from the minutes of the meeting of the Council of the .... Club held on Monday, December 10th, 1928:

The Treasurer called the attention of the Council to the fact that he anticipated being absent from the city for a period of several months and on motion duly made, seconded and carried, it was

VOTED that until further action of the Council, Messrs. ....
be each appointed to act, or sign for the Treasurer of the .... Club, and that each of them be and is hereby authorized to receive and disburse the funds of the Club and to execute in its name and behalf, any and all checks, drafts, notes or other negotiable instruments and to perform all other duties of the Treasurer, as provided for under the By-laws, in the absence of the Treasurer.

Attest:

Secretary

Seal.

FIFTH AVENUE OFFICE COMMITTEE
MINUTES OF MEETING

A meeting of the Fifth Avenue Office Committee was held at 475 Fifth Avenue, New York, on Thursday, April 19, 1928, at 9:30 A. M. The minutes of the last meeting were read and approved and the usual statements were examined. There being no further business the meeting adjourned.

Present: Mr. ...., Mr. ...., Mr. ...., Mr. ...., and Mr. ....

....
Vice President

MINUTES OF STOCKHOLDERS' MEETING

The Minutes of a Stockholders' Meeting generally include the following: the names of those present, how many shares they hold, which are represented in person and which by proxy, an alphabetical list of stockholders, proof of mailing of notice-of-the-meeting with affidavit duly acknowledged before notary, copy of proxy, oath of inspectors, nomination of officers, report of inspectors on votes cast, announcement of elections, approval of preceding minutes, all in great detail and formal order. These minutes are usually written by the Company attorney.

The following illustrates in detail the minutes of such a meeting:

> The annual meeting of the stockholders of The Greene Company, a Maine corporation, was held at the office of the Company, 240 Park Avenue, in the Borough of Manhattan, City, County and State of New York, on Monday, February 27, 1928, at 4:00 o'clock in the afternoon, pursuant to adjournment.

Mr. John Greene, President of the Company, called the meeting to order and Mr. W. A. Sands, its Assistant-Secretary, kept the minutes.

The Secretary presented the alphabetical list required by statute, of the stockholders entitled to vote at the meeting and, after comparing the list with the proxies presented and after ascertaining the stockholders present in person, reported that the following stockholders whose stock had not been transferred on the books of the Company within twenty (20) days next preceding the meeting, holding the number and kinds of shares indicated opposite their respective names and aggregating a total of 3,326 shares out of a total of 5,422 shares entitled to vote at this meeting, were present in person or represented by proxy and entitled to vote.

STOCKHOLDERS PRESENT IN PERSON

Name of Stockholder	*1st Pref. . . Sec. Pref. . . Common*
(Names)	(Number of shares held by each)

STOCKHOLDERS REPRESENTED BY PROXY

Name	*Name of Proxy*	*No. of Shares*
		1st Pref. Sec. Pref. Common

The alphabetical list of stockholders referred to above is attached.

The Chairman thereupon announced that a quorum was in attendance at the meeting.

The Secretary presented and read a copy of the notice-of-the-meeting together with proof of the due mailing thereof to each stockholder of the Company at least ten (10) days before the meeting, as required by the by-laws.

On motion, it was unanimously

  RESOLVED that the original affidavit of mailing notice of this meeting together with the copy of said notice, the form of proxy and the list of stockholders thereto annexed, be kept among the records of the Company and that copies thereof be incorporated in the minutes of this meeting.

Following are copies of said affidavit of mailing said notice of this meeting, said form of proxy and said list of stockholders.

THE GREENE COMPANY
Affidavit of Mailing Notice
of
ANNUAL MEETING OF STOCKHOLDERS

STATE OF NEW YORK }
COUNTY OF NEW YORK } ss.:

 VIRGINIA WHYTE, being duly sworn, deposes and says that she is over the age of twenty-one years.

 That on February 9th, 1928, at about 11:45 A.M., she placed in a mail-chute maintained by the United States Post Office, at No. 240 Park Avenue, in the Borough of Manhattan, City, County and State of New York, securely sealed, post-paid envelopes addressed to the persons and at the addresses set forth upon the annexed "List of Stockholders"; that each of said envelopes contained a copy of the "Notice of Annual Meeting of Stockholders," of which another copy is hereto annexed.

Virginia Whyte

Sworn to before me this
9th day of February, 1928

   Mary Heald
    Notary Public,
   New York County Clerk's No. 483
   New York County Register's No. 8262
   Commission expires March 30th, 1929

(Mary Heald)
Notary Public)
(New York, N. Y.)

253

THE GREENE COMPANY
NOTICE OF ANNUAL MEETING
of
STOCKHOLDERS

TO THE STOCKHOLDERS OF THE GREENE COMPANY

NOTICE IS HEREBY GIVEN pursuant to the by-laws of The Greene Company (a Maine Corporation) that the annual meeting of its stockholders will be held at the office of the Corporation at No. 240 Park Avenue, New York, N.Y., on Monday, February 27th, 1928, at 11:00 o'clock in the forenoon.

1. To elect a Board of Directors;
2. To ratify, approve and confirm previous action of the stock-holders, the Board of Directors and the officers of the Corporation and act on any reports of the officers made on said meeting;
3. To take action on any other matters that may properly come before the meeting.

W. A. SANDS
Assistant Secretary

New York, N. Y.
February 9, 1928.

If you do not expect to be present in person, please sign the accompanying proxy and return it at once.

THE GREENE COMPANY

PROXY

First Preferred Shares.........
Second Preferred Shares.......
Common Shares ....
Total ....

KNOW ALL MEN BY THESE PRESENTS that the undersigned stockholder of THE GREENE COMPANY, a Maine Corporation, does hereby constitute and appoint attorneys, agents and proxies, and each of them attorney, agent and proxy, for the undersigned and in the name, place and stead of the undersigned, with full power of substitution and revocation, to vote upon and act as proxy of the undersigned in respect of all preferred stock and all common stock, or either, of THE GREENE COMPANY held by or standing in the name of the undersigned (hereby revoking any proxy or proxies heretofore given by the undersigned in respect of such stock or any thereof), at the annual meeting of stockholders of said Corporation to be held at its office, No. 240 Park Avenue, New York, N.Y., on February 27th, 1928, at eleven o'clock in the forenoon, and at any and all adjournments thereof, upon all matters that may come before said meeting, including the election of a Board of Directors and the ratification, approval and confirming of all previous action of the Board of Directors and officers of said Corporation, according to the number of votes the undersigned would be entitled to vote if then personally present. A majority of such of said attorneys, agents, and proxies as shall be present at the meeting (or, if only one be present, then that one) shall have and may exercise all the powers of all of them hereunder.

February   , 1928

_____(L.S.)
Stockholder's Signature

WITNESS:

_____

LIST OF STOCKHOLDERS OF THE GREENE COMPANY
TO WHOM NOTICE OF ANNUAL MEETING OF
STOCKHOLDERS WAS SENT ON 2/9/28

Names   *Addresses*

The Chairman announced that the next business before the meeting was the election of directors to hold office until the next annual meeting of the stockholders and until the election and qualification of their respective successors.

Miss Edna Payne and Mr. A. F. McMillan, (neither of them being a candidate for the office of director) were appointed inspectors of election and took the oath required by law, of which the following is a copy:

255

THE GREENE COMPANY
Oath of Inspectors of Election

STATE OF NEW YORK
County of New York ⎰ss.:

EDNA PAYNE and A. F. McMILLAN, being duly sworn upon their respective oaths, do severally promise and swear that they will faithfully, honestly and impartially perform the duties of inspectors of election for all votes that may be cast at the annual meeting of stockholders of The Greene Company, held on February 27, 1928, at the office of the Company, No. 240 Park Avenue, in the Borough of Manhattan, City, County and State of New York, and make true reports of said votes.

EDNA PAYNE
A. F. McMILLAN

Subscribed and
sworn to before me
this 27th day of
February, 1928.

MARY HEALD
Notary Public
New York County Clerk's No. 483
New York County Register's No. 826₂
Commission expires March 30th, 1929

(Mary Heald ⎱
(Notary Public ⎰
(New York County)

Thereupon, the following were duly nominated as directors to serve until the next annual election and until the election and qualification of their respective successors.

John Greene
F. G. Huyler
L. D. Louis
A. P. McLaren
R. T. Porter
E. O. Reynolds
W. A. Sands

The nominations having been closed, the polls were opened and the stockholders prepared their ballots and delivered them to the inspectors. Thereupon the polls were closed.

The inspectors having canvassed the votes for directors, prepared a report in writing of which the following is a copy:

THE GREENE COMPANY
Report of Inspectors

We, the subscribers, inspectors of election, appointed by the stockholders of The Greene Company, at the annual meeting of said stockholders, held this day at the office of said Company at No. 240 Park Avenue, in the Borough of Manhattan, City, County and State of New York, do report that, having taken an oath impartially to conduct the election of directors and all other votes at said meeting, we did receive the votes of the stockholders by ballot.

We report that 3,326 votes were cast and that the following persons received the number of votes set opposite their respective names:

John Greene	3,326
F. G. Huyler	"
L. D. Louis	"
A. P. McLaren	"
R. T. Porter	"
E. O. Reynolds	"
W. A. Sands	"

all of which is respectfully submitted, this 27th day of February, 1928, at New York, N. Y.

> Edna Payne
> A. F. McMillan
> Inspectors.

The Chairman then announced that Messrs. John Greene, F. G. Huyler, L. D. Louis, A. P. McLaren, R. T. Porter, E. O. Reynolds and W. A. Sands had been elected directors of the Company to serve until the next annual election and until the election and qualification of their respective successors.

There being no further business, the meeting, thereupon, on motion, adjourned.

_____
Secretary.

_____
Chairman

The program for a Directors' Meeting usually includes the following:

ROLL CALL
MINUTES OF LAST MEETING
REPORT OF THE PRESIDENT
REPORT OF THE TREASURER (or FINANCE COMMIT-
    TEE)

UNFINISHED BUSINESS (Under this are put items which
    are left over from preceding meetings; progress reports
    from committees appointed or their final reports, etc.)
NEW BUSINESS (any new business matters coming up since
    the last meeting.)
ADJOURNMENT

In general the matters coming up at the Board meeting are those involving large capital expenditures affecting the policies of the company.

Report of the President. This usually gives a resumé of the outstanding events of the past month, including amount of business done, outlook for the next month or the next quarter, and any recommendations the president may wish to make in regard to these matters.

Report of the Treasurer. This gives the financial position of the company in cash and securities, and reports on any new investments made. It also gives any figures on earnings and expense required with statistics showing comparison with previous year or years.

MINUTES OF A MEETING OF THE BOARD
OF DIRECTORS OF THE BLANK COMPANY
HELD AT THE OFFICES OF THE COMPANY,
240 PARK AVENUE, NEW YORK, N. Y., ON
MONDAY, MARCH 26, 1928, AT 9:30 A. M.

The following directors were present: Messrs. Black, Greene, Reade, Sands, and White. Mr. Sands acted as Chairman and Mr. Greene as Secretary.

The secretary presented a notice of the meeting that had been mailed to all directors on March 12.

The minutes of the meeting of Friday, March 23, were read and approved on motion duly made, seconded and unanimously carried.

THE WRITING OF MINUTES

The Secretary reported that at the meeting of the stockholders on February 27 the following directors had been elected for the ensuing year: F. H. Greene, W. A. Sands, B. L. Thomas, H. O. Vance, G. F. White, L. K. Wilde, and J. S. Zimmerman. The Chair then announced that the first business of the meeting was to elect officers and the following nominations were duly made and seconded:

President—W. A. Sands
Vice President—L. K. Wilde
Vice President—J. S. Zimmerman
Secretary—F. H. Greene
Treasurer—B. L. Thomas
Assistant Secretary—R. P. Mitchell

There being no further nominations it was moved, seconded and unanimously carried that the ballots be closed and the above officers be declared duly elected to serve until their successors be duly elected and qualified.

The President then read a report which was accepted and filed with the minutes of the meeting.

It was moved by Mr. Greene and seconded by Mr. Thomas and unanimously carried that the thanks of the Board be expressed to Mr. Vance for his services to the Company as Vice President during the several years of his occupancy of that office.

There then followed a discussion of several of the matters covered in the President's report without formal action.

It was moved by Mr. Thomas and seconded by Mr. Wilde and unanimously carried that a regular dividend of $6.00 per share and an extra dividend of $1.50 per share upon the Common Stock of the company be declared for the second quarter of the calendar year 1928 payable in equal monthly payments to Common Stockholders of record on the last day of each month.

There being no further business, on motion duly made, seconded and unanimously carried the meeting adjourned at 10:30 A. M.

F. H. Greene,
Secretary-of-the-Meeting

REFERENCE

CHURCH, ARTHUR F. *The Training of a Secretary.* J. B. Lippincott Company, 1922.

CHAPTER VI

THE FRAMING OF RESOLUTIONS

Resolution writing generally follows conventional lines. It is usually a formal expression, couched in almost legal phrasing, consisting of two parts: the reasons for the resolution, preceded by *Whereas,* and the resolution itself, preceded by *Be it resolved;* in case of more than one resolution, *Be it further resolved.*

A more informal type, increasingly used in modern writing, is a straightforward statement of the occasion for taking action, whatever it may be, followed by the action taken, without the use of *Whereas* or *Be it resolved.* This form is particularly suitable for resolutions to be passed by an organization which wishes to indicate its stand on certain subjects. It also seems more appropriate on the death of a prominent citizen, as it offers a wider scope for individual expression of appreciation and gives the impression of greater sincerity. Such resolutions are characterized by dignity, simplicity, and good faith.

Resolutions are framed for various purposes, some of which are the following:

1. To express appreciation for courtesies received
2. To do honor to one who has achieved distinction
3. To commemorate a distinguished service
4. To indicate action taken by an association on certain topics
5. To express regret at the resignation of an official
6. To offer congratulations on the promotion of an individual
7. To express appreciation of the life of a prominent citizen who has recently died, and to extend sympathy to his family

THE FRAMING OF RESOLUTIONS

Illustrations of various types of resolutions follow:

RESOLUTION EMBODIED INTO A FAMOUS PACT

CALVIN COOLIDGE
PRESIDENT OF THE UNITED STATES OF AMERICA

To all to whom these presents shall come, greeting:

Know ye, That Whereas a treaty between the President of the German Reich, the President of the United States of America, his Majesty the King of the Belgians, the President of the French Republic, his Majesty the King of Great Britain and the British Dominions beyond the seas, Emperor of India, his Majesty the King of Italy, his Majesty the Emperor of Japan, the President of the Republic of Poland and the President of the Czechoslovak Republic, declaring in the names of their respective peoples that they condemn recourse to war for the solution of international controversies, and renounce it as an instrument of national policy in their relations with one another, was signed by their respective plenipotentiaries at Paris on the twenty-seventh day of August, one thousand nine hundred and twenty-eight, the original of which treaty, in the French and English languages, is hereto annexed;

And Whereas, The Senate of the United States, by their resolution of Jan. 15, 1929 (two-thirds of the Senators present concurring therein) did advise and consent to the ratification of the said treaty,

Now Therefore, Be it known that I, Calvin Coolidge, President of the United States of America, having seen and considered the said treaty, do hereby, in pursuance of the aforesaid advice and consent of the Senate, ratify and confirm the same and every article and clause thereof.

In Testimony Whereof, I have caused the seal of the United States to be hereunto affixed.

Done at the City of Washington, this seventeenth day of January, in the year of Our Lord one thousand nine hundred and twenty-nine, and of the Independence of the United States of America, the one hundred and fifty-third.

(Seal) CALVIN COOLIDGE

By the President.

FRANK B. KELLOGG,
Secretary of State

THE SECRETARY'S HANDBOOK

FORMAL RESOLUTIONS
Adopted by Members of the American Council of Learned
Societies.

Sociological Society

Chicago, Jan. 10, 1925.

Professor William F. Osburn, as delegate of our society to
the American Council of Learned Societies, made a report to
our nineteenth annual meeting of the public-spirited action of
The New York Times in making possible the preparation
and publication of the Dictionary of American Biography.

As an expression of the appreciation felt by our members at
this generous contribution toward an enterprise of scholarship
the following resolution was unanimously passed:

The American Sociological Society in its nineteenth annual
meeting assembled desires to express its enthusiastic apprecia
tion of the munificence and rare wisdom displayed by Mr.
Adolph S. Ochs and the New York Times Company in under
writing to the extent of five hundred thousand dollars the
authoritative work on American biography projected by the
American Council of Learned Societies.

E. W. BURGESS, Secretary

Political Science Association

Madison, Wis., Jan. 9, 1925

As Secretary of the American Political Science Association, I
take pleasure in forwarding to you the following copy of a
resolution unanimously adopted at the recent meeting of the
association in Washington. Permit me to say, personally, that
your benefaction is deeply appreciated by scholars in the field
of political science, as indeed in all branches of learning.

Upon being informed of the gift of $500,000 by the New
York Times Company to promote the preparation of a Dic
tionary of American Biography under the auspices of the
American Council of Learned Societies, devoted to Humanis
tic studies, the Political Science Association, in session in Wash
ington, D. C., Dec. 29, 1924, adopted the following by unani
mous vote:

Whereas, in the opinion of the members of this association
the projected dictionary is a much-needed work of reference;
and

Whereas, it is imperative that the dictionary be prepared under such direction as will guarantee its high scholarly character; be it

Resolved, That the American Political Science Association take note of the benefaction of Mr. Adolph S. Ochs and the New York Times Company and express alike its appreciation of so signal an act of generosity toward an enterprise of scholarship and its endorsement of the plan whereby the preparation of the manuscript of the dictionary will be under the control of the societies represented in the American Council.

Resolved further, That the Secretary be instructed to send a copy of these resolutions to Mr. Ochs personally, as well as to The New York Times Company and also to Dr. J. Franklin Jameson, Chairman of the council committee in charge of editorial and publishing arrangements.

FREDERIC A. OGG, Secretary

A Letter Containing a Resolution of Appreciation

Passed at a meeting of an Executive Committee of the Charity Organization Society of the City of New York.

Dear Miss Burrows:

At a very well attended meeting of the Executive Committee I presented your resignation and there were expressions of regard for you on the part of a number of those present who are acquainted with you. The Executive Committee thereupon adopted a resolution and the minutes will read as follows:

The Secretary reported that in her fortieth year of service Miss Sarah F. Burrows has resigned from the service of the Society and that in announcing her retirement to the district secretaries and heads of bureaus he had sent the following notice:

"In her fortieth year of faithful service to the Charity Organization Society, Miss Sarah F. Burrows has retired and carries with her the affectionate good-will of all those who have known her.

"Miss Burrows has filled almost every place in the family work department of the Society, having been for many years district secretary, and for years assistant to the director. During all these years of service Miss Burrows brought to the Society the affection of many persons, young and old, whom she served and the affection and esteem of many for whom she acted as almoner.

"For many years the Society was an Institutional Member of the Red Cross and in that capacity and on its own behalf it was first in the field when any disaster occurred of fire, flood or shipwreck. In some of these cases Miss Burrows did the major part of the work and in most of them she played an important part. When the great fire took place in San Francisco and Dr. Devine directed the activities of the Red Cross, at a moment's notice Miss Burrows went to San Francisco and served the people in distress with intelligence and sympathy. It was a hard service faithfully performed."

It was thereupon resolved that this record be spread upon the minutes and that the Executive Committee thereby records its appreciation of the service rendered by Miss Burrows and its hope that she may long enjoy such activities as may be congenial and helpful to others.

Sincerely yours,

Lawson Purdy,

Secretary

Reprinted by permission of the Charity Organization Society.

RESOLUTIONS PASSED BY THE STATE CHARITIES AID ASSOCIATION IN PRAISE OF THE FUND FOR THE HUNDRED NEEDIEST CASES

George F. Canfield, president of the State Charities Aid Association, forwarded resolutions adopted by the board of managers of the association, as follows:

Whereas, *The New York Times,* at the beginning of the Christmas season, by editorial comment and news articles and by publication of the tragedies and problems of one hundred families and individuals in dire need of help from their fellow-citizens, has stirred to action the generous impulses of a large number of persons, and

Whereas, *The New York Times,* in so doing, has widened public understanding of the problems and needs of those who, by reason of sickness and misfortune, must rely upon the generosity of others, and

Whereas, the public has responded whole-heartedly to the peculiar needs of each case and has also, by its generous contributions, endorsed the wise and kindly method by which the appeal is carried out,

Resolved, That the Board of Managers of the State Charities Aid Association warmly commends this call for aid to the Hundred Neediest Cases, both because of its direct and vital help to the sick and poor in distress, and because of its great benefit to the community, and expresses to *The New York Times* its deep gratitude for the insight and skill with which this human and personal appeal has been directed, wisely assuring the greatest good to those who, at this season of good-will, most desperately need succor from their more fortunate brothers.

SEECTIONS FROM THE RESOLUTIONS ADOPTED AT THE NATIONAL EDUCATIONAL ASSOCIATION MEETING IN BOSTON, MARCH 1, 1928

The Department of Superintendence of the National Education Association at its meeting in Boston on March 1, 1928, adopted the following resolutions:

The Curtis-Reed Bill

1. The welfare of the children now enrolled in the schools of the United States is dependent upon our ability to make available to boards of education, to superintendents of schools, and to teachers throughout the nation the results of current practise, of experiments wherever they are conducted, and of the results of scientific investigation.

The Federal Government has long accepted responsibility for conducting inquiries and disseminating information concerning the public schools.

We hold that economy and efficiency demand that the activities of the Federal Government dealing with education be consolidated in a Department of Education under the leadership of a Secretary with a seat in the President's Cabinet. We urge that adequate support be provided for this department in order that it may conduct such inquiries and disseminate such information as will make for the highest degree of efficiency in all of our schools. We know that this service can be rendered without in any way interfering with the constitutional right of the several states to control, administer, and supervise their own schools. We, therefore, urge the Congress to pass the Curtis-Reed Bill which embodies the program which this Association has consistently advocated throughout its history.

HIGHER STANDARDS FOR ADMISSION TO AMERICAN CITIZENSHIP

Appreciating the cooperation now existing between the Bureau of Education and the Bureau of Naturalization, and recognizing that training for citizenship is a phase of adult education necessary for candidates seeking naturalization, the need of closer coordination of effort on the part of the Federal Bureau of Naturalization, the local courts, and the public school appears urgent. There should be a closer alignment of these three agencies to the end that the requirements for admission to American citizenship shall include a reading as well as a speaking knowledge of English and that there shall be an appreciable understanding of American history, American institutions, and American ideals on the part of aliens seeking citizenship in the United States of America. These standards should be nationwide.

APPRECIATION OF COURTESIES

For the delightful hospitality and efficient management that have made this fifty-eighth annual meeting of the Department of Superintendence a notable success we wish to extend our cordial thanks to the state of Massachusetts, to the Governor, to the Mayor, to the city of Boston and its citizens, to the officials, teachers, and pupils of the schools, to the churches, to the public press, and to all the many individuals and organizations that have so effectively given of their best efforts in our behalf.

APPRECIATION OF CURRICULUM COMMISSION

On motion of Superintendent S. Monroe Graves of Wellesley Hills, Massachusetts, it was resolved to spread upon the records of the Department of Superintendence an expression of deep appreciation for the work which was done by Chairman Broome and the Commission on the Curriculum in its four years' study of curriculum problems.

MEMBERS OF THE COMMITTEE

Members of the Committee on Resolutions were: Mr. A. L. Threlkeld, superintendent of schools, Denver, Colorado, chairman; Mr. J. R. Barton, superintendent of schools, Oklahoma City, Oklahoma; Commissioner A. B. Meredith, State Department of Education, Hartford, Connecticut; Mr. Charles L. Spain, deputy superintendent of schools, Toledo, Ohio; Dr. John W. Withers, dean, School of Education, New York University, New York City; Miss Ada York, county superintendent of schools, San Diego County, California.

Reprinted by permission of the National Educational Association.

THE FRAMING OF RESOLUTIONS

Resolutions Adopted May 10, 1928, at a General Session of the United States Chamber of Commerce, Robert P. Lamont, Chairman of the Committee on Resolutions

"The Chamber of Commerce of the United States declares its confidence in the general integrity and sound ideals of modern business. These are brought into high relief by recent disclosures of individual violation of established business practices.

Business Jealous of Good Name

"American business is jealous of its good name, insists upon protecting its professional status by the maintenance of the highest standards, and intends scrupulously to discharge its collective responsibilities. Chief among such responsibilities is that of purging business of all those who indulge in commercial and political corruption, and through resort to unclean or unworthy practices bring business into disrepute and shock the sensibilities of all decent citizens.

"The Chamber declares that the moral turpitude of corrupters of public servants is even greater than that of those whom they debauch.

"The Chamber emphasizes its principle of business conduct, which provides that 'corporate forms do not absolve from or alter the moral obligations of individuals.' It maintains that stockholders of corporations owe it to themselves, to the Government and to the profession of business publicly to repudiate those who misrepresent them. Such stockholders cannot accept the profits flowing from corruption and escape the moral stigma which inheres in such profits. Neither can they permit those who act for them to profit personally through corrupt corporate transactions or shield others who do."

Newspaper Item

From the Annual Report of The City Library Association of Springfield, Massachusetts
For the Year Ending April 30, 1928.

In Memoriam

George Walter Vincent Smith

It was the happy lot of our late associate, George Walter Vincent Smith, to make for himself a fortunate life, and to be given the satisfaction of knowing that the ample fruits of his labors were to remain for the enrichment of this community. Over years far beyond the scriptural span of life, Mr. Smith was permitted the joy that lay in his unselfish quest after objects of high artistic merit. It was a service rich in results for education and craftsmanship in the present and the future. How surpassing was his spiritual and cultural achievement is revealed by the treasures in the Art Museum, as is the thoughtfulness of his generosity by the fund provided for their care. Fitly placed under his direction, these fine possessions are to be studied and enjoyed to the profit of our people, whose gratitude, it is pleasant to remember, was often expressed during the life of the giver.

Impressive in its suggestiveness to the men and women who seek enduring ways of serving their fellows, was our friend's exceptional accomplishment. The City Library Association of Springfield has been fortunate in its appeal to wisely generous benefactors, and never more so than in this conspicuous instance. The members of the Board of Directors pledge themselves and their successors to constant and sympathetic nurture of this noble gift, by which Mr. and Mrs. Smith are to benefit the public to an extent beyond reckoning.

Adopted by the Board of Directors, April 17, 1928.

Reprinted by permission of the City Library Association of Springfield, Mass.

In Memoriam

Samuel Bowles, 3d

With profound sorrow, the Directors of the City Library Association record the death of one of its most earnest and zealous friends—Samuel Bowles, 3d. Mr. Bowles, succeeding his father in 1878, was for thirty-seven years a member of the Association, during twenty-four of which he was active in its Board of Directors. In the Springfield which he so loved and served, the City Library Association in a peculiar degree claimed his interest and support. He was ever ready to advance its usefulness by material contributions toward its buildings, as well as by wise counsel and enthusiasm for its aims. His high conception of the mission of public library and museums in enlightening and safeguarding a democratic community was not only felt in this city, but through the columns of the Springfield Republican became of far-reaching influence.

With the sense of community-loss is mingled deep sympathy for the members of his family.

Adopted by the Board of Directors, March 27, 1915.

Reprinted by permission of the City Library Association of Springfield, Mass.

Resolution Passed at the Death of a Prominent Citizen

Resolution passed by The Vocational Guidance Association at Boston on the death of Mr. Frederick J. Allen.

"In recognition of the long and untiring services of Frederick J. Allen in the field of vocational guidance, the National Vocational Guidance Association at its annual meeting in Dallas, Texas, on February 25, 1927, wishes to express its sense of personal loss in the death of Mr. Allen, and its appreciation of his services as a member and officer of the Association.

"From the earliest beginnings of vocational guidance in the United States, Mr. Allen has been identified with constructive research in educational and vocational guidance. At the time of his death he was the only member of the Association who had worked intimately with Frank A. Parsons, the father of vocational guidance in the United States.

"Perhaps his most distinguished service to the Association was his work as Editor of *The Vocational Guidance Magazine,* which was brought by his unusual vision and diligence from a modest and occasional publication to its present high standard of editorial and mechanical perfection.

"Be it therefore resolved, that this expression of appreciation be sent to the family of Mr. Allen and to Harvard University, also that it be spread upon the minutes of this meeting."

Reprinted from the *Vocational Guidance Magazine.*

Resolution Included in a Letter

January 9, 1926.

My dear Professor Seager:

I have the honor of informing you that the following resolution was passed at the Annual Meeting of the Archæological

Institute of America at Ithaca, New York, on December 29, 1925:

On the death of Richard Berry Seager, by Stephen B. Luce:

In the sudden and untimely death of Richard Berry Seager, at Candia, Crete, on May 12, 1925, America has lost one of her foremost archæologists. His success in scientific excavation won for him the respect, and his warm heart and enduring qualities the affection, of all that knew him. This is proved by the fact that the citizens of Candia tendered him a public funeral, a distinction offered to the memory of only the most distinguished citizens. Seager's name will always be identified with Crete, as one of the pioneers in the opening to the world of the marvellous civilization of the Minoan Age. His first work was done for the University of Pennsylvania, when he was associated with Mrs. Harriet Boyd Hawes at Gournia; and most of his subsequent excavations were conducted under the same auspices. His name is also associated with the American School at Athens, in connection with his excavations on the island of Mochlos. His residence at Pachyammos, in Eastern Crete, was always open to the stranger, and his hospitality there unbounded. During the World War, he served with great distinction as an officer in the Red Cross, in Italy and Greece. As long as archæology is studied, so long will his monographs on Vasiliki (in the volume on Gournia), Pseira, and Mochlos be indispensable to the student.

The Council of the Archæological Institute of America desires to spread upon its records its keen sense of personal loss in Seager's untimely death, and the feeling that professionally this loss can never be replaced or made good. With every prospect of a life of continued usefulness and brilliance before him, he was taken away from us before his forty-third year had ended. To such as he there is no successor.

Yours very truly,

———————————

Recorder

THE FRAMING OF RESOLUTIONS

Adopted at a meeting of the Commission held May 20th, 1904, signed by all the original members of the Commission, and forwarded to Andrew Carnegie

WHEREAS, Mr. Andrew Carnegie by his deed of gift, dated March the 12th, 1904, and witnessed by Mrs. Louise Whitfield Carnegie, has with more than princely generosity set aside from his fortune the sum of five millions of dollars for the purpose of recognizing in a suitable manner heroic efforts to save human life made by those following peaceful vocations, to relieve those injured in making such efforts, and to provide for their widows and orphans in cases where life may have been sacrificed, and to aid to some extent those who may be injured by accident in future great catastrophies or disasters, and

WHEREAS, Mr. Andrew Carnegie has named the undersigned as the first members of the Carnegie Hero Fund Commission, charged by him with the important duty of administering the trust created by him for the purposes above mentioned; therefore be it

Resolved, That we express to Mr. Carnegie our grateful appreciation of the high honor which he has conferred upon, and the confidence reposed in, us in entrusting the execution of his plans and purposes to our keeping and thus permitting us and our successors in the trust to share with him to some extent in the inestimable privilege of doing good to our fellow men.

Resolved, That we individually and collectively desire to express to Mr. Carnegie our sense of the great benevolence displayed by him in this gift, which for the purposes designated is altogether without parallel in the history of human beneficence.

Resolved, That we believe the action of Mr. Carnegie is calculated to foster in the minds of the people of the countries named in the deed of gift, a sense of their brotherhood and to promote among them the spirit of self-sacrifice, which is one of the most exalted traits of the highest civilization.

Resolved, That we appreciate the nobility of his purpose in confining the operations of this Fund to those who have shown true heroism in the peaceful walks of life, by which act he consistently testifies to his ardent desire for the coming of that

[1] Reprinted by permission.

better day when men shall forget the arts of war and shall seek for peace and good-will throughout the earth.

Resolved, That in accepting this trust we pledge ourselves to the sincerest endeavor to administer it according to the best of our knowledge and ability and with the purpose of realizing, so far as possible, the hopes and aims of the generous founder of the Fund.

A LETTER CONTAINING A FORMAL RESOLUTION OF APPRECIATION

My dear Miss Jacopraro:

It gives me great pleasure to inform you that at the last meeting of the Board of Directors of the Woman's Roosevelt Memorial Association the following resolution was unanimously passed:

"WHEREAS, the co-operation of the principals and teachers of the public schools of Greater New York having made possible the success of the meeting of Affiliated Roosevelt Clubs at Town Hall on the sixty-seventh anniversary of Theodore Roosevelt's birth, be it

"RESOLVED, that the Board of Directors of the Woman's Roosevelt Memorial Association take this means of expressing their thankfulness to the afore-said principals and teachers and members of the Affiliated Roosevelt Clubs for their generous co-operation."

Sincerely yours,
Ellen C. Lambert
(Mrs. Alexander Lambert)
Secretary

Resolution presented to Congress, January 25, 1929, to express gratitude to heroes of the S.S. *America,* in saving the crew of the S.S. *Florida.*

Whereas, the world is again thrilled with the heroic rescue of the entire crew of the Italian freighter, S. S. Florida, by Captain George Fried, Chief Officer Henry Manning and eight members of the crew of the United States Lines ship America; and

Whereas, in that rescue these eight sailors, under the doughty Chief Officer Manning, risked death in darkness and mountainous seas; and

Whereas, a grateful nation remembers the rescue three years ago of the crew of the British freighter Antinoe by the same Captain George Fried, then commanding the S. S. President Roosevelt of the United States Lines; now,

Therefore, be it resolved by the House of Representatives (Senate concurring) that in gratitude for the precious intrepidity, unblanching courage and splendid seamanship of these valiant officers and men, the thanks of Congress be expressed to the said Captain George Fried, Chief Officer Manning and the eight members of the crew.

CHAPTER VII

THE FRAMING OF CONSTITUTIONS

A committee on framing a constitution should study those of similar organizations for arrangement, material, and phraseology. Most constitutions include articles divided into sections which embody the following topics, the order depending upon the decision of the committee.

1. Name and purpose of the organization.
2. Membership and dues.
3. Names and duties of officers.
4. Committees.
5. Time of meetings.
6. Amendments.
7. By-laws.

The By-laws are made up of a set of rules subordinate to those of the constitution. They often contain the rules of order to be followed, the order of business, and the duties of officers if they have not already been treated.

A constitution should be so written that there is no question as to its meaning or interpretation. The style should be formal. The sentence structure should have little variety, as most follow the same form. The statements should be concise, clear, and definite.

The following pages afford a model for those who are given the task of drafting a constitution. The form, the phraseology, and the content are typical of those ordinarily used.

VOCATIONAL GUIDANCE ASSOCIATION OF NEW YORK CITY

CONSTITUTION

ARTICLE I

Name

Section 1. The name of this association shall be the VOCA. TIONAL GUIDANCE ASSOCIATION OF NEW YORK CITY

Section 2. This association is organized as a constituent local organization of the Vocational Guidance Association of the United States.

ARTICLE II

Objects

Section I. The objects of the Association shall be:

a—To unite in one local organization those persons who are engaged or interested in any phase of vocational guidance in New York City and vicinity.

b—To correlate closely the vocational guidance work being performed by public and private agencies in New York City and vicinity.

c—To act as a central agency through which will clear information relating to the vocational guidance work being conducted in New York City and vicinity.

d—To formulate standards and principles for vocational guidance work in New York City and vicinity.

e—To encourage legislation and public support of vocational guidance in New York City and vicinity.

275

ARTICLE III

MEMBERS—*Qualifications and Admission*

Section 1. Any person engaged or interested in vocational guidance in New York City or vicinity may apply for membership.

Section 2. Any person may become a member of the association *whose name has been approved by the committee on membership* and on the payment of the annual dues of the local Association, together with those of the Vocational Guidance Association of the United States, to the treasurer of the organization.

ARTICLE IV

Officers, Trustees, and Annual Meeting

Section 1. The officers of this association shall be:
President
First Vice President
Second Vice President
Secretary
Treasurer
all of whom shall be members in good standing in the local organization.

Section 2. The Board of Trustees shall consist of the president, vice presidents, secretary and treasurer and nine other members.

ARTICLE V

Election of Officers and Trustees

Officers and Trustees shall be elected at the annual meeting of the Association.

In the case of a vacancy of office, the board of trustees shall have power to fill the same until the next annual meeting.

ARTICLE VI

Amendments

Amendments to the constitution or the by-laws of this Association shall be made only at a regular meeting thereof, by a two-thirds vote of the members present. No proposition to amend shall be acted upon unless written notice thereof has been given to the secretary at least thirty days prior to the meeting. A copy of such a proposition shall be embodied in the call for the next regular meeting, and a copy sent to every member of the Association at least 10 days before the date of the next regular meeting at which the amendment is to be voted upon.

BY-LAWS

ARTICLE I

OFFICERS

****

President

Section I. It shall be the duty of the president to preside at all meetings and to enforce all laws and regulations relating to the administration of the Association.

Section 2. He shall call meetings of the Association or board of trustees when he deems it necessary, or when requested so to do by the executive committee, or upon written request of at least one-fourth of the constituent societies for a meeting of the Association, or one-fourth of the trustees for a meeting of the board of trustees.

He shall appoint all standing committees.

Vice President

Section 3. In the absence of the president, one of the vice-presidents named by the president, or failing this, designated by the board of trustees, shall have all the powers and prerogatives of the president, provided that if the president be absent from the annual meeting of the Association the chairman shall be appointed from the vice presidents by the board of trustees.

Chairman Pro Tempore

Section 4. In the event of the absence of the president and vice-presidents from any meetings of the Association or board of trustees, one of the members present shall preside.

Secretary

Section 5. All resolutions and proceedings of meetings, whether of the Association or of the board of trustees, shall be entered in proper books by the secretary. The secretary shall conduct all correspondence relating to the Association, shall issue all notices of meetings, and shall perform all duties pertaining to the office of secretary. The secretary shall keep a register of the members of the Association.

Treasurer

Section 6. All moneys payable to the Association shall be paid to the Treasurer of the Association. All moneys payable by the Association shall be paid by checks signed by the Treasurer.

He shall report at each meeting of the Association the condition of the treasury.

Board of Trustees

Section 7. It shall be the duty of the board of trustees to take the initiative in determining the policies of the Association. They shall also be responsible for the relations of the local branch to the National Vocational Guidance Association.

It shall be their duty to take charge, control and management of all the property belonging to the Association.

They shall keep a record of their proceedings and make a report thereof in writing to the Association at the annual meeting.

The board of trustees shall appoint an executive committee consisting of the president of the Association as chairman, the secretary, the treasurer and the chairmen of the program and membership committees. It shall be the duty of this committee to supervise the finances of the Association and audit all bills prior to the payment thereof.

Section 8. The office of a member of the board of trustees may be vacated by his absence from two consecutive meetings of the board, without good and sufficient reason satisfactory to the board of trustees.

Committees

Section 9. There shall be three standing committees of the Association:

The Program Committee shall make all plans and arrangements for the regular meetings of the Association.

The Membership Committee shall receive applications for membership, pass on such applications and make recommendations to the Association.

The Nominating Committee shall prepare a slate of officers for the succeeding year.

Committee chairmen shall attend all trustees' meetings.

ARTICLE II

Meetings of the Association—Regular

Section 1. The annual meeting of the Association shall take place on the third Tuesday of May of each year. There shall also be at least four other regular meetings from September to May at times to be set by the Program Committee. Notices of meeting shall be sent out ten days prior to such meeting direct to each member. The place at which meeting shall be held shall be determined by the Program Committee.

Special Meetings

Section 2. Special meetings may be called at any time with the approval of the president of the Association.

Board of Trustees Meetings

Section 3. There shall be two regular meetings of the board of trustees to take place in May and October of each year. Other meetings may be called by the president.

Ten days' notice of a meeting of the board of trustees shall be given to each member, mailed to him at his usual or last known address, and such notice shall, as far as practicable, contain a statement of the business to be transacted at such meeting.

Committee Meetings

Section 4. All committees shall be subject to the call of their respective chairmen.

Quorum

Section 5. A representation of a majority of the members of this Association shall constitute a quorum authorized to transact any business duly presented at any meeting of the Association.

Seven trustees shall constitute a quorum of the board of trustees; a majority of any and all committees shall constitute a quorum of such committees.

ARTICLE III

Representation at Meetings of Vocation Guidance Association of the United States

Section 1. Delegates and alternates to the annual meeting of the Vocational Guidance Association shall be elected prior to such meeting, the number to be in proportion to the membership of the New York Association.

ARTICLE IV

Nomination and Election of Officers and Delegates

Section 1. The Nominating Committee shall present a slate at the annual meeting for the following officers:

President	Secretary
First Vice-President	Treasurer, and
Second Vice-President	Nine trustees

except as otherwise provided in Section 2.

Any member of the Association may make additional nominations from the floor.

Section 2. At the first election under these laws three of the nine trustees referred to in the preceding section shall be elected for one year, three for two years each, and three of them for three years each. At every succeeding annual meeting thereafter three trustees shall be elected for a term of three years each.

Section 3. Election shall be by ballot when necessary. A chairman and two tellers shall be appointed to receive the ballots for each officer and trustee. They shall canvass the ballots so cast and announce the result to the presiding officer, who thereupon shall declare the members receiving the majority of the votes cast elected to the respective offices.

Section 4. In case of no choice on the first ballot for any one or more officers or trustees, a new election shall take place at once for the particular case or cases in which there had been no choice, until a choice be made.

ARTICLE V

Initiation Fees and Dues

Section 1. The dues for each fiscal year ending December 31, shall be two dollars and a half ($2.50), one dollar and a half ($1.50) of which shall be paid to the treasurer of the Vocational Guidance Association of the United States.

Section 2. Such dues shall be due and payable annually in advance of November 30 of each year, or at the date of a member's election or admission to membership, and until such payment thereof, no certificate of membership shall be issued.

ARTICLE VI

Rules of Order

Section 1. The rules of parliamentary procedure as laid down in "Robert's Rules of Order" shall govern all meetings of the Association.

Reprinted by permission of the Vocational Guidance Association of New York City.

CHAPTER VIII

THE WRITING OF REPORTS

Reports may be defined as "careful and accurate presentations of facts or statistics compiled, or conditions or operations studied, for the purpose of informing those desiring such information." [1]

The purpose in writing a report is to present matter clearly and impersonally and to make such explanation as is necessary for a complete understanding of the subject.

Perhaps the most important principle of writing which the report-writer should observe is that formed in Herbert Spencer's famous dictum of style in his essay, *The Philosophy of Style:*

> The reader has at each moment but a limited amount of mental power. To study the economy of words, of sentences, of figures of speech, of suggestion, of association, is to have the means of writing positively, directly, and vigorously. The more simple and the better arranged in parts, the greater will be the effect produced.

A report-writer follows this suggestion "of economizing the reader's attention." He views his material in a right prospective. He knows how to present his points in their true proportion and finds the best possible arrangement.

In long reports a table of contents usually follows the title page. This is a guide to what follows. It contains the principal subjects or the names of the chapters, if divided into chapters. Main subjects are usually preceded by Roman numerals fol-

---

[1] *Training for Secretarial Practice.* Taintor, S. A. McGraw-Hill Book Co., Inc.

lowed by subtopics indented from the beginning of the line. Page numbers to these subjects or chapters are written in Arabic numerals.

The parts of a report are these: introduction, discussion, and conclusion. The introduction may be formal or informal. It should state clearly the nature of the report, the scope, the purpose, and, if necessary, the circumstances under which it has been made.

Such an introduction is often embodied in a formal letter of transmittal preceding the report, illustrations of which follow:

March 1, 1928.

Mr. Oliver C. Billings, *Chairman,*
Committee of Arrangements,
New York Stock Exchange.

Dear Sir:

In the accompanying report of the Personnel Department for 1927 an effort has been made to present as concisely as possible the "Human Relationship Policy" of the Stock Exchange. Observations made in many sections of the country lead me to believe that the public in general looks upon our institution simply as a great organization whose sole interest is concerned with finance.

It is hoped that this report may be a means of conveying to the members of the Exchange an adequate conception of the scope of the work, as evidenced by the interest of the management in the individual employee.

The hearty cooperation of many governors and other members of the Exchange and leaders in the financial world in appearing as special lecturers before our Institute has been of material assistance in the advancement of our educational program.

During the past year the members of the Exchange have taken to their offices an increasing number of our employees —an indication of their high regard for the character and intelligence of the youth in our employ.

The Personnel Department wishes to acknowledge its appreciation to the President, the Committee of Arrangements, and the members of the Exchange and to the officers and employees for their cooperation during the past year.

Respectfully submitted,
CAMERON BECK,
Personnel Director

Reprinted by permission of the Personnel Department of The New York Stock Exchange.

October 1, 1925.

Mr. Oliver C. Billings, *Chairman,*
Committee of Arrangements,
New York Stock Exchange.

Dear Sir:

In submitting the accompanying report, an effort has been made to present as concisely as possible a review of the activities of the year. Much more might be written of the constant unselfish service of the Governors and members of the Exchange in the individual welfare of the employees. It is hoped, however, that the graphs, tabulations, and text will convey to those who may be interested, an accurate picture of the human side of the nation's greatest financial institution.

The adoption on July 1 of this year of "The Stock Exchange and Affiliated Companies Employees Retirement Plan" marks the successful culmination of four years' exhaustive study on the part of the special Committee on Pensions. The adoption of this Retirement Plan, in addition to the Group Insurance Plan now in operation, is but another indication of your desire to free the mind of the employee and his dependents from the perplexing problem of financial stability at the time of retirement from active service or at the time of death.

The hearty cooperation of the Governors and leading members of the Exchange in the educational work of the New York Stock Exchange Institute has been of great help in developing an intelligent and capably trained staff of employees. A direct result of this service is that an increasing number of employees are being offered responsible positions in the offices of Stock Exchange firms. A number of these former employees are now members of the Stock Exchange or partners of members.

The statement of our President in a recent address—"that the employment of workers is a sacred and patriotic trust"—is reflected in the attitude of the management of the Exchange in its dealing with all "human relationship" problems. The faithful and loyal service of the employees is an indication of the appreciation of the treatment they have received. Mutual confidence is therefore a reality.

The Personnel Deparment wishes to express its appreciation to the President, the Committee of Arrangements, the members, the executive officers and to the employees for their cordial cooperation during the past year.

Respectfully submitted,

CAMERON BECK,
Personnel Director

Reprinted by permission of the Personnel Department of The New York Stock Exchange.

Sometimes in place of the formal letter of transmittal, a *Foreword,* which serves the same purpose, precedes the text. Two illustrations follow. The first embodies in tabular form a program of work illustrated and explained in the text of the report.

BULLETIN PUBLISHED BY
THE WOMEN'S MUNICIPAL LEAGUE OF BOSTON

FOREWORD

What is the significance to the practical work of the League of the ideas of municipal housekeeping and municipal homemaking which it embodies, and which the City Institute will develop actively in the different neighborhoods?

1. Cleanliness is essential in every home.

The Department of Streets and Alleys and Waste Disposal is accomplishing visible results in cleaning the city through the coöperation of the housewives, the expert engineer and the public officials.

2. Decent Housing Conditions are necessary for any home.

The Department of Housing has already effected important ameliorations in the housing conditions of the city, but in order to secure radical and permanent improvement, an aroused public opinion is needed which shall put an end to this disgrace of Boston,—twenty thousand of *us* living in houses unfit for human habitation—in *our* home. A conservative estimate.

3. Public Health means personal health in the home.

The Department of Public Health has incorporated into its work the Habit Clinics for Children of Pre-School Age. Clinics for adults who are supposedly well are being carried on at the Blossom Street Health Unit in coöperation, by the Department of the League and the city.

4. The Foreign Born are our guests; we must make them our friends in our home.

The Department of the Foreign Born and the Community House at North Brighton have been largely helpful in many different ways in making the strangers who come to live here feel at home in our house.

5. The Service of Trained Women is needful in every home.

The Training School for Women in Public Service is focussing and organizing the public opinion of women to demand that they be allowed the opportunity to render their trained service to the community as police women to prevent evil before it becomes crime, as school attendance officers to care for the children, and as sanitary inspectors to help the housewives.

6. The Upbringing of the Children is the responsibility of every home.

The Children's City Club is being organized by the League in close coöperation with the teachers of the public schools, and at their request, in order that the women of the community, with the teachers, may share the responsibility of leading the children to understand the obligations and duties as well as the pleasures and privileges of their great home, the city. The Vacant Lot Gardens and the work in the Playgrounds during the summer, have brought to the children a little of the beauty and vital stimulation that should come to all children in their own homes.

The second illustration of a Foreword states briefly what is to follow.

FOREWORD

The number of requests that have come to the Exchange regarding policies, methods, and procedure in the handling of personnel problems has been increasing. In this report we have explained in detail our method of handling these problems now confronting others with the thought that our own experience may be of value to many. We are confident that our threefold approach to the employee, namely, in his daily work, in his mental training, and in his play, together with the encouragement given to our program by the management of the Exchange has been in no small measure the reason for any success we have obtained in the handling of personnel problems.

Reprinted by permission of the Personnel Department of The New York Stock Exchange.

A brief summary, following the Letter of Transmittal or the Foreword, often precedes the report. It contains a digest of the main points, including the results of the investigation and the recommendation made for the benefit of the reader who does not have the time to read the whole.

The body of a report presents the carefully outlined study of the subject logically organized and concisely expressed. Headings, subheads, and every other device that will make the subject clear, show relationship of parts, emphasize the main points, or give an outlined view of the whole, should be inserted.

The conclusion of a report ordinarily consists of a brief summary of results obtained, or of points presented, or of recommendations made, in the light of data studied.

An illustration of a general summary follows, taken from a Report of the Westchester Park Commission, 1925.

General Summary

The projects herein recommended will provide the following:

Suitable areas for not less than 4 public golf courses, one of which is already partly developed.

Space for scores of baseball fields, playgrounds, tennis courts and other field and water sports.

Wide areas of picturesque lands for picnicking and general park use.

Several thousand acres in the northerly part of the County for individual and group camps and general reforestation purposes.

The protection of important municipal water supplies, so vitally necessary to our built-up communities.

The opening up of the Sprain Valleys and securing therein large recreation areas at moderate cost. These valleys are now almost inaccessible and the increase in value, following the proposed improvements will stimulate development that will shortly pay the cost of the improvements.

Parkways through the easterly side of the County where the rapidly increasing population now has available only one through road from New York City to the Connecticut line.

A main cross-road parkway connecting the north and south systems and connecting the most important communities in the County without passing through their congested centers.

Secondary cross-county and diagonal connections between valleys and main parkways.

Then follows a schedule of the projects recommended.

The report is concluded by the following:

The Commission respectfully requests favorable consideration from your Honorable Board of the projects recommended herein.

Respectfully submitted,
WESTCHESTER COUNTY PARK COMMISSION
By William Delavan Baldwin,
President

Sometimes in order to make conclusions emphatic, important points are arranged in an original way as in the report of the Women's Municipal League Bulletin of Boston, which sums up the ideals of the League.

WHAT WE ALL WANT!

Clean Streets
Decent Houses
Mutual Understanding among All Races

Work and Recreation for Health and Happiness
The Best Interests of the Children

The League is trying to make these things possible for every member of our great family, and especially for the children.

BECAUSE

We all TOGETHER owe to each child the opportunity for healthy and happy development.

JOIN THE LEAGUE!

LET US WORK TOGETHER!

Reports in Letter Form

Some reports, such as those to Boards of Trustees, to the President of a University, or to Stockholders, are often made in letter form. The introduction is brief and formal, admitting of little variation.

The following excerpts illustrate various ways of beginning reports in letter form:

REPORT OF THE
PRESIDENT OF COLUMBIA UNIVERSITY

For the year ending June 30, 1928

To the Trustees:

The annual Report on the condition and needs of the University as prescribed by the Statutes is submitted herewith. The various activities, happenings and future plans of the several parts of the University's vast educational system are presented and discussed in the accompanying reports of the deans and directors. These documents are of the highest importance not only because of their contributions to our academic history, but because of the reflections which they offer and the hopes for future improvement which they express. They are earnestly commended to the attention of the Trustees and the appropriate committees, as well as to that larger public which has formed the fortunate habit of following with interested attention the development of the work of Columbia University.

THE SECRETARY'S HANDBOOK

To the President of the University

Sir:

I have the honor to present herewith the report of University Extension for the year 1925-1926.

The body of the report in letter form is organized in much the same manner as that of other reports. It presents the chief features in narration or exposition without too much detail.

The letter report is concluded by appropriate remarks and signed by the writer with his official position.

Two illustrations follow: the first from the Annual Report of the President made to the Trustees of Columbia University, 1926; the second from the Annual Report of the Director of University Extension made to the President of Columbia University, 1926.

This is the twenty-fifth Annual Report to be submitted over the present signature. The record of the University's steady progress during that period toward the accomplishment of its ideal of Scholarship and Service is surely one to rejoice the hearts of Samuel Johnson, first President, whose pen wrote the advertisement of May 31, 1754, of Alexander Hamilton of the Class of 1777, who drafted the Report of 1784, of Williams Betts of the Class of 1820, chief author of the Report of 1858, and of Frederick A. P. Barnard, tenth President, who plead with patient and continuing eloquence for such policies as have been now justified by their results.

Nicholas Murray Butler,
President

Our prominent educators are lamenting the greater pride which college students take in achievements on the athletic field rather than in the class room and are looking for means of arousing interest in the things of the intellect. The contrast as shown in the disposition of students in University Extension is startling, for they are possessed with a desire to pursue an intellectual life and the problem before us is how we may gratify their desire in the most satisfactory manner. Why should we not speak of such students with enthusiasm for they do not hesitate to devote day and night to their purpose of attaining an education in the adult period of life. They say with the

Psalmist "Day unto day uttereth speech and night unto night showeth knowledge."

Respectfully submitted,

JAMES C. EGBERT

REPORT IN LETTER FORM

REPORT OF NATIONAL COMMITTEE OF AWARD THEODORE N. VAIL MEDALS 1927

May 7, 1928.

To the Trustees,
Theodore N. Vail Memorial Fund

In the reports of the fifty-four Theodore N. Vail bronze medal awards made by Committees of Award of the Bell System Associated Companies for 1927, and the many other cases considered by these Committees, this Committee finds inspiring evidence that the men and women of the Bell System are carrying out the high ideals which Mr. Vail held as to public service and that they cheerfully accept special responsibilities in times of emergency.

The Committee feels that to be selected for National Vail Medal recognition an act must have for its objective the accomplishment of something of real value in the public interest through the medium of Bell System facilities, organization, training or experience, and must reveal to a high degree many, if not all, of the positive qualities of intelligence, initiative and resourcefulness, and usually courage, endurance and fortitude. The Committee believes that in making its selections it has recognized acts which meet these requirements.

During the year the Mississippi Valley was inundated by one of the worst floods in its history and extensive sections of the telephone plant operated by the Southwestern Bell Telephone Company, the Southern Bell Telephone and Telegraph Company and the Long Lines were not only crippled but rendered almost inaccessible for days and in some cases for weeks. Throughout this emergency the entire organizations of these companies in the affected areas, together with many others called from different sections, rendered conspicuously outstanding public service in maintaining and restoring telephone service under well-nigh impossible conditions.

The Committee welcomes this opportunity to commend in the most unqualified terms the initiative and resourcefulness, loyalty and devotion, courage and endurance displayed by these great groups of telephone men and telephone women in the manner in which they carried on throughout this distressing period.

This outstanding service was essentially the result of group organization and effort and accordingly does not offer the opportunity for individual awards as did the New England flood where, although the group performance was equally noteworthy and outstanding, the suddenness of the onset made emergency individual action vital before group action could be organized.

The National Awards for 1927 follow:

Reprinted by permission.

A SECRETARY'S REPORT
VOCATIONAL GUIDANCE ASSOCIATION
1926-27

During the past year the officers of the National Vocational Guidance Association have not been able to have a regular meeting, but they have kept in touch with each other through correspondence. At the joint meeting of the National Vocational Guidance Association and the American Vocational Association held in Louisville early in December, four of the trustees and the Chairman of the Program Committee were present and held several informal conferences. The Philadelphia Branch of the National Vocational Guidance Association arranged for the vocational-guidance program held during the August meeting of the National Education Association in Philadelphia. Mr. Edgerton was chairman of the vocational-guidance programs which were an important part of the meetings of the American Vocational Association convention in Louisville in December.

Shortly after the Washington conference, the secretary communicated with the local secretaries of the various branches requesting that they vote on the new ruling for the collection of dues passed at the Washington meeting. Only one branch has not given its approval of the ruling,—the New England Branch objecting to Section "e," which provides that there shall be no refund to local chapters when local chapters do not collect dues and the national treasurer secures this payment from local members. Since the Washington meeting one new branch has been affiliated with the National Association,—the North Carolina Branch with headquarters at Winston-Salem, North Carolina. Local branches to the present date number fifteen. Within the last few weeks there have been four requests from local groups who wish to form associations and apply for national membership,—Washington; Detroit, Michigan; Shreveport, Louisiana; and Drake University, Iowa. Two communications have been sent to our 1650 membership list during the year: One in December—a preliminary announcement of the convention—and a more recent announcement which included a hastily prepared mimeographed program (inasmuch as the official programs were delayed by the printer). Announcements of the Dallas conference were also sent to large numbers of educational journals and to school systems of the central, southern, and western states.

A secretary's report should not close without mentioning the great amount of interest shown in the National Association and its program as indicated by the hundreds of letters that have come to her office during the past year. It is hoped that there may be an even greater interest expressed in the years to come through the addition of new chapters in parts of the United States where we are not as yet represented.

Mary P. Corre, *Secretary*

Reprinted by permission from the *Vocational Guidance Magazine.*

The following represents one type of report, including its parts and contents, the graphs only being omitted:

STUDENT'S REPORT ON MARKETING MADE BY MARIE KONZELMAN, COLUMBIA UNIVERSITY, 1927

CONTENTS

III. Appendix
  A. Charts
  B. Graphs
  C. Bibliography
  D. Outline of Report

I. INTRODUCTION

A. SYNOPSIS

The report on "Marketing" which is submitted below is divided into four general discussions. Under the heading of "Marketing Functions" the general services performed by marketing agencies are outlined. In the second section the development of the various forms of retailing organizations is traced. A discussion of the general, specialty, department, and chain stores and of the mail-order house is included. Another section deals with the four most common forms of middlemen. The marketing problems of the manufacturer are outlined in the final section, as well as the present trends in the solution of these problems.

B. FOREWORD

In recent years more emphasis has been placed upon the importance of marketing than formerly, and it is because of this widespread interest that the investigation resulting in the report which follows was undertaken.

The standardization of production within the past two decades has enabled the manufacturer to turn his attention toward the problem of distribution and, as a result, marketing has become the outstanding problem. The present report is concerned with this problem, as it affects the business organization. The purpose of the investigation has been to trace the development of marketing.

As a result of this investigation, some general recommendations concerning the future of marketing are embodied in the conclusion of the report.

II. TEXT OF REPORT

A. PURPOSE OF REPORT

The aim of this investigation and of the presentation of this report has been primarily to indicate the nature of the marketing problems which confront the modern business organization. A discussion of the development of the various branches of the modern distributing mechanism has been given. The secondary purpose has been to show present trends toward a solution of these various problems.

B. DISCUSSION

PART ONE: MARKETING FUNCTIONS

Assembling and Grading
The primary function of marketing is the assembling and grading of merchandise preparatory to its distribution to the consuming public.

Assembling is of two general types. Its aim may be either the concentration in one central locality of great quantities of one particular commodity or the concentration of a sufficient variety of commodities to effect the most economical distribution. The specialty store is an example of the former type while the department store possesses the characteristics of the latter. Both these types are common not only in the retailing field, but also in the field of the jobber and of other wholesale agencies.

Grading is a function of marketing that has developed more fully in recent years. It has tended to enlarge markets by making sales by description possible and it has tended to reduce the cost of marketing by lowering the percentage of spoilage and of unsalable goods.

Grading is based upon a large variety of characteristics, varying with the type of product and the demand of the consumer. Such factors as quality, size, quantity, variety and packing methods are among the more common bases of distinction.

Storing
The storing function is one which is present in all branches of marketing. There are a great many products which are not immediately consumed and for which, therefore, storage facilities must be provided. This function is performed by one or more of the following, according to the special requirements of the product concerned: the producer, the middleman and the consumer.

In the case of some products, especially those of an agricultural nature, the supply is seasonal, i.e., production is limited to certain periods of the year. For this reason, some adequate method of storage must be provided to cover these seasonal inequalities. In still other cases there is sectional inequality of production. (See Appendix, Figure 1)

As a result of these types of inequality, the storage function in marketing has developed. Storage not only adjusts the supply of commodities and broadens markets, but it also reduces waste and thereby increases profits.

Transportation
The function of transportation is also present in all stages of marketing. In the manufacturing field raw material must be transferred to the plant and the finished product shipped to the distributing agency employed. The jobber must, in turn, transfer the goods to dealers; and, finally, the retail delivery to the consumer must be made.

Transportation costs have a direct effect upon the extent of the producing area and upon the size of the potential market. Rail, highway, and water transportation play an important part in distribution.

The transportation problem which confronts the manufacturer is essentially that of developing an efficient traffic department. The retailer's problem is concerned chiefly with the choice of that type of transportation which provides adequate service for the consumer. (See Appendix, Figure 2)

Financing and Risk Taking
The importance of the financing function in marketing varies directly with the length of the period of time between production and consumption. The ordinary methods used in connection with marketing are bank loans and deferred payments. Manufacturers, middlemen, retailers and consumers take advantage of these methods of financing.

Risks are either covered by insurance or price margins. Definite risks such as those of a physical nature are usually provided for by resort to insurance, while those of an indefinite nature, such as the possible losses attendant upon the carrying of style goods, are taken care of in the price margin.

Creation of Demand

Demand is of three general types: seasonal, class and sectional. The function of creating a demand is largely that of the producer and of the retailer. By the use of demonstrations, premiums, special sales, etc., the producer can appeal directly to the consumer. The retailer appeals to the consumer through price policies and the rendering of services. The most effective demand creation is that based upon a knowledge of buying motives and an effective utilization of this knowledge.

Advertising plays an important part in the creation of demand. By this means an attempt is made to fix the product firmly in the mind of the buying public and to arouse an active demand. The effectiveness of demand creation depends to a large extent upon the choice of advertising copy and media.

Merchandising

Merchandising is complementary to the creation of demand. It consists of the transferring of the title of goods from the manufacturer, the jobber, or the retailer, to the customer. The methods employed vary with the article since some commodities "sell themselves" while others, such as services, are intangible and therefore require a distinct merchandising plan.

One aid to the merchandising of products is display. This method is usually employed by the retailer. The latter also resorts to demonstrations. The manufacturer, on the other hand, makes use of samples and premiums in an effort to promote sales.

Another part of the merchandising function is stock-keeping and inventory. The manufacturer keeps his record in the form of a control on material and supplies, while the retailer or wholesaler keeps the record as an indication of stock turnover.

PART TWO: THE DEVELOPMENT OF RETAILING

Commodity distribution originally took the form of direct barter. It was not until the time of the Civil War that retailing ceased to be a system of bargaining. Then a new system developed. The department store, the chain store, and the mail-order house sprang up as remedies for the inefficiency of the prevailing system.

Specialization founded on either need or service has greatly increased and the present tendency is toward a still greater increase in retailing types. (See Appendix, Figure 3)

The General Store	The present tendency is toward a decline in the number of general stores. The decline of this type is due to defective management rather than to any essential inefficiency as a means of distribution. The proprietor of the general store usually knows nothing of purchasing plans or of the importance of stock turnover.
	The chief competitor of the general store is the mail-order house on the one hand, and the larger stores of the adjacent communities made accessible by the use of automobiles.
The Specialty Store	The specialty store was the first improvement of the general store. Merchandising in this type is confined to one or a few lines. The term is applied to both the small neighborhood store and to the small exclusive, city store.
	The buying problem of the specialty store is particularly difficult since, in most cases, merchandise must be better than, or at least as good as, that carried by the department store.
	The tendency, at present, is toward an increase in the numbers of the specialty store.
The Department Store	The department store is one form of large-scale merchandising. It is the result of an attempt to supply the principles of large-scale production to retail selling problems.

The general purchasing policy of the department store is to buy directly from the manufacturer in large quantities, taking advantage of the discounts for cash payment.

The advertising of the department store is generally based on a definite price policy with emphasis on the effectiveness of display.

The functions of the department store are highly specialized since each function is under the management of a specialist. In addition to buying and selling, the chief functions are accounting and finance and personnel management. The latter is subdivided into problems of employment, training and relations with employees. (See Appendix, Figure 4)

The
Chain
Store

The chain store movement began after the close of the Civil War. The number of chain stores has increased rapidly in recent years. The chain store is an example of standardization in retailing. The application of standardization to all of its activities enables this type of organization to undersell its competitors.

The chief advantage of the chain store over the individual proprietor store is its ability to undersell competitors due to the economies it effects through standardization.

Its great disadvantage lies in the fact that there is a great loss due to the fact that employees are in charge of branches and for this reason the personal contact with customers, which plays such an important part in the individual store, is usually lacking.

The
Mail-Order
House

The mail-order house is another illustration of the tendency shown by all large-scale retailers. In addition to utilizing the economies made possible by large-scale buying and selling, it has introduced the instalment plan of payment for its customers. It has also developed the use of the mails for selling purposes to their highest extent.

Developing its own private brands as an advertisement is another step taken by the mail-order house.

The rapid expansion of railroads and the introduction of the parcel post system were largely responsible for the development of the mail-order system of retailing.

PART THREE: THE MIDDLEMAN

The Jobber The jobber assumes for the manufacturer the problems of assembling, grading, financing and distribution to the dealers. Manufacturing costs are relatively higher than distributing costs, and for this reason, the manufacturer concentrates his efforts on a reduction in producing costs, leaving the problem of distribution to some outside agency.

Jobbers are of various types. There is the agent who deals in a variety of lines, the agent who specializes in one line, and also the agent who is a manufacturer as well as a distributor.

The jobber usually maintains a warehouse for storing products in time of slack demand. In this way he assists in stabilizing production.

Advertising by a jobber is a difficult problem, since he does not come in direct contact with the consumer. When, however, he makes use of the private brand, he indulges in one form of advertisement. His chief means of creating demand is through dealers' catalogues.

The Broker In some lines of business, the jobber has not completely satisfied the need for a specialist in distribution. Thus, the broker has arisen in answer to a definite need. "Brokers as middlemen may be divided into three groups:

1. The broker who functions between the producer and other middlemen.
2. The broker connected with one phase of a particular business.
3. The broker on the organized exchange."

All classes of brokers merely act in the name of a principal. The broker does not possess goods but deals in orders. He has no discretionary power in making sales. Brokers usually specialize either in selling or buying.

There has been some discussion as to the necessity of the broker's existence. Despite the fact that a large amount of the work formerly done by brokers has been taken over by co-operative marketing agencies, the broker still exists in large numbers. This fact seems to justify his position in the economic field.

Organized Exchanges   An organized exchange is an association of those who deal in a certain type of commodity. These concentrate in a specified locality and function according to set regulations.

Sales on an organized exchange are made either by sample or by the use of a standard system of grading. The organized exchange is a development of the market place. It is merely a specialization of the original form.

In order to establish an organized exchange certain conditions must be met. The volume of potential business must be large enough to justify the adoption of regulations and the commodity, itself, must be suitable.

"Brokers as middlemen may be divided roughly into three groups:

1. The broker who stands between producer and other middlemen, commonly called the merchandise broker. He is active in lines of business where there is a large number of small producers and widely extended markets, such as textiles, canned goods, fruits, etc.

2. The broker who has come into existence because of the peculiar circumstances connected with the trade channels of a particular line of business. He deals in a highly specialized commodity, such as insurance, foreign exchange, or real estate.

3. The broker on the organized exchange who deals in stocks and bonds and in grain, cotton, sugar and other commodities." [1]

The article should be a staple, capable of being graded and not highly perishable. The exchange is justified economically despite the fact that certain defects in its organization and operation still require correction.

The chief cause for complaint on the part of the public lies in the fact that it exists chiefly for speculation and consequently disturbs prices.

Co-opera-
tive
Marketing

Co-operation in marketing is effected for the purpose of securing for small units the advantages of large-scale selling. The co-operative organization assumes the functions of the more common types of middlemen. It limits its operation, however, to the primary market.

The modern movements are organized on the basis of product rather than locality. Short term contracts are made with small producers to turn over their total production capacity to the co-operative organization. This organization assumes all the functions of marketing. It establishes standards and grades: it finances the producer and it creates demand through advertising.

The co-operative marketing movement has developed rapidly in recent years and has been particularly successful in Denmark. The agricultural industries in California have also been organized on this basis.

PART FOUR: MARKETING PROBLEMS

Market
Analysis

Market analysis deals with the product, the market and the means of bringing them together. In general, it may be said, that market analysis is the application of the principles of research to marketing. It has had a recent development simultaneous with that of scientific management in industry. Market

[1] White, Percival & Hayward, Walter S., *Marketing Practice*, p. 176.

analysis is conducted either by a research department within the organization or by an outside agency, specializing in that type of work.

The procedure in making an analysis includes first of all a study of the product to be marketed with special consideration of its uses. A survey of the potential market is also made by means of interviews and questionnaires. The purpose of this survey is to determine what the line of appeal should be and how to adjust it to various sections and classes of the consuming public. (See Appendix, Figures 5 and 6.)

Sales Planning and Promotion by the Manufacturer

Planning in its application to the many branches of business was the most important contribution of the scientific management movement. The planning of sales is based upon market research and co-ordinated with production schedules. Its object is to predict sales possibilities and to co-ordinate the various branches of an organization with reference to its research.

Sales promotion connects sales planning and advertising. It is really the carrying out of sales plans. An important part of this work is obtaining the proper momentum for sales campaigns. (See Appendix, Figure 7)

Sales Management

The importance of salesmanship in marketing is so great that a great deal of emphasis is placed upon the function of sales management. The first step in sales management is the choice of a sales organization suitable to the type of product manufactured and to the character of the potential market. Sales may be controlled either centrally through one large organization or territorially by means of district branches.

Problems growing out of this primary choice are the selection and training of salesmen, the assignment of territory to each individual, and developing a system of reports for the purpose of maintaining contact with the sales force. Upon the proper co-ordination of these matters of sales policy with the character of the product and market depends the success of the organization.

The
Advertising
Campaign

The primary purpose of the advertising campaign is to increase the demand for a product. The secondary purpose is to familiarize the consumer with the name of the organization manufacturing that product.

The advertising campaign is based upon a market analysis the purpose of which is to determine in what sections and among what classes the potential market lies. Advertising copy is then adapted to the character of the market. The choice of media is the result of a careful analysis of the probable effectiveness of each of the available forms.

The advertising agency is of great importance to the average organization since only the largest companies can effectively finance an advertising department. The agency has developed from a broker of space to an organization equipped to take over the entire management of a client's campaign. Modern advertising methods and policies have evolved during the past twenty years.

PART FIVE: CONCLUSION

The direct effect of marketing policies upon other branches of an industrial organization, as shown in the foregoing discussion, is so great that marketing has become, within the past two decades, the most important problem confronting the modern business institution.

In his search for more economical methods of distribution, the business man will undoubtedly bring about a standardization of marketing similar to that effected in the field of production. This cannot, however, be achieved until certain obstacles are overcome. Foremost among these is the apparent duplication of effort prevailing in many of the distributing functions.

The tendency seems to be toward standardization but it is doubtful whether the degree of standardization in marketing will reach that attained in production.

BIBLIOGRAPHY

CLARK, FRED E. *Principles of Marketing*. New York, Macmillan, 1925, 570 pp.

CONVERSE, PAUL D. *Marketing Methods and Policies*. New York, Prentice-Hall, Inc., 1921, 650 pp.

DOUGLAS, A. W. *Merchandising*. New York, Macmillan, 1918, 151 pp.

MORIARTY, W. D. *Economics of Marketing and Advertising*. New York, Harper & Bros., 1923, 592 pp.

WHITE, PERCIVAL. *Market Analysis*. New York, McGraw-Hill Book Company, 1921, 340 pp.

WHITE, PERCIVAL and HAYWARD, WALTER S. *Marketing Practice*. New York, Doubleday, Page & Co., 1926, 577 pp.

OUTLINE OF REPORT

I. *Introduction*

    A. Synopsis of Report
    B. Foreword

II. *Text of Report*

    A. Purpose of Report
    B. Discussion

        1. Marketing Functions
            a. Assembling and grading
            b. Storing
            c. Transportation
            d. Financing and risk taking
            e. Creation of demand
            f. Merchandising

        2. The Development of Retailing
            a. The general store
            b. The specialty store
            c. The department store
            d. The chain store
            e. The mail-order house

        3. The Middleman
            a. The jobber
            b. The broker
            c. Organized exchanges
            d. Co-operative marketing

4. The Marketing Problems of the Manufacturer
    a. Market analysis
    b. Sales planning and promotion
    c. Sales management
    d. The advertising campaign

III. *Appendix*

A. Charts
B. Graphs
C. Bibliography

REFERENCE BOOKS

BAKER, RAY PALMER. *The Preparation of Reports, Engineering, Scientific, Administrative.* The Ronald Press Company.

CALLOWAY, LEE. *Office Management, Its Principles and Practice.* The Ronald Press Company.

HOTCHKISS and KILDUFF. *Advanced Business Correspondence.* Harper & Brothers.

KILDUFF, EDWARD JONES. *The Private Secretary.* The Century Company.

LEE, JAMES MELVIN. *Language for Men of Affairs,* Vol. II, *Business Writing.* The Ronald Press Company.

McNAMARA, EDWARD L. *Secretarial Training.* The Ronald Press Company.

TAINTOR, SARAH AUGUSTA. *Training for Secretarial Practice.* McGraw-Hill Book Company, Inc.

CHAPTER IX

PREPARATION OF MANUSCRIPT

1. Typewrite manuscript to be sent to a publisher or printer. It will present a better appearance and will be easier to read. Type in double-space.

2. Leave margins as follows: one and a half inches at the top, one and a half inches at the left, one at the right, and one at the bottom.

3. If possible keep the number of lines on each sheet the same. This will enable the printer to estimate the amount of space the copy will take.

4. Use good bond paper, eight and a half by eleven inches. Write on one side of paper only.

5. Number all sheets consecutively, not separately by chapters.

6. If you wish to include additional pages, note on the margin of the page after which the insert is to be made, the number of pages to be inserted; as, *Insert 8a-8c,* and write on the following pages, *8a, 8b, 8c.*

7. Do not pin inserts to a sheet, but paste them carefully in their proper places.

8. Fasten the sheets of a manuscript by clips or pins. Do not sew or tie them together, as they are likely to be torn.

9. Begin new chapters at the top of a sheet. Clip all pages together belonging to a chapter.

10. Footnotes should be placed directly below that part of the text to which they refer. They should be typed in single space and should have lines drawn across the page above and below them.

11. Write in the text after the punctuation mark (if any), a superior figure to correspond with the figure preceding the footnote.

12. Number footnotes consecutively throughout a chapter or an article. If there are several footnotes to appear on one page, write them one below the other, so that they will read down.

13. Spell out in full all references to periodicals. When more than one reference to the same work is made, abbreviations may be used after the first one.

14. Number chapters, charts, plates, and graphs consecutively throughout. Most writers use Roman numerals.

15. Make the index after the page proof has been returned from the printer. (See page 325.)

16. Do not roll manuscript. Send it flat in a box or a strong envelope. Mark on the outside the author's name and return address. It is best to insure the manuscript or register it if sent by mail.

17. Read a manuscript through carefully before submitting it to anyone for consideration. Edit it critically to be certain that it contains no incorrect usage and no inexact punctuation. Be sure that the sentence conforms to the best rhetorical principles, that the paragraphing is clear and defined, and that the manuscript contains no errors.

18. Always send the original copy to the publisher as it is clearer in type than a carbon. Retain a carbon copy for reference and as protection against loss of the original.

A GLOSSARY OF TERMS

The following list of definitions of terms commonly used in bookmaking and publishing is adapted through the courtesy of *The Publishers' Weekly* from a longer glossary published serially by that journal through the months of July and August, 1924.

I

BOOK PLANNING AND PRODUCTION

bastard title.—The name of a book standing by itself on the leaf preceding the title-page. Also known as *"fly title"*—not to be confused with *"half title."*

book sizes.—

Size	Approximate dimensions in inches
Atlas folio	16 x 25
Elephant folio	14 x 20
Folio	12 x 15
4to (quarto)	9 x 12
8vo (octavo)	6 x 9
12mo (duodecimo)	5 x 7½
16mo	4½ x 6¾
18mo	4 x 6¼
24mo	3½ x 6
32mo	3½ x 5
48mo	2½ x 4
64mo	2 x 3

The common book-trade designation of sizes was based originally on their relation to a sheet of paper measuring 19 x 25. When folded to 8 leaves and trimmed, each 6 x 9 inches, it is the standard dimension of an 8vo. When folded to make 16 leaves it is a 16mo. With the present infinite variety of paper sizes all dimensions are approximate.

bulk.—The thickness of a book without its covers.

cancel.—A leaf reprinted and inserted in consequence of an error or defect on the leaf replaced.

caption.—A heading, as of a chapter, table, etc. Caption is sometimes used to designate the title of an illustration or the brief description printed immediately below it. *See* LEGEND.

cut.—A term commonly used to mean either a half-tone engraving or zinc etching. Also the block or plate from which it is printed.

cut-in side note.—A note set into the side of a page of printed matter.

dummy.—Unprinted paper, folded, trimmed or untrimmed, bound or unbound, to show size, bulk, and general appearance of a projected publication.

electrotypes.—Facsimile plates for use in printing made by taking an impression in wax or other substance, depositing in this mold a thin shell of copper or other metal by an electrotyping process, and backing it with type metal. Electrotypes are made for books which are to have a large printing or a second printing. The plates will stand more wear than the original type and can be more easily stored. Moreover, new electrotypes can be made from "molders" (electrotypes used as patterns only) or from type kept standing.

end papers.—Strong sheets, sometimes decorated, pasted on the interior of the cover.

fly leaves.—Unprinted leaves at front and back of books, between the lining papers and body of book.

format.—The general make-up of a book as to size of page, margin, binding, etc.

front matter.—The pages preceding the first chapter of a book, known as "front matter," include the following, frequently in the order named:

Bastard title
Frontispiece (facing title-page)
Title-page
Copyright notice and printer's imprint
Dedication
Preface (or foreword)
Table of contents
List of illustrations
Introduction
Half title

Each to begin on a right-hand or odd-numbered page, excepting the frontispiece which faces the title-page and the copyright which appears on the verso of title.

frontispiece.—A picture or plate facing the title-page.

half title.—A short title heading the text of a book or a one-line title on a full page introducing a subdivision.

head margin.—The blank space above the first line on the page. Usually planned at half the width of the bottom margin. *See* MARGINS.

initial letter.—A large capital or decorated letter sometimes used to begin a chapter or section of a book.

inserts or insets.—Illustrations, maps, or other material not part of the printed sheets, included when binding a pamphlet or book.

jacket.—The printed or unprinted paper placed around a bound book. Sometimes called the wrapper.

layout.—Practically, the working diagram for the printer to follow. Usually marked to show the general grouping of a job, and specifying the sizes and kinds of type to be used.

leaders.—Dots or dashes set in succession so as to lead the eye, as in the table of contents.

legend.—The title or short description printed under an illustration, not to be confused with *caption* (q. v.).

list price, or published price.—The price to the individual consumer as set by the publisher.

margins.—The proportional width of the margins is a very important element in a properly balanced book page. A good ratio is: top margin, 2; outside, 3; bottom, 4; inside, $1\frac{1}{2}$.

net; net price.—"Not subject to discount or reduction."

plates.—Illustrations printed on special paper and inserted separately in the binding of a book. *See also* INSERTS; ELECTROTYPES.

reprints.—A new printing of a book.

royalties.—A compensation paid by a publisher to the owner of a copyright for the right to act under it.

running head; running title.—The line which appears across the top of a printed page. Usually the title of the book is run on the left-hand page while the chapter title is on the right-hand page.

sheets; "in sheets."—Printed pages of a book, either flat or folded, but unbound. English term is "In Quires."

subtitle.—An additional or second title to a book; an under-title. For example, "Fundamentals of Pedagogy: *A Textbook for Teachers.*"

title-page.—A page at the beginning of a book always on the right, giving its title, its author, if acknowledged, and its publisher, with place and date of publication. *See* FRONT MATTER.

type sizes.—

This is 4½ point, old name "Diamond"

This is 5 point, old name "Pearl"

This is 5½ point, old name "Agate"

This is 6 point, old name "Nonpareil"

This is 7 point, old name "Minion"

This is 8 point, old name "Brevier"

This is 9 point, old name "Bourgeois"

This is 10 point, old name "Long Primer"

This is 11 point, old name "Small Pica"

This is 12 point, old name "Pica"

This is 14 point, old name "English"

This is 18 point, old name "Great Primer"

REFERENCE BOOKS

LEE, JAMES MELVIN. *Language for Men of Affairs,* Vol. II, *Business Writing.* The Ronald Press Company, 1920.

MAWSON, C. O. SYLVESTER. *Style-Book for Writers and Editors.* Thomas Y. Crowell Company, 1926.

CHAPTER X

MAKING A BIBLIOGRAPHY

Bibliographical lists are frequently made in the following order:

1. Name of the author in capitals, last name first, followed by first and second names or first name and middle initial, or according to the custom of the author.

2. Title of book in italics, name of place of publication, name of publisher, date of publication. A comma follows each of the first two items; a colon follows the place of publication, and a period, the date.   *Manual of Style*

> WESEEN, MAURICE H., *Crowell's Dictionary of English Grammar and Handbook of American Usage,* New York: Thomas Y. Crowell Company, 1928.

3. When listing more than one work by the same author, do not repeat the name, but use a line to represent it as follows:

> KRAPP, GEORGE PHILIP, *A Comprehensive Guide to Good English,* Chicago: Rand, McNally & Co., 1927.
> ——— "Is American English Archaic?" *Southwest Rev.,* XII. 292-303.
> ——— *The Knowledge of English,* N. Y.: Holt and Company, 1927.

4. When making a definite reference to a book for a bibliographical list, write as follows:

> OPDYCKE, JOHN B., *The Literature of Letters: Famous Literary Letters, as Related to Life, to the History of Literature, and to the Art of Literature:* Humor, 206-245, New York: Lyons and Carnahan, 1925.

5. When a reference to the same work is repeated immediately, use the abbreviation *ibid.* (*ibidem, in the same place*) as follows:

> NOYES, ALFRED, *The New Morning*, "Victory," p. 10, New York: Frederick A. Stokes Company, 1919.
> *Ibid.*, "The Lost Battle," pp. 94-95.

6. The following illustrates the manner of listing a subtitle:

> WELLS, H. G., *The Outline of History: Being a Plain History of Life and Mankind*, New York: The Macmillan Company, 1921.

7. When referring to articles in magazines use quotation marks around the name of the article and write the name of the periodical in italics.

> LOWELL, ABBOTT LAWRENCE, "Self-Education in College," *The Forum*, Vol. 79, No. 4, pp. 519-526, April, 1928.

8. When referring to a Government Bulletin, list as follows:

> TUCKER, W. A., "Wearing Apparel in Chile," *U. S. Department of Commerce, Bureau of Foreign and Domestic Commerce Bulletin* 168, Washington: 1918.

9. When referring to a report, list as follows:

> *Annual Report of the Directors to the Stockholders* for the Year Ending December 31, 1925, New York: 1925.
> *The Metropolitan Museum of Art, Fifty-Fifth Annual Report of the Trustees*, New York: 1924.
> *Annual Report of the Trustees*, 49 pp., New York: 1924.
> EGBERT, JAMES C., *Annual Report of the Director of University Extension, Columbia University*, New York: 1925.

VARIOUS WAYS OF MAKING BIBLIOGRAPHIES

SUGGESTED BOOKS ON SECRETARIAL TRAINING

CENTER, STELLA S., and HERZBERG, MAX J., *Secretarial Procedure*, New York: The Ronald Press, 1929.
CHURCH, ARTHUR L., *The Training of a Secretary*, Philadelphia: J. B. Lippincott Company, 1922.

KILDUFF, EDWARD JONES, *The Private Secretary,* New York: The Century Company, 1919.

MCNAMARA, EDWARD J., *Secretarial Training,* New York: The Ronald Press Company, 1927.

MEYER, ELIZABETH, *The Social Secretary,* New York: Brentano's, 1919.

SORELLE, RUPERT, and GREGG, JOHN ROBERT, *Secretarial Studies,* New York: The Gregg Publishing Company, 1922.

TAINTOR, SARAH AUGUSTA, *Training for Secretarial Practice,* New York: McGraw-Hill Book Co., Inc., 1926.

SUGGESTED BOOKS ON VOCATIONAL INFORMATION

(Note periods after names of authors and books.)

BLAKE, MABELLE BABCOCK. *Guidance for College Women: A Survey and a Program for Personal Work in Higher Education.* New York, D. Appleton & Co., 1926.

BERNAYS, EDWARD L., Ed. *An Outline of Careers: A Practical Guide to Achievement by Thirty-Eight Eminent Americans.* New York, George H. Doran Company, 1927.

HATCHER, O. LATHAM, Ed. *Occupations for Women.* Richmond, Virginia, Southern Women's Educational Alliance, 1927.

LORD, E. W. *The Fundamentals of Business Ethics.* New York, The Ronald Press Company, 1926.

LYON, L. S., and BUTLER, A. M., Eds. *Vocational Readings.* New York, The Macmillan Company, 1927.

PLATT, RUTHERFORD H., Jr., Ed. *The Book of Opportunities, What 3000 American Occupations Have to Offer.* New York, G P. Putnam's Sons, 1927.

SUGGESTED LIST OF BOOKS ON ADVERTISING

Author	*Title*	*Publisher*
Adams, H. F.	Advertising and Its Mental Laws	Macmillan
Agnew, H. E.	Cooperative Advertising by Competitors	Harper
Allen, F. J.	Advertising as a Vocation	Macmillan
Barton, H. A.	How to Write Advertising	Lippincott
Brewster, A. J.	Introduction to Retail Advertising	Shaw

Author	Title	Publisher
Bull, A. E.	Business Man's Guide to Advertising	Pitman
Calkins and Holden	Modern Advertising	Appleton
Cherington, P. S.	Advertising as a Business Force	Doubleday, Page
Cherington, P. S.	Consumer Looks at Advertising	Harper
Chase, S., and Schlink, F. L.	Your Money's Worth	Macmillan
Durggins, W. A.	Layout in Advertising	Harper
Durstine, R. S.	This Advertising Business	Scribner
Farroe, G. P.	How Advertisements Are Built	Appleton
Hall, S. Roland	Writing an Advertisement	Houghton, Mifflin
Hall, S. Roland	Advertising Handbook	McGraw-Hill
Higham, C. E.	Advertising; Its Use and Abuse	Holt
Hollingworth, H. L.	Advertising and Selling	Appleton
Larned, W. L.	Illustration in Advertising	McGraw-Hill
Nixon, H. K.	Attention and Interest in Advertising	Columbia University Press
Opdycke, John B.	The Language of Advertising	Pitman
Scott, Walter Hill	The Psychology of Advertising	Small
Starch, Daniel	Principles of Advertising	Shaw
Sheldon, G. H.	Advertising, Elements and Principles	Harcourt
Tupper, Hollingworth, Hotchkiss and Parsons	Advertising, Its Principles and Practices	Ronald

MAKING A BIBLIOGRAPHY

A LIST OF BOOKS ON OFFICE MANAGEMENT

(Illustrating library methods of capitalization)

Barrett, H. I.   Modern methods in the office, Harper, 1918.

Beck, Cameron.   Youth, the beginning of right relations in management, American Management Association, 1926.

Cahill, M. F.   Junior office practice, Macmillan, 1926.

Galloway, Lee.   Office management, Ronald Press, 1919.

Mac Donald, J.   Office management, Prentice-Hall, 1927.

Schulze, J.   Office administration, McGraw-Hill, 1917.

Tead, Ordway.   Course in personnel administration; syllabus and questions, Columbia University Press, 1923.

REFERENCE BOOKS

Manual of Style. University of Chicago.

United States Catalog. H. W. Wilson Company.

MUDGE, ISADORE. *New Guide to Reference Books.*

CHAPTER XI

PROOFREADING

Proofreading requires accuracy, alertness, and judgment. Errors should be carefully sought out and corrected in the first reading. The resetting of even a line in the page proof is costly to the author.

Writers and their secretaries should be familiar with commonly accepted marks of proofreading and with their actual use on proofs.

Kinds of Proofs

Galley Proofs, about the length of a newspaper column, are the first proofs made by the printer. They are usually revised and cleared of all apparent errors before being sent to the author.

An author's proofs are those corrected and revised from the first Galley Proof and sent to him for correction. The author may ask for a second Galley Proof before the material is finally set into page form.

Page Proofs are those made from the Galley Proofs as they are to appear in regular page form. These should be corrected with great care, as any changes are at additional cost. The proofreader should observe closely the headings, subheads, numbering of pages, footnotes, and all other parts of the page to be sure that all are correct. The author seldom receives a second Page Proof; unless the corrections on the first page proofs have been many and complicated.

After corrections have been made by the author on the Page Proof, the pages are then locked up for the press. Sometimes another proof, known as the Foundry Proof, is taken, which is sent to the author at his request for his final approval.

The Plate Proof is the final proof furnished to the publisher, but not usually sent to the author.

GENERAL DIRECTIONS FOR PROOFREADING

1. Read all proof slowly, letter by letter, in order to detect every error.

2. Read through the proof several times with a definite point in view. Consider carefully punctuation, correct usage, typographical errors, general alignment, spacing, general effect.

3. Make all corrections in ink of a color contrasting with that used by the professional proofreader.

4. Put all corrections in the margin near the word marked. If several are made, place them in the order of their appearance with a slanting line between them; as, *wf/tr/sc/*.

5. Do not erase a correction made which you have found unnecessary. Draw a line through the correction and write *stet,* which means *Let it stand*. If necessary, rewrite a correction.

6. Underline three times a word or words to be written in large capitals and write "caps" in the margin; underline twice to indicate small capitals and write "s. c." in margin.

7. When a word is incorrectly capitalized, draw a line through the letter and write "l. c." in the margin to indicate "lower case."

8. Underline a word once to indicate that it is to be italicized, and write "ital" in the margin.

9. Place a circle in the margin around a period or colon to be inserted. To indicate a comma write ⁣/or⁀; to indicate an apostrophe write ⱱ; to indicate quotation marks write ⱱⱱ.

10. To indicate that a word or expression should be removed draw a line through the word or expression and write in the margin the sign ⍺ (dele), which means *Take out.*

11. Write in the margin all new material to be inserted and indicate by caret (∧) where it is to be placed.

12. Write in the margin a double (=) to show that a hyphen is to be placed where indicated by a caret sign.

13. Use the space sign ♯ to indicate that more space is needed where indicated by the caret.

14. Use the sign ◠ to indicate that space between letters or words is to be eliminated.

15. Be careful to answer all queries made by the publisher's proofreader. To indicate your approval, cross out the question mark and allow the correction to stand. To show disapproval of the correction suggested, cross out the question or answer it in full.

The following list represents with little variation proofreader's marks used in most printing offices.

SIGNS USED IN CORRECTING PROOFS

⍐	Push down the lead which is showing with the type.
⍺	Delete; take out.
⍩	Turn inverted letter right side up.
stet ····· }	Let it remain; change made was wrong.
▫	Indent one *em*.
⊙	A period.
‖	The type line is uneven at the side of the page; straighten it.
✕	A broken letter.

.	A hyphen.
ital.	Use italics.
◡	Join together; take out the space.
ℬ	Take out letter and close up.
center	Put in middle of page, or line.
≡	Straighten lines.
⌄	Insert an apostrophe.
⩗	Insert a comma.
⌐ ¬	Raise the word or letter.
⌊ ⌋	Lower the word or letter.
⊏	Bring matter to the left.
⊐	Bring matter to the right.
#	Make a space.
lead	A thin metal strip used to widen the space between the lines.
space out	Spread words farther apart.
¶	Make a paragraph.
no ¶	Run on without a paragraph.
cap.	Use a capital.
l.c.	Use the lower case (small type), *i.e.* not capitals.
s.c.	Small capitals.
w. f.	Wrong font — size or style.
font.	Kind of type.
tr.	Transpose.
rom.	Use roman letter.
overrun	Carry over to next line.
∧	Indicates where an insertion is to be made.
Qy. or (?)	Doubt as to spelling, etc.

Indicates CAPITAL letters.

Indicates SMALL CAPITAL letters.

Indicates *italic* letters.

Indicates **black type** letters.

Indicates **BLACK CAPITALS.**

Indicates **BLACK SMALL CAPITALS.**

Indicates ***black italic.***

PROOF SHOWING CORRECTIONS

cap.   ADᴅRESS AT GETTYSBURG

Fourscore and seven years ago our fathers brought

forth on this continent a new nation conceived in

liberty, and dedicated to the proposition that all

men are created equal. Now we are engaged in a

great civil war, testing whether that nation or any

nation so conceived and so dedicated, can long

endure. We are met on a great battlefield of that

war. We have come to pedicate a portion of that

field as a final resting-place for those who here here

l.c. gave their lives that that Nation might live. it is *cap.*

altogether fitting and proper that we *should* do this. *rom.*

But, in a larger sense, we cannot dedicate — *lead*

we cannot consecrate — we cannot hallow this

ground The brave men, living and dead, who

struggled here, have consecrated it far above our

poor power to add or detract. The world will

little note nor long remember what we here say *tr.*

but it can never forget what they did here.

no ¶ It is for us, the living, rather, to be dedicated

w.f. here to the unfinished work which they who fought

(Address at the dedication of the Gettysburg National Cemetery, *ital.*

ital. Nov. 19, 1863. Reprinted, by permission of The Macmillan Company, *s.c.*

from Abraham Lincoln, the Man the People, by Norman Hapgood.) *of /*

PROOFREADING

CORRECTED PROOF
ADDRESS AT GETTYSBURG

Fourscore and seven years ago our fathers brought forth on this continent a new nation, conceived in liberty, and dedicated to the proposition that all men are created equal.

Now we are engaged in a great civil war, testing whether that nation, or any nation so conceived and so dedicated, can long endure. We are met on a great battlefield of that war. We have come to dedicate a portion of that field as a final resting-place for those who here gave their lives that that nation might live. It is altogether fitting and proper that we should do this.

But, in a larger sense, we cannot dedicate — we cannot consecrate — we cannot hallow — this ground. The brave men, living and dead, who struggled here, have consecrated it far above our poor power to add or detract. The world will little note nor long remember what we say here, but it can never forget what they did here. It is for us, the living, rather, to be dedicated here to the unfinished work which they who fought here

(*Address at the dedication of the Gettysburg National Cemetery, Nov. 19, 1863.* Reprinted, by permission of THE MACMILLAN COMPANY, from "Abraham Lincoln, the Man of the People," by Norman Hapgood.)

CHAPTER XII

MAKING AN INDEX

The purpose of an index is to present a means of ready reference. An index should offer to the reader an opportunity to find quickly what he wishes without reading more than is necessary. It is essential, then, for an indexer to know what the average reader may want to refer to and under what headings he will naturally look. One or two may not be enough.

Chapter headings, subheads, subjects, and even minor subjects may be included in the index. Cross references should be made wherever possible. The indexer should list topics under as many headings as he thinks necessary.

There are several typographical forms for indexing. If a given form is not required by a publisher, an author may select a type which he considers suitable to the content or nature of his work.

In the form selected, he should observe the capitalization, spacing, indention, punctuation, and phrasing of topics, and follow that form rigidly.

The making of an index begins usually after the return of the page proofs from the printer. The author may have anticipated this by writing on separate library cards or on small slips of paper uniform in size, subjects which he has decided should be indexed. If he has not done this, his work begins when the page proof is put into his hands.

In order to be sure that all important subjects are indexed, it would be well to start at the beginning and read through all pages consecutively, writing on separate cards each subject or name important enough to be indexed. One main subject only

MAKING AN INDEX

should be written on a card. Subentries, indented a few spaces
to the right, alphabetically arranged, may be included on the
same card. If more subentries are to be indexed than there is
space for, the main subject is repeated on a new card with the
word *Continued* following it. Often it is necessary to make
subentries under subentries. This is done by double indention.

When all subjects are completely and carefully indexed and
cross references made under suitable headings, the cards should
be alphabetized. From these the index, a complete list of all
entries on the cards, may then be made in its final draft.

Every reference should be checked to see whether the index
reference corresponds to the page quoted. This is most important, as errors frequently creep in, particularly in the proof.

SUGGESTIONS FOR INDEXING NAMES

In indexing proper names write the last name first, followed
by a comma, then the Christian or given name, followed by a
comma and page number.

> Carlyle, Jane, 20
> Conrad, Joseph, 116

The following illustrate ways often observed in making an
index: by column form with indention and sub-indention; by
paragraph form for all topics; by the use of main entries only;
by the use of the dash to indicate subentries.

Index with indention and sub-indention:

> Secretary, the business training of, 8
>   cultural training of, 5-7
>   definition of, 2-3
>   duties of, 3
>   efficient, the, 61-62
>   from point of view of employment
>   managers, 57-60
>   of man, 64
>   of woman, 65
>   general qualities of, 17-18
>   history of, 72-81
>   hundred per cent secretaries, 65-66
>   in architectural offices, 45, 68

in authors' offices, 47-49
in editorial offices, 46-47
in educational offices, 51-55, 69
in engineers' offices, 43
in executive secretary's office, 71

From *Training for Secretarial Practice.*

Paragraph form for extensive index

Subjects, of letters, acceptance, 225; accident, 368; advice, 218; arrest, 353; art, 388; authorship, 231; autobiography, 34, 56, 106, 435, 457; bank, 290; biography, 372, 432; business, 402-411; butcher, 132; cats, 216, 241; character, 124; charity, 281; clothes, 409; condolence, 256, 320, 346; congratulation, 283; contribution, 281; convalescence, 228, 233; cottage, 247; *cries of London,* 297; criticism, 250, 305, 308, 310, 311, 312, 313, 318, 340, 372, 393, 417, 440, 453, 462; dancing, 207; declination, 237, 264; delivery, 408; despair, 262; disappointment, 107; dogs, 162, etc.

From *The Literature of Letters.*

Index for main entries:

From *Secretarial Studies.*

The use of the dash to indicate sub-entries:

From *A Manual of Style*.

CHAPTER XIII

RULES FOR ALPHABETICAL FILING

Used in Business Offices

GENERAL DIRECTIONS

1. Entries on cards, lists, etc., should always be placed in the following order:

1. Surname
2. Comma
3. Christian name (or initials)
4. Comma
5. Title (in parenthesis) Stewart, George D. (*Dr.*)

2. Many names are pronounced exactly alike but spelled differently:

(1) File exactly as spelled.
(2) When spelling differs only at the end of the word, no cross reference is necessary, since one spelling would follow immediately after another:

Smith	Conner
Smithe	Connor

When spelling differs in the beginning of a word, make blanket cross-references from one form of name (surname only) to the other:

Monroe .... *see also* Munroe
Munroe .... *see also* Monroe
Conolly .... *see also* Connolly
Connolly .... *see also* Conolly

Illustration of Alphabetic Divisions Found on Filing Guides

25 Divisions	40 Divisions	60 Divisions
A	A	AA-AM
BA-BL	BA	AN-AZ
BO-BY	BE-BI	BA
CA-CL	BL-BO	BE
CO-CZ	BR-BY	BI-BL
D	CA-CE	BO
E	CH-CL	BR
F	CO-CZ	BU-BY
G	DA-DE	CA-CE
HA-HE	DI-DY	CH-CL
HI-HY	E	COA-COP
I-J	FA-FL	COR-COZ-CR-CZ
K	FO-FY	DA-DE
L	GA-GL	DI-DO
MA-MC	GO-GY	DR-DY-EA-EK
ME-MY	HA	EL-EZ-FA
N-O	HE-HI	FE-FL
P-Q	HO-HY	FO-FY
R	I-J	GA-GE
SA-SE	KA-KI	GI-GO
SH-SO	KL-KY	GR-GY
SP-SY	L	HAA-HAP
T-U-V	MA	HAR-HAZ-HEA-HEK
WA-WH	MC	HEL-HEZ-HI
WI-WY-X-Y-Z	ME-MI	HO
	MO-MY	HU-HY-I
	N-O	J
	PA-PH	KA-KE
	PI-PY-Q	KI-KY
	RA-RI	LA
	RO-RY	LE-LI
	SA-SC	LO-LY
	SE-SK	MAA-MAN
	SL-SQ	MAR-MAY
	ST-SY	MC
	T	ME
	U-V	MI-MOA-MOO
	WA-WE	MOR-MOZ-MU-MY
	WH-WI	N
	WO-WY-X-Y-Z	O
		PA-PEA-PEM
		PEN-PEZ-PF-PH-PI
		PL-PY-Q
		RA-RE
		RH-RI-ROA-ROG
		ROH-ROZ-RU-RY
		SA
		SC
		SE-SH
		SI-SM
		SN-SQ-STA
		STE-STY
		SU-SY-TA-TE
		TH-TY
		U-V
		WA
		WE
		WH
		WI
		WO-WY-X-Y-Z

3. File *Mc* as if spelled *Mac*.

> Mackey, Thelma
> MacLaren, Frank
> MacLean, Samuel
> McMahon, Agnes
> McNab, Robert
> McNaughton, Maude

4. When filing a group of one surname, alphabetic order, bear the following in mind:

(1) Nothing stands before something.

(2) Initials always precede names beginning with the same letter.

> Lord, (Mrs.)
> Lord, A. F.
> Lord, A. Frances
> Lord, Augustus

5. Hyphenated names should be indexed under the first name, and, when necessary, a cross-reference made from the second:

> Thoburn-Arzt, James
> Quiller-Couch, Arthur T.

Cross-references:

> Arzt, James Thoburn—See Thoburn-Arzt, James
> Couch, Arthur T. Quiller—See Quiller-Couch, Arthur

FOREIGN NAMES

6. Foreign names commencing with *da, de, della, di, du, la, le, van, von,* etc., are filed alphabetically as they are spelled. The prefix is considered as part of the name, not separately.

> Da Costa, Carl
> De Kosa, L. A.
> Della Fazia, Aneilo
> De Stefano, Adolfo
> Des Verney, Kenneth
> De Takacs, Maria
> Di Bari, Lorenzo
> Du Bois, Paul
> La Barre, Emily
>
> La Bell, W.
> Le Blanc, Jean
> Van Loon, Hendrik
> Van Ness, George
> Von Bremen, Fritz
> Von Burg, Karl

7. When names beginning with *La* or *Le* are family names (as *Le Roy, Le Bolt,* etc.) they follow the foregoing rule, but when *La* or *Le* is used in place of *the,* disregard the *La* or *Le* and alphabetize by the word following:

> Barre Realty Corp., La.
> Barton Mfg. Co., Le

Make blanket references from *La* and *Le*.

> La Barre Realty Corporation
> Le Barton Mfg. Co.

D' should be alphabetized without regard to the apostrophe.

> D'Agnostina, Albert
> Dagnosturo, George
> Dagood, Holding Corp.
> D'Elia, Louis J.

Names such as, *El Comercio, El Mora,* etc., are alphabetized under the article as one name.

> El Caso Apts.
> El Comercio Co.
> Elcus, John
> Elmhurst Land Co.
> El Mora

If the entire name is in Spanish and *El* stands in place of *the,* disregard *El* and alphabetize the word following.

> El Diario de la Marina

Make blanket cross references from *El,* as follows:

> *El* (used as *the*)

See the first word of title.

> Diario de la Marina, E

8. Names that begin with *Van, Van Den, Van Der, von, von den,* should be alphabetized as one word.

> Van Arsdale, James   Van Dyke, John
> Vanasco, Robert   Von Hagen, Otto
> Van Auken, Amy   Vonhausen, Fritz
> Van Beuren, Alice   Von Hoffman, L. R.
> Vandenberg, I. R.   Von Ost, Felix

9. Foreign titles are indexed strictly according to title, disregarding *El, La,* and *Le*. Make as many cross-references as may be necessary for identification.

> Société Anonyme des Cycles Peugeot, La
> Make cross-reference under *Peugeot*.

COMPANY NAMES

10. If a *company* is a customer, enter under the company's title, with name of officer following:

> Best & Co.,
> Strickland, W., Manager
> Stetson Shops, Inc.,
> Interman, K. M.

If the *officer* himself is the customer, enter under his name in care of the company:

> Brown, Joseph A.,
> Credit Manager, Stewart & Co.

11. Great care must be taken to ascertain whether the first part of a company's name is a Christian name or a surname: (See Sec. 22, p. 335).

> Simon & Company, Franklin, *not* Franklin Simon & Co.

12. Every word of a title is to be taken into consideration when alphabetizing except *a, an,* and *the,* when they precede the title.

> First National Bank of Lewiston, The
> Mayflower, The
> Tailored Woman, The

If there is any doubt about strict alphabetical order, place one title directly under the other and imagine all the letters run together, as follows:

> Cent a Minute Mining Co., The
> Centaminute
> Cent and a Cup Water Co., The
> Centandacup

13. Names that begin with numbers should be indexed as if spelled out.

> File
> > 1st National Bank, as
> > First National Bank
>
> File
> > 3rd Presbyterian Church, as
> > Third Presbyterian Church
>
> File
> > 14th Street Curiosity Shop, as
> > Fourteenth Street Curiosity Shop

14. Company names should be alphabetized under the first name and the names following in strict alphabetical order, with cross-reference from the second name when necessary.

> Canadian Pacific Railway Company
> Cross-reference
> Pacific Railway Company, Canadian

15. When there are a large number of titles of the same name, these should be alphabetized according to names of towns in the address.

> American Can Company, Allentown, Pa.
> American Can Company, Memphis, Tenn.

16. Companies with initials or Christian names should be filed (1) by surname, (2) by Christian name or initial, (3) by remainder of title (& Co., Bros., etc.).

> Ryan, A.   Ryan, Edward, & Bros.
> Ryan, B., & Co.   Ryan, Henry, & Son
> Ryan, Bernard   Ryan & Co.

17. When companies of one name are followed by the words *Bros., Co., Inc., Sons,* etc., the titles are filed as though they were Christian names:

> Patton, Abner   Patton Co.
> Patton Bros.   Patton, Inc.

18. But if the titles are *& Bros., & Sons* (without initials or Christian names), etc., they are filed at the end of the list.

Patton, Abner	Patton & Bro.
Patton Bros.	Patton & Small
Patton, Edwin, & Bros.	Patton & Sons
Patton, Warren	

This last rule is illogical but since the greater number of authorities use it, a difference in the files results in confusion and delay.

Names written in the possessive come after the foregoing list:

Patton's Carpet Co.	Patton's Costume Co.

MISCELLANEOUS NAMES

19. When filing titles of a state, county, or city, file according to importance of government divisions; or they may be filed according to alphabetical sequence of geographic district (city, county, state), other names and titles following in alphabetic order.

> a. Washington (State)
> "   (County) Conn.
> "   (City) Conn.
> "   (City) D. C.
> "   (County) Fla.
> "   (County) Tenn.
> "   (City) Tenn.
> "   Assurance Corporation
> "   , Booker T.
> "   Candy Corporation
> "   Coffee Co., G. (cross reference)
> "   , George
> "   Heights Battery Service
> "   Hotel Co., Martha
> "   , Martha
> "   Pipe and Foundry Co.
> "   Square Book Shop

20. Titles beginning with *Mt., New, Pan, Rock, St., Saint, San, Santa,* etc., are alphabetized as distinct names.

Mt. Carmel	Rock Island R. R.
Mt. Vesuvius Lumber Co.	St. Agnes Day Nursery
Mt. Zion Cemetery	Saint Joseph's Union
New Lenox Market	Saintsbury, George
New Life Co.	San Francisco Chronicle
New Orleans Refining Co.	San Joseph, Harold
Pan American Society of U. S.	Sanka Coffee House
Pancoast Co.	Santa Fe Co.
Rockefeller, John D.	Santangelo Bros.

21. Churches are filed as the name appears.

> Cathedral of St. John the Divine
> > Cross-reference under *St. John the Divine*
> St. Patrick's Cathedral

CORPORATE TITLES

22. Institutions or societies beginning with a Christian name should be filed under the first name, with a cross-reference from the surname when necessary. (See Sec. 11, p. 332.)

> Benjamin Franklin Hotel
> Johns Hopkins University
> Katharine Gibbs School
> Russell Sage College
> Theodore Roosevelt High School

23. When titles are composed of two or more names joined by *and,* the & is alphabetized without regard to comma or hyphen.

> American & Canadian Flour Corporation
> American-Canadian Property Corporation
> American-Russian Chamber of Commerce

24. When points of the compass are part of the name, index under *north, south,* etc.

> North Chicago, Ill.
> South Boston, Mass.

North West, North Western, etc., are alphabetized as if spelled as one word.

> North River Savings Bank
> Northwest Paper Company
> Northwestern Chemical Company

The same rule applies to words that are sometimes hyphened.

> Co-operative
> Inter-state

25. Titles beginning with descriptive words should be inverted, so that the main entry will come first.

> Trustees of Cornell University
> should be
> Cornell University, Trustees of
> Estate of Chauncey M. Depew
> should be
> Depew, Chauncey M., Estate of

REFERENCE BOOKS

HUDDERS, E. R. *Indexing and Filing: A Manual of Standard Practice.* The Ronald Press Company, 1920.

SORELLE and GREGG. *Secretarial Studies.* Gregg Publishing Company, 1923.

WALLACE, EUGENIA. *Filing Methods.* The Ronald Press Company, 1924.

CHAPTER XIV

SOURCES OF INFORMATION USEFUL TO SECRETARIES

BIOGRAPHICAL DATA

Who's Who. A biographical dictionary issued annually, devoted mainly to English people of note.

Who's Who in America. A biographical dictionary of contemporary men and women of note in America, with addresses, lists of works of authors, pronunciation of difficult names, educational statistics, and geographical index.

Wer ist's? A German *Who's Who,* including some Austrian, Dutch, and Swiss names.

Qui êtes vous? A French *Who's Who* of contemporary men and women of note.

Who's Who in Art. A biographical dictionary of contemporary artists, included in the *American Art Annual.*

American Catholic Who's Who. A biographical dictionary of prominent Catholics of the higher rank of the priesthood and those distinguished in some particular line of work, as author, scientist, missionary.

Who's Who in Finance. A biographical dictionary of bankers, capitalists, and those engaged in finance in the United States and Canada.

Men of Science and Industry. Biographical data of scientists, engineers, inventors, and physicians.

Dau's Blue Books. A directory issued in principal cities, containing names and addresses of persons living in residential sections.

The Social Register. A directory containing names of men and women of social rank and prominence living in and near

New York; includes names of all members of the family, city and country addresses, names of colleges attended, and club memberships.

The Blue Book, issued in other cities of the United States, contains information similar to that of the *Social Register.*

The Directory of American Society. A directory of those socially prominent throughout the United States.

(The Secretary will find that other countries and other parts of our country have their own *Who's Who.*)

Who's Who in the National Capital.
Who's Who in New York.
Who's Who in New England.
Who's Who in Science.
Who's Who in Engineering.
Who's Who in Music.
American Labor's Who's Who.
Century Cyclopedia of Names.

REFERENCE BOOKS CONTAINING BIOGRAPHICAL DATA OF THE NOBILITY OF GREAT BRITAIN AND THE CONTINENT

Burke's Peerage. A genealogical and heraldic history of the Royal Family; Peerage and Baronetage; Archbishops and Bishops; Foreign titles of nobility held by British subjects; Knightage, Companionage, and Privy Council; Order of Precedence; Orders of Knighthood.

Whitaker's Peerage, Baronetage, Knightage, and Companionage.

Titles. (*Armiger*) A manual containing concise information about the orders of nobility in England, the correct manner of addressing them, order of precedence, etc.

Kelly's Handbook to the Titled, Landed and Official Classes.

Almanach de Gotha. A genealogical annual containing information of the royal and princely families of Europe; authoritative lists of executive, legislative, diplomatic, consular, and other officials of the different countries of the world.

SOURCES OF USEFUL INFORMATION

Official Congressional Directory for the Use of the United States Congress. Authoritative information of all legislative, judicial, and executive departments at Washington; lists of members of all departments of the diplomatic and consular service of the United States and to it, etc.

U. S. Bureau of the Census. *Official Register of the United States.* Official list of all Government employes.

U. S. Bureau of Education. *Educational Directory.* Lists of national and state educational officials, county, town, and district superintendents, college presidents, professors and superintendents in training schools, educational boards, and federations of women's clubs, officers of education in foreign countries, etc.

Handbook of American Private Schools. Lists of schools, camps, lists of educational directors, articles on educational literature and progress.

Minerva. (German) A yearbook of the learned world. Contains names of universities, colleges, libraries, etc., and lists of officials, professors, etc.

Athena. A yearbook of the learned world for English-speaking races.

Handbook of Learned Societies and Institutions of the Carnegie Institution of Washington. Contains names, addresses, history, objects, membership of all such societies in North and South America.

Yearbook of the Churches. A book of current statistical and directory information compiled for the Federal Council of the Churches of Christ in America.

U. S. Bureau of Census. *Religious Bodies.* Statistical information of the church membership, building, Sunday Schools, missionary activities, etc.

Official Catholic Directory. A directory and compilation of statistical information concerning the clergy, churches, religious orders, etc., of the Catholic Church in the United States and its possessions, in Great Britain, Canada and other parts of British America, in Cuba, and in Mexico.

American Jewish Year Book. A directory and compilation of statistical information, biographical sketches of Rabbis, welfare workers, and other prominent Jews.

Official Register and Directory of Women's Clubs in America. A register of clubs, names of presidents, number of members, and officers of state federations with addresses and dates of organization.

Kelly's Directory of Merchants, Manufacturers, and Shippers. A guide to the export, import, shipping, and manufacturing interests. Contains official lists, consuls, glossaries of foreign trade terms with English equivalents.

Bradstreet's and *Dun's Directories.* Financial rating books.

Moody's Manual. A manual of names of officers, directors, and capitalization of corporations, with statements of income, assets, and liabilities.

Directory of Directors. A book containing names of directors and of corporations with dates of meetings.

New International Year Book; A Compendium of the Year's Progress.

American Year Book. A record of events and progress in various fields, particularly in the United States.

Statesman's Year Book (published in England). Concise and authoritative information about the governments of the world. Information given about the ruler, constitution, government, population, religion, finance, industry, commerce, money and credit, diplomatic representatives, etc.

World Almanac. Most comprehensive of American Almanacs. Contains statistics of industry, politics, governments, finance, religion, education, etc.

Whitaker's Almanac. Statistical information relating to Great Britain particularly.

Brooklyn Eagle Almanac.

Chicago Daily News Almanac.

SOURCES OF USEFUL INFORMATION

New Guide to Reference Books. ISADORE MUDGE. A guide to all important reference books.

United States Catalog. An index of all books in print in the United States in 1928, with author's name, short title, edition, date, publisher, price, and paging.

Cumulative Book Index. An index issued monthly except August, containing names of all publications of the year and forming an annual supplement to the United States Catalog.

Publishers' Weekly. American book-trade journal containing lists of books announced for publication and the new publications for the week.

New York Times Index. An index made quarterly of references to articles and names appearing in *The New York Times,* with date, page number, and column.

Readers' Guide to Periodical Literature. An index to cultural and scientific articles found in a selected list of periodicals.

Industrial Arts Index. An index to a selected list of engineering and trade journals.

Public Affairs Information Service. The combination of a subject index to the current literature in its field: books, documents, pamphlets, articles in periodicals, multigraphed material, etc., and a digest of recent events and developments in the fields of sociology, political science, and economics, particularly the practical side of these subjects.

Business Digest. An index to business periodicals and digests of articles relating to advertising, and sales promotion, foreign trade, banking and investment, executive management, manufacturing, store management, accounting and office methods.

MISCELLANEOUS REFERENCE BOOKS

Roget's Thesaurus of English Words and Phrases. Arranged according to ideas rather than alphabetically. Helpful in finding exact words or expression for a given idea, together with idiomatic combinations peculiar to it.

Allen's Synonyms and Antonyms.
Crabb's English Synonyms.
Fernald's English Synonyms and Antonyms with Notes on the Correct Use of Prepositions.

STYLE BOOKS

Style Manual of the Government Printing Office.
Manual of Style of the University of Chicago.
Style-Book for Writers and Editors, C. O. Sylvester Mawson.
Style Book of The New York Times.
Text, Type and Style, a Compendium of Atlantic Usage.

ATLASES

Lippincott's Gazeteer of the World.
London Times Atlas.
Phillipp's Mercantile Marine Atlas.
Rand & McNally's Atlas.

GUIDES

U. S. Official Postal Guides.
International Postal Guide.
Bullinger's Post Office, Express, and Freight Guide.
Blue Book of American Shipping.

CHAPTER XV

CITATIONS

Citations made by President Butler of Columbia University in conferring honorary degrees: [1]

John St. Loe Strachey—

Trained, broadened and deepened at Balliol College under the guidance of the powerful personality of Benjamin Jowett; scholar, historian, man of letters and journalist; conducting for a full generation, under the shadow of the names of Addison and Steele, the most noteworthy journal of opinion in the English speaking world; careful and sympathetic student of American history, institutions and life; and interpreter of them with insight and understanding to all who use the speech of Shakespeare and Milton, of Franklin and Lincoln, I gladly admit you to the degree of Doctor of Letters in this University and confer upon you all the rights and privileges which belong thereto. In token whereof I hand you this diploma.

Alfred Emanuel Smith—

Born on Manhattan Island and trained in the hard school of its many-sided cosmopolitan life; since manhood a constant and eager public servant in posts of steadily growing importance and authority; sometime Speaker of the Assembly, member of the Constitutional Convention of 1915, three times chosen by the people of a truly imperial State to be their Governor; alert, effective, public-spirited and courageous, constantly speaking the true voice of the people; on this one hundredth anniversary of the Commencement at which your great predecessor, De Witt Clinton, received like honor, I gladly admit you to the degree of Doctor of Laws in this University, and confer upon you all the rights and privileges which belong thereto. In token whereof I hand you this diploma.

[1] Reprinted by permission.

The Rt. Hon. and Rt. Rev. Arthur Foley Winnington-Ingram—

Lord Bishop of London, Dean of the Chapels Royal, and Prelate of the Order of the British Empire; fortunately trained, with high honors, at Marlborough College and at Keble College, Oxford; passing steadily and quickly from one post to another of ecclesiastical usefulness, influence and distinctions; now administering the vast work of the Church of England in the capital city of the British Commonwealth of Nations; eager in service, constant in labor, guided always and everywhere by deep insight into human nature and keen sympathy with the inspiration and activities of youth, I gladly admit you to the degree of Doctor of Sacred Theology in this University, and confer upon you all the rights and privileges which belong thereto. In token whereof I hand you this diploma.

John Bassett Moore—

Native of Delaware, graduated at the University of Virginia with the Class of 1880; quickly entering the public service in the Department of State and serving there until appointed Hamilton Fish Professor of International Law and Diplomacy in 1891; called from time to time by the Government to serve either in high and responsible office in the Department of State or as special envoy or as delegate to numerous international conferences; signally honored in many lands; first of living authorities on international law and procedure; profound in scholarship and unwearied in industry; member of the Permanent Court of Arbitration at the Hague since 1913 and Judge of the Permanent Court of International Justice since 1921, I gladly admit you to the degree of Doctor of Laws, in this University and confer upon you all the rights and privileges which belong thereto. In token whereof I hand you this diploma.

A citation made by President Thomas of Rutgers University in conferring the degree of LL.D. upon Dr. James C. Egbert, 1928.[1]

James Chidester Egbert,

Alumnus and Doctor of Philosophy of Columbia University; distinguished scholar and teacher in the field of Roman Archæology and sometime President of the Archæological Institute of America;

[2] Reprinted by permission.

builder of the outstanding Summer Session of American Universities;

director of the world's greatest enterprise in adult education, through whose leadership the privileges of learning have been extended to many thousands whose educational needs and possibilities had been unnoticed, whereby the institutions of higher learning in America have been brought to a new and inspiring realization of their responsibilities in a democracy;

Rutgers University, Columbia's next of kin, confers upon you the degree of Doctor of Laws.

A citation made by Theodore S. Woolsey, LL.D., of Yale University, in presenting Mr. Henry Drysdale Dakin for an honorary degree, 1918: [1]

English born, widely trained in the chemistry of the human body, skilled in research, Dr. Dakin's studies peculiarly fitted him to aid in the development of surgical practice in the present war.

In both French and British services he has been a pioneer in the new surgery and his discoveries in antiseptic treatment have saved life and limb to many a broken soldier.

In response by President Hadley:

As a pioneer in the work of discovery, important in all times, but doubly important in war times, we confer upon you the degree of Doctor of Science.

Honorary degree of LL.D. conferred upon Herbert Hoover by Princeton University in 1917. The following citation was made by Dean West in introducing Mr. Hoover.[1]

HERBERT CLARK HOOVER, geologist and engineer, student and writer on mining; developer and director of large enterprises in Australia, China, Burma and Siberia, our first authority on the history and economics of mining; at the outbreak of the war relieving the stranded hordes of Americans in London with swift succor; then head of the Commission for Relief of Belgium and there fighting a hard fight to shelter the homeless, to cover the naked and "to deal bread to the hungry"; chief master of the problem of producing, dividing and using our national food supply to feed all who need it; a true son of the

[1] Reprinted by permission.

people, a youth in heart, a giant in vast achievement; swift, sleepless and resistless, bending all to one great purpose—to save and not to destroy.

Citation made by President Lemuel H. Murlin of Boston University, in conferring the degree of LL.D. on behalf of the Trustees (December 12, 1924) on Mrs. Calvin Coolidge:[1]

Student, university graduate, teacher; daughter, wife, mother; in every station exemplifying the finer qualities of mind and heart we most admire in women; your own works praise you; you have gained the confidence, admiration and love of the American people. Upon the recommendation of the University Council, I have been authorized by the Board of Trustees of Boston University to admit you to the degree of Doctor of Laws.

Citations made by President Daniel L. Marsh of Boston University.[1]

CLARENCE WALKER BARRON, editor, publisher, spokesman of industrial America to the investing public of the United States, promulgator of the doctrine that the laws of happiness are the laws of service, by the authority vested in me, I admit you to the degree of Doctor of Commercial Science of Boston University and to all the rights, privileges and distinction belonging thereto, and in testimony thereof I present to you this diploma bearing the seal of the University and the inscriptions of its proper officers.

HAMILTON HOLT, President of Rollins College, educator, publicist, constructive advocate of international good-will and world-peace, foe of war and by the same token friend of humanity, by the authority vested in me, I admit you to the degree of Doctor of Humanities of Boston University and to all the rights, privileges and distinction belonging thereto, and in testimony thereof I present to you this diploma bearing the seal of the University and the inscriptions of its proper officers.

Granting of an honorary degree to Charles A. Lindbergh at the University of Wisconsin, presentation made by Professor Paxson.[1]

[1] Reprinted by permission.

CITATIONS

Mr. President:

When Dr. Franklin visited the court of France, as the sort of ambassador who serves his country by making friends, he was characterized by a famous line: *Eripuit caelo fulmen, sceptrumque tyrannis;* He has snatched the lightning out of Heaven and the sceptre from the tyrants. Since the days of Dr. Franklin no other American has reached his eminence in friendship. But *Charles Augustus Lindbergh* offers him today a genuine rivalry. There has been no sceptre for the new ambassador to grasp, no tyrant to displace, and the lightnings have long since been harnessed. But he has mastered the currents of the air, giving to mankind a new dimension; and he has done it with restraint and power that have enhanced the dignity of our manhood. As a representative of American good-will to all the world he has served us well. And Wisconsin takes real pride in the feeling that he is one of us.

Upon recommendation of the Faculty and by vote of the Regents I present *Charles Augustus Lindbergh* to receive the honorary degree, Doctor of Laws.

Conferring of the Degree of Doctor of Laws by President Frank.

Colonel Lindbergh, the degree that the University of Wisconsin to-day confers upon you is the outward sign of its recognition of acts and careers that represent distinguished and socially significant leadership. It is the ribbon of the University's Legion d'Honneur.

The receiving of honors is no novelty to you. Kings and commoners have competed in admiration and acknowledgment of your achievements. But this recognition comes to you at a later stage of your adventure, and for a different reason than animated your initial honors. And I venture to think that this latest honor recognizes the most significant aspect of your service. The University of Wisconsin to-day accords to you its highest honorary degree, not for your flawless flight of the Atlantic—stirring and significant as that was—but for what you have done with the priceless power of public interest that came to focus on that flight. By a magnificent feat of psychological engineering, you have transformed what might have been an evanescent mood of hero-worship into the motive power of a program of development of civil aviation that promises to write a new chapter in human history.

And so—

Because the subtle chemistry of your courage changed the very climate of our spirits until we all felt capable of heroism.

Because, with quiet dignity, you have refused to capitalize the affectionate plaudits of a planet for personal advantage.

Because, as a Modern Mercury, you are the flying symbol of a future America that shall be emancipated from slavery to distance.

Because you are an able representative of that technical statesmanship which promises increasingly to supplement political statesmanship in this machine age.

Because—as I said to you on another occasion—both in the winning and in the wearing of your laurels, you have displayed that intelligent daring, that emotional control, and that effective coordination of brain and body which are the first fruits and final justification of an authentic education.

Because you have given the nation an idol whose feet are not of clay.

But above all because of the genuine qualities of leadership you have displayed in the conversion of your personal popularity into a social asset to the future of American civilization, I am happy to confer upon you the honorary degree of Doctor of Laws.

Citation made in conferring posthumously a Distinguished Service Cross upon Richard D. Johnson.

Richard D. Johnson (Army serial No. 275890), sergeant, Company E, 127th Infantry, 32d Division, American Expeditionary Forces. For extraordinary heroism in action near Cierges, France, July 30, 1918. Coming unexpectedly upon a German machine gun, he threw himself upon it as it started firing, being himself killed but preventing any casualties among the members of his own platoon, the enemy gunners being made prisoners. Next of kin: Carl Johnson, brother, 1416 Birch Street, Eau Claire, Wis. Residence at enlistment: Eau Claire, Wis.

Citations made in conferring posthumously, a Distinguished Flying Cross.

Hawthorne C. Gray, captain, Air Corps, United States Army. For heroism while participating in aerial flights. On March 9, 1927, he attempted to establish the world's altitude record for aircraft, but due to faulty oxygen apparatus he fainted at an altitude of 27,000 feet, recovering consciousness after 52 minutes, when his balloon, having overshot its equilibrium point, descended to an atmosphere low enough to sustain life. Undaunted by this experience, Captain *Gray,* on May 4, 1927, made a record attempt when he attained an altitude of 42,470 feet, higher than any other earth creature has ever gone. On his descent, however, his balloon failed to parachute, and it was necessary for him to descend from 8,000 feet in a parachute. With faith still unshaken, and displaying great courage and self-reliance, Captain *Gray,* on November 4, 1927, made the third attempt, which resulted in his making the supreme sacrifice. Having attained an altitude of 42,000 feet he waited for 10 minutes, testing his reactions, before making a last rapid climb to his ceiling and a more rapid descent to safe atmosphere. Undoubtedly his courage was greater than his supply of oxygen, which gave out at about 37,000 feet. Residence at enlistment: 1050 South Hope Street, Los Angeles, Calif. Nearest relative: Mrs. Marion Maddux Gray, widow, Box 173, R. F. D., No. 5, Santa Rosa, Calif.

Citations made in conferring Congressional Medals of Honor.

An Act Providing for the promotion of Lieutenant Commander Richard E. Byrd, United States Navy, retired, and awarding to him a congressional medal of honor.

Be it enacted by the Senate and House of Representatives of the United States of America in Congress assembled, That the President of the United States be, and he is hereby, authorized to advance Lieutenant Commander Richard E. Byrd, United States Navy, retired, to the grade of commander on the retired list of the Navy, to date from May 9, 1926, with the highest retired pay of that grade under existing law.

SEC. 2. The President of the United States is hereby authorized to present, in the name of Congress, a medal of honor to the said Richard E. Byrd for distinguishing himself conspicuously by courage and intrepidity at the risk of his life in demonstrating that it is possible for aircraft to travel in continuous flight from a now inhabited portion of the earth over the North Pole and return.

Approved, January 5, 1927.

An Act Providing for the promotion of Floyd Bennett, aviation pilot, United States Navy, and awarding to him a congressional medal of honor.

Be it enacted by the Senate and House of Representatives of the United States of America in Congress assembled, That the Secretary of the Navy is hereby authorized to appoint Floyd Bennett, aviation pilot, United States Navy, to the grade of machinist in the Navy from May 9, 1926.

SEC. 2. The President of the United States is hereby authorized to present, in the name of Congress, a medal of honor to the said Floyd Bennett for his gallant service to the Nation as a member of the Byrd Arctic expedition, which medal, when presented, shall entitle him to the benefits provided by the Act approved February 4, 1919.

Approved, January 5, 1927.

An Act Authorizing the President of the United States to present in the name of Congress a medal of honor to Colonel Charles A. Lindbergh.

Be it enacted by the Senate and House of Representatives of the United States of America in Congress assembled, That the President of the United States be, and he is hereby, authorized to present in the name of Congress, a medal of honor to Colonel Charles A. Lindbergh, United States Army Air Corps Reserve, for displaying heroic courage and skill as a navigator, at the risk of his life, by his nonstop flight in his plane, the Spirit of Saint Louis, from New York city to Paris, France, on May 20, 1927, by which he not only achieved the greatest individual triumph of any American citizen, but demonstrated that travel across the ocean by aircraft was possible.

Approved, December 14, 1927.

Citation made in presenting the Congressional Medal of Honor upon Lieutenant Frank Schilt, USMC.

On 9 April 1928, the President of the United States presented the Congressional Medal of Honor to Lieutenant Schilt at the White House, in the presence of high ranking officials of the Army, Navy and Marine Corps. The citation read as follows:

For extraordinary heroism distinguished by conspicuous gallantry and intrepidity at the risk of his life above and beyond the call of duty. On the 6th, 7th, and 8th of January, 1928, at Quilali, Nicaragua, Lieutenant Schilt, then a member of a marine expedition which had suffered severe losses in killed and wounded, volunteered under almost impossible conditions to evacuate the wounded by air and transport a relief commanding officer to assume charge of a very serious situation.

CITATIONS

Lieutenant Schilt bravely undertook this dangerous and vitally important task and by taking off a total of ten times in the rough, rolling street of the partially burned village, under hostile infantry fire on each occasion, succeeded by almost superhuman skill, combined with personal courage of the highest order, in accomplishing his mission, thereby actually saving three lives and bringing supplies and succor to others in desperate need.

Citations made by Hermann Hagedorn for the Roosevelt Memorial Association in conferring the Roosevelt Medal for Distinguished Service.[1]

(1)

For the medal for distinguished service in the administration of public office and in the development of public and international law, I have the honor, Mr. President, to present the name of one who has served the nation in many capacities, and always served her well; a public investigator, clear-minded and relentless; a governor, upright and brave; a brilliant judge; an advocate, eloquent in defense and attack; a statesman in the field of foreign affairs who has won the admiration of the world by his resourcefulness, his courage, his intellectual power, the nobility of his vision, the determination and the enthusiasm of his pursuit. His country is richer by his life and a world-peace is nearer because of his labors.

Charles Evans Hughes

(2)

For the medal for distinguished service in the promotion of the study of natural history, Mr. President, I have the honor to present a name which is beloved wherever in America, in school or home, the birds are permitted to come down from the treetops to be the companions of men; a writer and lecturer of persuasive charm, who has taught a nation to see, to know, to love and to protect the entrancing and forever mysterious familiars of its daily life; a creative innovator in methods of exhibition and of ornithological research; a scientist, wise and unsatisfied, whose laboratory is a wilderness of Andean peaks, where fluttering wings betray to him things secret since the beginning of time—

Frank M. Chapman

[1] Reprinted by permission of the Roosevelt Memorial Association.

351

(3)

For the medal for distinguished service in the leadership of youth and the development of American character, I have the honor, Mr. President, to present the name of one who flew out of clouds and darkness into the heart of mankind; a master of the tumultuous air, who finds his way securely also on the earth, in crowds, and alone along dizzy crests; an emissary of good will, in whose presence the fears and hatreds of men withdraw for an hour abashed, confronting not a boy but irresistible youth itself; a boy, a man; a sword, a bugle; a burst of ringing laughter in the face of the money-changers and the sellers of doves; to an older generation, a symbol of forgotten day-dreams for once triumphant over the stubborn fact; to boys and girls their own best selves made manifest, his achievements and his triumphs a presage of the glories that shall be theirs.

Charles A. Lindbergh

Citations made by the American Telephone and Telegraph Company in conferring the Theodore N. Vail Medal.

Fred F. Brown
The Connecticut Valley Telephone

Foreman
Bradford, Vermont

Citation

For courage, initiative and resourcefulness in restoring vital telephone service in a serious emergency, in the face of grave personal danger.

When the unprecedented rains in Northern Vermont in early November 1927 had turned the rivers into torrents of destruction which paralyzed activities in that section of the state, Foreman Brown and two fellow-employees set out on November 5 to clear at least one toll line into Montpelier, the capital city, which had been isolated.

After driving twenty miles over back roads and high ground, they found that the lines were crossed where the Wells River had washed out a pole and left the tie wires tangled in the toll circuits. The cross could not be shaken out and, although the river was a rushing torrent filled with logs, trees and other debris, and a fall would have meant almost certain death, Brown hooked his safety strap over the four wires and rode out on what was then a two hundred and sixty foot span, untangled the ties which caused the cross and, when one wire broke as he started back, rode the remaining three back to the pole in safety.

The circuit which he restored was immediately put in service for official use of the state authorities and was of vital importance in the organization of the relief work and in giving accurate news to the outside world.

Patrick B. McCormick   Agent
New England Telephone and   Becket, Mass.
   Telegraph Company

Citation

For fortitude, initiative and devotion to public service despite grave personal danger.

Unprecedented rains in Western Massachusetts early in November 1927 had swelled the rivers and streams to torrents and it was feared that the dams in the vicinity of Becket would go out and cause great destruction. About four o'clock in the morning of November 4, when McCormick was notified that the nearest dam a mile above the town would doubtless fail, he notified every subscriber in the valley, warned them to leave, and asked them to notify those who had no telephones. He sent his own family to safety in the hills and, realizing that some of the residents would remain despite his earlier warning, stayed at the switchboard in his home, in constant telephone communication with people at the dam, to receive and transmit the final warning.

The dam went out at six o'clock, and after notifying all who had remained, he started warning all the towns in the path of the danger. This task completed, his escape was cut off and he was forced to remain, while houses and trees were torn up and carried past, and his own home was flooded and the switchboard put out of order.

As soon as the water began to recede he climbed a pole, cut in on the toll line with his test set, and gave to the outside world the first call for relief.[1]

Citation made by the Carnegie Hero Fund Commission in conferring a Medal for an Heroic Act.[2]

[1] Reprinted by permission.
[2] Reprinted by permission from the *Report of the Carnegie Hero Fund Commission*, 1928.

2122 | **Susan Ruth Sherwood,** aged eleven, school-girl, saved Dale B. Smith, aged twelve, from drowning, Lakeside, Ohio, July 1, 1925. Dale, who could not swim, got on a small raft and paddled with his hands until he was a hundred and fifteen feet from shore. He then became frightened and jumped into water seven and a half feet deep. Susan, who was a poor swimmer, waded fifty feet toward Dale carrying a life-belt. She then rested on the life-belt and swam sixty feet to Dale through deep water. He put his arms around her arms and body, and a struggle followed before she could regain the use of her arms. Susan struck him on the temple with her fist and then swam twenty feet toward shore with Dale holding around her waist and his head resting on the life-belt. A swimmer met them and took Dale to shore. | Bronze Medal and $1,600 for educational purposes as needed.

2181 | **Frederick G. Michaelis,** aged fifty-five, foreman (bridge-builder), saved Arlie G. Berry, aged two, from being killed by a train, Randall, Minn., July 22, 1924. Arlie walked onto a track, on which a train was approaching at a speed of forty miles an hour. Michaelis, who was recovering from recent operations on his feet and walked with great difficulty, ran two hundred and forty feet to Arlie, lifted him with one hand, and ran from the track, clearing the track when the train was only a few feet distant. | Bronze Medal and $1,000 for a worthy purpose as needed.

CHAPTER XVI

INSCRIPTIONS

On the Post Office at Washington, D. C.

Carrier of news and knowledge, instrument of trade and industry, promoter of mutual acquaintance, of peace and good-will among men and nations.

Messenger of sympathy and love, servant of parted friends, consoler of the lonely, bond of the scattered family, enlarger of common life.

On the Post Office, Eighth Avenue and Thirty-third Street, New York City.

Neither snow nor rain nor heat nor gloom of night stays these couriers from the swift completion of their appointed rounds.

On the Union Station, Washington, D. C.

He that would bring home the wealth of the Indies must carry the wealth of the Indies with him. So it is in travelling —a man must carry knowledge with him if he would bring home knowledge.

A frieze of inscriptions in the Detroit Public Library.

Books are the most enduring monuments of man's achievement. Through them, civilization becomes cumulative.

Read not to contradict and confute, nor to believe and take for granted, but to weigh and consider.

Through seas of knowledge we our course advance, discovering still new worlds of ignorance.

To promote self-development by ample facilities for wide reading in an atmosphere of freedom and morality.

Inscriptions at the north and south ends of Detroit Public Library, respectively.

Consider what nation it is whereof ye are; a nation not slow and dull, but of a quick, ingenious and piercing spirit, acute to invent, subtle and sinuous to discourse, not beyond the reach of any point the highest that human capacity can soar to.

355

Reading, trying all things, assenting to the force of reason and convincement; what wants there to such towardly and pregnant soil, but wise and faithful laborers to make a knowing people, a nation of prophets, of sages, and of worthies.

Inscription on No. 1 Broadway New York City.

ADJOINING THIS SITE WAS THE FIRST DUTCH FORT ON MANHATTAN ISLAND KNOWN AS FORT NEW AMSTERDAM. THE FIRST HOUSE WAS ERECTED HERE BEFORE 1664. IN 1771 CAPTAIN ARCHIBALD KENNEDY BUILT HERE HIS RESIDENCE WHICH WAS USED IN 1776 BY GENERAL WASHINGTON AS HIS HEADQUARTERS AND LATER BY GENERAL HOWE DURING THE BRITISH OCCUPATION. IT WAS LATER USED AS A HOTEL. TORN DOWN IN 1882, IT WAS REPLACED BY THE WASHINGTON BUILDING WHICH WAS TRANSFORMED IN 1920-21 INTO THIS BUILDING FOR OCCUPANCY BY ITS OWNERS THE INTERNATIONAL MERCANTILE MARINE COMPANY AND KNOWN AS

NO. 1 BROADWAY

Inscription in a room entered through the east portal of the Amphitheater at Arlington near the tomb of the Unknown Soldier. Taken from the oration of President Harding delivered at the dedication.

THE NAME OF HIM WHOSE BODY LIES HERE TOOK FLIGHT WITH HIS IMPERISHABLE SOUL. WE KNOW NOT WHENCE HE CAME, BUT ONLY THAT HIS DEATH MARKS HIM WITH THE EVERLASTING GLORY OF AN AMERICAN WHO DIED FOR HIS COUNTRY. WE DO NOT KNOW THE EMINENCE OF HIS BIRTH, BUT WE DO KNOW THE GLORY OF HIS DEATH. HE DIED FOR HIS COUNTRY, AND GREATER DEVOTION HATH NO MAN THAN THIS. HE DIED UNQUESTIONING, UNCOMPLAINING WITH FAITH IN HIS HEART AND HOPE ON HIS LIPS THAT HIS COUNTRY SHOULD TRIUMPH AND ITS CIVILIZATION SURVIVE.

INSCRIPTIONS

Inscription on tomb of Unknown Soldier in Westminster Abbey, London.

Beneath this stone rests the body of a British Warrior
Unknown by name or rank
Brought from France to lie among
The most illustrious of the land
And buried here on Armistice Day
November 11th, 1920, in the presence of
His Majesty, King George V,
Ministers of State,
The chiefs of the forces,
And a vast number of the nation.
Thus are commemorated the many
Multitudes who during the Great War
of 1914-1918 gave the most that
Man can give, life itself,
For God
For King and country,
To loved ones, home, and empire,
To the sacred cause of justice, and
The freedom of the world.
They buried him among the kings
Because he had done good toward God
And toward His house.

Inscription within Lincoln Memorial, Washington.

IN THIS TEMPLE
AS IN THE HEARTS OF THE PEOPLE
FOR WHOM HE SAVED THE UNION
THE MEMORY OF ABRAHAM LINCOLN
IS ENSHRINED FOREVER

Panels in the Northeast Pavilion of the Library of Congress contain the following inscriptions:

On Treasury and State Seals

'TIS OUR TRUE POLICY TO STEER CLEAR OF PERMANENT ALLIANCES WITH ANY PORTIONS OF THE FOREIGN WORLD.

—Washington

357

LET OUR OBJECT BE OUR COUNTRY, OUR WHOLE COUNTRY, AND NOTHING BUT OUR COUNTRY.

—Webster

On War and Navy Seals

THE GREATEST HAPPINESS OF SOCIETY IS, OR OUGHT TO BE, THE END OF ALL GOVERNMENT. TO BE PREPARED FOR WAR IS ONE OF THE MOST EFFECTUAL MEANS OF PRESERVING PEACE.

—Washington

On Agriculture and Interior Seals

THE AGRICULTURAL INTEREST OF THE COUNTRY IS CONNECTED WITH EVERY OTHER, AND SUPERIOR IN IMPORTANCE TO THEM ALL.

—Jackson

LET US HAVE PEACE.—*Grant*

On Justice and the Post Office Seals

EQUAL AND EXACT JUSTICE TO ALL MEN, OF WHATEVER STATE OR PERSUASION, RELIGIOUS, OR POLITICAL; PEACE, COMMERCE, AND HONEST FRIENDSHIP WITH ALL NATIONS, ENTANGLING ALLIANCES WITH NONE.

—Jefferson

Inscription in the ceiling encircling the Great Seal of the United States.

THAT THIS NATION, UNDER GOD, SHALL HAVE A NEW BIRTH OF FREEDOM, AND THAT GOVERNMENT OF THE PEOPLE, BY THE PEOPLE, FOR THE PEOPLE, SHALL NOT PERISH FROM THE EARTH.

—Lincoln

Inscriptions encircling the dome in the National Academy of Sciences, Washington.

AGES AND CYCLES OF NATURE
IN CEASELESS SEQUENCES MOVING
TO SCIENCE, PILOT OF INDUSTRY, CONQUEROR OF DISEASE, MULTIPLIER OF THE HARVEST, EXPLORER OF THE UNIVERSE, REVEALER OF GOD'S LAWS, ETERNAL GUIDE TO TRUTH.

INSCRIPTIONS

Inscriptions in the Reading Room of the Library of Congress.

Religion
WHAT DOTH THE LORD REQUIRE OF THEE, BUT
TO DO JUSTLY, TO LOVE MERCY, AND TO WALK
HUMBLY WITH THY GOD?—*Micah* VI:8.

Commerce
WE TAKE THE SPICES OF ARABIA, YET NEVER
FEEL THE SCORCHING SUN, WHICH BRINGS THEM
FORTH. *Considerations on East India Trade.*

History
   ONE GOD, ONE LAW, ONE ELEMENT,
   AND ONE FAR-OFF DIVINE EVENT,
   TO WHICH THE WHOLE CREATION MOVES.
—Tennyson

Art
AS ONE LAMP LIGHTS ANOTHER, NOR GROWS
LESS, SO NOBLENESS ENKINDLETH NOBLENESS.
—Lowell

Philosophy
THE INQUIRY, KNOWLEDGE AND BELIEF OF
TRUTH IS THE SOVEREIGN GOOD OF HUMAN
NATURE.
—Bacon

Poetry
HITHER, AS TO THEIR FOUNTAIN, OTHER STARS
REPAIRING, IN THEIR GOLDEN URNS, DRAW LIGHT
—Milton

Law
OF LAW THERE CAN BE NO LESS ACKNOWL-
EDGED THAN THAT HER VOICE IS THE HARMONY
OF THE WORLD.
—Hooker

Science
THE HEAVENS DECLARE THE GLORY OF GOD
AND THE FIRMAMENT SHOWETH HIS HANDI-
WORK.
—Psalms XIX

Inscriptions on the walls of the Union Station, Washington.
Selected by President Eliot of Harvard University.

In the Waiting Room
     WELCOME THE COMING
     SPEED THE PARTING GUEST.

> VIRTUE ALONE IS SWEET SOCIETY
> IT KEEPS THE KEY TO ALL
> HEROIC HEARTS AND OPENS YOU
> A WELCOME IN THEM ALL

Over the State Entrance

> LET ALL THINGS THOU AIMEST AT BE
> THY COUNTRY'S—GOD'S AND TRUTH'S.

> BE NOBLE AND THE NOBLENESS THAT
> LIES IN OTHER MEN—SLEEPING, BUT
> NEVER DEAD—WILL RISE IN MAJESTY TO
> MEET THINE OWN.

Dedicatory Inscriptions for the Chimes of Bells in Mitchell Tower, University of Chicago, in Memory of Alice Freeman Palmer.

Bronze Tablet

> JOYFULLY TO RECALL
> ALICE FREEMAN PALMER
> DEAN OF WOMEN IN THE UNIVERSITY
> 1892–1895
> THESE BELLS MAKE MUSIC

INSCRIPTIONS

Lines on Individual Bells

A GRACIOUS WOMAN RETAINING HONOR

.   .   .   .

EASY TO BE ENTREATED

.   .   .   .

ALWAYS REJOICING

.   .   .   .

MAKING THE LAME TO WALK AND THE BLIND
TO SEE

.   .   .   .

GREAT IN COUNCIL AND MIGHTY IN WORK

.   .   .   .

ROOTED AND GROUNDED IN LOVE

.   .   .   .

FERVENT IN SPIRIT

.   .   .   .

GIVEN TO HOSPITALITY

.   .   .   .

THE SWEETNESS OF HER LIPS INCREASES
LEARNING

.   .   .   .

IN GOD'S LAW MEDITATING DAY AND NIGHT

Inscription on the East Wall of the Reynolds Club Theater,
University of Chicago.

MEN MUST KNOW THAT IN THIS THEATER OF
MAN'S LIFE IT IS RESERVED FOR GOD AND ANGELS
TO BE LOOKERS-ON.

Inscription on the West Wall of the Reynolds Club Theater.

THUS WE PLAY THE FOOLS WITH THE TIME
AND THE SPIRITS OF THE WISE SIT IN THE CLOUDS
AND MOCK US. GOD GAVE US WISDOM THAT HAVE
IT; AND THOSE THAT ARE FOOLS, LET THEM USE
THEIR TALENTS.

361

Inscription on Tablet to President Harper, University of Chicago.

TO HONOR THE MEMORY OF
WILLIAM RAINEY HARPER
FIRST PRESIDENT OF THE UNIVERSITY OF
CHICAGO
Born 1856   Died 1906
THIS BUILDING WAS ERECTED
BY GIFTS OF THE FOUNDER OF THE UNIVERSITY
MEMBERS OF THE BOARD OF TRUSTEES
AND FACULTIES

A Dedicatory Inscription on the Wall of the Frank Dickinson Bartlett Gymnasium, University of Chicago.

To
THE ADVANCEMENT
OF PHYSICAL EDUCATION
AND THE GLORY OF MANLY SPORTS
THIS GYMNASIUM IS DEDICATED
TO THE MEMORY OF
FRANK DICKINSON BARTLETT
A. D. 1880–1900

Inscriptions carved on exterior of Boston Public Library.

On the Dartmouth Street side
THE PUBLIC LIBRARY OF THE CITY OF BOSTON.
BUILT BY THE PEOPLE AND DEDICATED TO
THE ADVANCEMENT OF LEARNING
A. D. MDCCCLXXXVIII.
On the Boylston Street side
THE COMMONWEALTH REQUIRES THE EDUCA-
TION OF THE PEOPLE AS THE SAFEGUARD OF
ORDER AND LIBERTY.
On the Blagden Street side
MDCCCLII. FOUNDED THROUGH THE MUNIFI-
CENCE AND PUBLIC SPIRIT OF CITIZENS

Inscription over the Dexter Memorial Gate, Harvard University.

ENTER TO GROW IN WISDOM
DEPART TO SERVE BETTER THY COUNTRY AND
THY KIND

INSCRIPTIONS

Inscription on the Library of Columbia University.

KING'S COLLEGE FOUNDED IN THE PROVINCE OF NEW YORK—BY ROYAL CHARTER IN THE REIGN OF GEORGE II—PERPETUATED AS COLUMBIA COLLEGE BY THE PEOPLE OF THE STATE OF NEW YORK—WHEN THEY BECAME FREE AND INDEPENDENT—MAINTAINED AND CHERISHED FROM GENERATION TO GENERATION—FOR THE ADVANCEMENT OF THE PUBLIC GOOD AND THE GLORY OF ALMIGHTY GOD

Inscription at the entrance of Reading Room, New York Public Library.

A GOOD BOOK IS THE PRECIOUS LIFE BLOOD OF A MASTER SPIRIT, EMBALM'D AND TREASUR'D UPON PURPOSE TO A LIFE BEYOND LIFE.

Inscription on a Tablet to John Pierpont Morgan in the Metropolitan Museum of Art, New York.

ERECTED BY THE MUSEUM
IN GRATEFUL MEMORY OF
JOHN
PIERPONT
MORGAN
From 1871 to 1913
As Trustee, Benefactor and President
He·was·in·all·respects
A·great·citizen··He
helped·to·make·New·York
The·True·Metropolis
of··America··His·interest
In·art·was·lifelong
His·generous·devotion
To·it·commanded
Wide·appreciation
His·munificent·gifts·to
The·museum·are·among
Its·choicest·treasures
Vita·plena
laboris
M C M X X

Inscription on St. Louis Public Library.

> SPEAK LOW, TREAD SOFTLY, THROUGH THESE
>   HALLS:
> HERE GENIUS LIES ENSHRINED;
> HERE SLEEP IN SILENT MAJESTY
> THE MONARCHS OF THE MIND.

Inscription on a Tablet of the Young Men's Christian Association Memorial Building, New York.

> YOUNG MEN'S CHRISTIAN ASSOCIATION
> OF THE
> CITY OF NEW YORK
> WILLIAM SLOANE MEMORIAL BUILDING
> To Honor the Memory
> of
> WILLIAM SLOANE

and to be of service to young men, especially our soldiers and sailors to whom he gave his life in unselfish devotion.

Chairman, National War Work Council of the Young Men's Christian Associations from 1917 to 1921; Vice-Chairman International Committee from 1910 to 1919; Chairman Army and Navy Department of the International Committee from 1901 to 1917.

Born 1873   Died 1922

Inscription for the Walter Camp Memorial, Yale University.

> GIVEN BY
> AMERICAN COLLEGES
> AND SCHOOLS
> UNITED WITH GRADUATES OF YALE
> TO HONOR
> WALTER CAMP
> AND THE TRADITIONS
> OF
> AMERICAN COLLEGE SPORTS
> WHICH HE EXEMPLIFIED

INDEX

INDEX

INDEX

INDEX

369

INDEX

INDEX

Titles
  academic degrees, abbreviations of,
    131
  books, 22-23
  ecclesiastical, 225-232
  Esquire, 217
  Honorable, 217
  hyphen in, 61
  italics in, 76-78
  musical compositions, 23
  newspaper, 22
  personal names, capitalization of,
    3-6, 18-19
  of pictures, 23
  use in official letters, 207-237.
Trade names
  capitalization of, 25
Type sizes, 312

Undersecretary of State
  form of address in letters to, 209

Vail, Theodore N.
  medal conferred, 352
Verbs
  correct usage, 150
  principal parts, 148-150
  tenses, 146-150
Vice President
  form of address in letters to, 207

Weights, 85
West, Dean
  citation by, 345
Woolsey, Theodore S.
  citation by, 345
Words
  See Diction

373